D0233917

Born in 1909, the fourth of five children, George Thomas was educated at University College, Southampton, before going on to teach in the East End of London and then in Wales.

In a long and distinguished political career, George Thomas was appointed Joint Parliamentary Under-Secretary of State: Home Office, 1964–66; Minister of State: Welsh Office, 1966–67; Minister of State: Commonwealth Office, 1967–68; Secretary of State for Wales, 1968–70; and Deputy Speaker and Chairman of Ways and Means, House of Commons, 1974–76.

Elected Speaker of the House of Commons in 1976, George Thomas was MP for a Cardiff seat from 1945 until 1983 when he retired. Created First Viscount Tonypandy on his retirement from the Speaker's Chair in 1983, he now divides his time between the House of Lords and his duties as a Methodist lay preacher.

The publishers would like to thank the following organisations and individuals for the use of their photographs: Ramon Hunston, p. 2; Mrs Evans, p. 3 (T); Marit Press, p. 5 (B); Western Mail & Echo Ltd, pp. 6 (T), 7, 8 (B), 10 (B), 11, 12 (B), 30 (B); Three Star Press Agency, p. 6 (B); Daily Herald, p. 8 (T); Topix, pp. 13 (T), 18 (B); The Press Association, p. 13 (B); Financial Times, p. 14 (B); Sidney Harris Ltd, p. 20 (T); COI (Crown Copyright), pp. 20 (M), 24; United Press International (UK) Ltd, p. 22; Ben-Zvi, p. 25; The Times, p. 26 (B), 27 (B); Shuhei Iwamoto, p. 27 (T); Les Wilson, p. 28; National Children's Home, p. 29; Universal Pictorial Press, p. 32.

George Thomas, Mr Speaker

THE MEMOIRS OF
THE VISCOUNT TONYPANDY

ARROW

To the House of Commons, Westminster,
whose fellowship enriched my life

Arrow Books Limited
62-65 Chandos Place, London WC2N 4NW

An imprint of Century Hutchinson Ltd

London Melbourne Sydney Auckland
Johannesburg and agencies throughout
the world

First published by
Century Publishing Co. Ltd 1985
Arrow edition 1986

© George Thomas 1985

Printed and bound in Great Britain by
Guernsey Press Limited,
Guernsey, C.I.

ISBN 0 09 944590 5

Contents

Acknowledgements

I wish to express my heartfelt gratitude to all those who encouraged me to write my memoirs, especially my parliamentary colleagues, my friend Sir Julian Hodge, Richard Broyd of the Bodysgallen Hotel, Llandudno and Alecos Michaeliades of Paphos Beach Hotel, Cyprus. Much of this book was written in these two places.

I extend my particular thanks to Patrick and Mary Cormack, Giles Gordon, Miss Elsie Beaton MBE, my private secretary, and to David Tytler for all his help. I would also like to thank Stephen Marsden, Christopher Pryce and Fred Tyrell, my agent in Cardiff West, who has been an unfailing source of encouragement.

Foreword

When my memoirs were first published, the reaction of a handful of Parliamentarians caused great excitement. I was much surprised that some who had presented themselves as champions of open government protested that neither Parliament nor people should learn of the "behind the scenes" pressures to which Speakers of the House of Commons had been subjected.

The Speaker enjoys enormous power in Parliament, but his real authority springs from his total impartiality. This is as important a quality behind the scenes as it is in the public gaze when he sits in his chair in the Commons.

I have thought it right to reveal how difficult it can be for the Speaker to resist pressures that are put upon him. Others have writen trenchantly about the conduct of Cabinet Affairs in government and they have revealed much more than I have thought it necessary to do in writing of my life as Speaker.

My purpose in lifting just a corner of the veil that surrounds the Speaker's Office is to make life easier for my successors by showing the sort of background tensions that test the strength of character of the Speaker.

By far the easiest part of the Speaker's job is presiding over the proceedings in the Chamber. This comes out clearly in my memoirs.

It never was my intention to hurt individuals. I was sorry that some who are quite uninhibited in their criticisms of fellow Parliamentarians have proved highly sensitive when references are made to themselves. But my story could only be told by reference to people who played a major part in Parliament throughout my Speakership.

My book is directed to strengthening our Parliamentary Democracy by increasing protection for the impartiality of Speakers in the House of Commons.

I believe in our Parliamentary system with every fibre of my being. I honour and love the House of Commons, and I nourish enormous respect for the Office of the Speaker. My hope and belief is that these memoirs will serve to strengthen our democracy by shedding light on its proceedings. In this way I have tried to keep faith with Parliament and with the British people.

My heart is full of gratitude for the countless blessings I have received in my travel from our miner's cottage in the Rhondda Valley to the shining splendours of Speaker's House at Westminster.

I hope that the reader will capture something of the thankfulness I feel for all God's mercies to me.

George Thomas
Tonypandy
Cardiff 1986

CHAPTER ONE

Invitation to a Wedding

I have been very fortunate to have had high peaks in my life which have taken me to places and introduced me to people I could never have dreamed of as a boy in the Rhondda. Looking back now I can see how providence has guided my life on a path set by my mother who was the single most important influence in my life.

She introduced me to chapel and then into the growing Labour movement in Wales, of which she was a vital part all her life – known as Mam to all involved, at first in Cardiff and then at Westminster. When I first discussed with her my growing conviction that I was being called to be ordained as a Methodist minister but was only too aware of all the difficulties that would undoubtedly lie ahead, she reacted calmly and with love as she always did: "George, if that is what God intended, then the doors will open."

And doors did open. Not to the life of an ordained minister but to a public life which took me from backbench Labour MP to junior minister, to membership of the Cabinet, and then to one of the most historic offices of state in Britain, the Speaker of the House of Commons in the Palace of Westminster.

In my seven years in the Chair during a very difficult period in our history, with some of our age-old traditions and values being challenged at every turn, there were rich moments, any one of which would have been compensation enough for the darker patches of my life both inside and outside Parliament.

The beginning of one of those moments, which would have a far larger impact than I could ever have imagined, came one morning as I sat in my private lounge in Speaker's House at Westminster opening my letters. It was my rule that only I opened any envelope with the word private written on top. And a very good rule it was too.

I could see that this one was from the Archbishop of Canterbury, Robert Runcie, a man I had come to know well. The Archbishop had written to say that Prince Charles wanted me to read the lesson at his wedding to Lady Diana Spencer in St Paul's Cathedral on 29 July 1981. For someone who had spent his life in churches as a Methodist lay preacher, that word "the" caught my eye. It meant I was to read the only lesson. The Archbishop went on to point out that I was a Methodist, therefore could represent the Free Churches in St Paul's; I was the Speaker, therefore could represent Parliament; I was also Welsh, and after all, it was the wedding of the Prince of Wales.

As I read the Archbishop's words, I looked at my mother's picture on the mantelpiece and thought, if only you were here now. She would have been as moved as I was that the Prince of Wales, who could have asked any crowned head in the world to read the lesson at his wedding, had asked me, a miner's son, to do so.

I wrote to thank Prince Charles, who sent me a very moving letter in which he expressed the wish that I would do him the very great honour of reading the lesson. It was typical of Prince Charles but I knew very well who was giving the great honour.

On the Monday night before the wedding the Queen and Prince Philip gave a reception for Prince Charles and Lady Diana at Buckingham Palace and I remember thinking that it was a bit unlucky to have the reception before the marriage. But with a Royal wedding there is little choice because of the large number of people involved and the need for the couple to leave for the honeymoon almost immediately after the ceremony with the crowds waving and the television cameras poised.

When I climbed those steep stairs to the reception room at Buckingham Palace – and there are a lot of stairs in Buckingham Palace – I was met at the top by the Prince and Lady Diana. They were radiant, they were happy, and Prince Charles teased me about reading the lesson carefully. As I left them I said, "God bless you both." Neither of them knew what I was going to say but instinctively they both said exactly the same thing: "And God bless you, George," which touched me very deeply.

When I had finished speaking to them I moved on and saw the Queen, whom I had not noticed. I apologised to her but she simply said, "Well, it's their night. We are here to support them." A little further on was the Queen Mother, who had had a fall during the Trooping the Colour the previous month and had hurt her leg. I was anxious that if she stood too long at the reception she might not be able to go to St Paul's. It was a foolish thing even to think.

The Queen Mother's determination is incredible and nothing would have kept her away from her grandson's wedding. For there is undoubtedly a special bond between her and Prince Charles going back to his childhood when the young prince spent many months with his grandmother while his parents were away on various royal tours.

That night Buckingham Palace must have seen one of the happiest parties ever to have been held in its awe-inspiring rooms – with the establishment on parade but outshone by a great crowd of the wedding couple's young friends.

As I left I was both moved and thankful. The Prince and Princess of Wales are clearly a natural couple happy in themselves and with each other. I was rather surprised by the spontaneity of Lady Diana, who is naturally shy, and this was only the second time I had met her. I had, of course, known Prince Charles since 1969 when I was Secretary of State for Wales at the time of his investiture as Prince of Wales at Caernarfon Castle.

I had first met Lady Diana after a special Privy Council meeting attended by Commonwealth Prime Ministers and representatives from across the world called by the Queen to Buckingham Palace to hear the engagement announced. All the formal words were used, the Queen giving her son all his names, as she gave her official approval to her son "entering into a contract of marriage". I remember the phrase so well, but despite the formality there was no disguising the Queen's enormous pleasure.

When we came out of the Privy Council the Queen entertained us to lunch with the Prince and Lady Diana. To my great joy I sat next to Lady Diana and throughout lunch we were sharing jokes, talking and laughing as we discussed our mutual interest in children and the things they do. We both saw Prince Charles look across clearly wondering what we were talking and laughing about.

I am a believer in the traditions of our country, which would never have survived into the second half of the twentieth century had they not been good traditions, strong enough to withstand the battering and close examination by those who would sweep them away. I was never a republican and would certainly not have held a Cardiff seat for thirty-eight years had I expressed republican sentiments. When Royalty comes to visit, the people of Cardiff turn out in their tens of thousands.

In some ways, the idea of monarchy is illogical but it works well for

Britain, providing stability and a focal point for the affections of our people, keeping loyalty to the country, as embodied in the Queen as head of state, separate from loyalty to party politics, as represented by the Prime Minister of the day.

The argument in favour of the Crown is helped immeasurably by the nature of the present Royal family. Seen as dedicated and honourable, the Queen, as head of a strongly knit family, has done more than anybody else to secure British Royalty. Her sense of duty has been passed on to Prince Charles. But in recognising the debts owed to the Queen I also believe that Prince Philip has done more for the family and the country than many people either realise or are prepared to admit. Prince Charles has learned a lot from his father and often I have seen his father's character assert itself when Prince Charles suddenly speaks out. And why shouldn't they speak out?

The monarchy neither wants nor claims political power and the Royal family must steer clear of party politics, as they do. But I think it is absurd in the 1980s to expect British Royalty not to be free to express opinions – so long as they are not party political. It must be frustrating enough as it is to be as careful as they are. To inhibit them further would be to diminish them.

At the time of the wedding it was certainly not the Royal family who were diminished, but a handful of Labour MPs who announced they would not even be watching the wedding on television. They had better things to do, they said.

I thought that was really very silly, because they were clearly out of touch with the people they represented. Any Member of Parliament who said that his personal predilections came before those of his constituents was free to do so, but he certainly was not representative of the people as a whole. The country rejoiced in that wedding, many thousands of young people amongst those who packed the streets of London, turning the day into a national celebration and taking no notice of the handful who did not want to join in.

My own guess is that if the left wing came out openly and said they were against the monarchy, they would get even less support than they do at present, because the British public are not republican-minded. They take a real joy out of the Royal family and want to share in their celebrations, as was seen at the Queen's Jubilee, the Queen Mother's eightieth birthday and the wedding. I remember thinking at the time of his wedding that Prince Charles had a better understanding of how people feel than many of those on the far left.

But parliamentary business did mean that I was unable to attend the rehearsal the day before the Wednesday wedding. Tuesday was Prime Minister's Question Time in the House and as Speaker, Royal Wedding or not, I had to be there.

The rehearsal was full dress, with the Prince and Lady Diana, but my place was taken by my Secretary, Sir Noel Short. He always looked after me well and when he came back in the evening he said, "There are just two things you ought to know, Mr Speaker, but I will tell you tomorrow just before you go so that it will be fresh in your mind."

I went to bed rather late that night going over the arrangements for the following very special day, but when it finally came, I picked up my Bible to read a few passages as I had every morning for as long as I can remember. Only that morning it was Corinthians 13, the wedding lesson that would be heard by 750 million people across the world. And I read it out loud as I sat alone in my bedroom.

Then I put on my state uniform, the legal court dress of a Queen's Counsel, with knee breeches, long black stockings and buckled shoes, and went into the lounge to read the lesson out loud again. I reminded myself that I had read this lesson a thousand times, in different chapels and churches throughout the country, and in other countries too. If I could not read a lesson in a service without getting agitated, then there was something seriously wrong with me.

So I said a prayer, as I always do before major occasions, and in came Sir Noel, a fine upstanding man but not always seen as the answer to a prayer, to tell me the two things I would have to remember. He explained that because I was reading the lesson I would be sitting with the clergy in the stalls behind the choir. I would have to leave my seat while the choir was singing the Gloria and make my way across to the lectern and, in doing so, have to miss a formidable obstacle.

In St Paul's, as in many Anglican churches, there is a tall iron stand with an enormous display of flowers, and Sir Noel warned that unless I sidled past it very carefully, I would knock it over. I was a little subdued after hearing that. The Day the Speaker Knocked Over the Flowers could become the talking point of the wedding-watchers instead of the wedding itself. And that would never do.

Then came the second warning. There was, according to Sir Noel, an invisible step on the floor of St Paul's. If I failed to see it I would trip, fall flat on my face and join the flowers.

I paid good attention to the advice, and when the choir began to sing the Gloria, I edged past the flowers gently and gingerly. Suddenly the conductor got so excited he knocked the lampshade off one of the choir-stall lights. As he stooped down to pick it up I saw the step, so I was safe. Divine providence had intervened again. The Royal couple, just like any young couple about to be married, nervous no doubt but happy, were sitting right in front of me and as I came down to the lectern for the lesson they both gave me a smile. Naturally I was about to smile back when I realised that they had their backs to the cameras. I was facing the cameras, and I felt that people watching on television would think I had a nerve to be smiling at them, so I compromised and just gave them a brief acknowledgement.

There are two other very clear memories of the service: the beautiful singing of the New Zealand opera star, Kiri Te Kanawa, whom I could only hear, not see, in the obscured vastness of St Paul's, and the courage of Lady Diana's father, Earl Spencer, who had to make the long walk escorting his daughter from the main door to the high altar after a very serious illness which had left him unsteady on his feet. There was not a single guest in the cathedral who did not fear that he might fall, who willed him safely down that aisle, as did the millions who watched his uncertain progress on television.

But the Earl, a former attaché to the Queen, had a father's pride and love for his daughter that beat any physical weakness and helped to add to the overwhelming feeling in St Paul's that whatever else might be happening there, we were all taking part in a Christian family wedding service, a traditional and central part of British family life.

It was immediately on leaving my seat in the choir stalls that I had the first indication that the reading had gone well. Others were to follow in letters and requests to visit various churches; all I believe because people listening or watching understood that I believed in what I was reading. But the very first word came from the Roman Catholic Cardinal of Westminster, Basil Hume, who was behind me and whispered, "A-plus, George."

It had been a marvellous day, but there was still one small memory to come. I returned to Speaker's House, where like millions of others the staff had been watching the television broadcast of the service, in time to see the bride and groom in their carriage decorated with balloons go on their way to Waterloo and Lord Mountbatten's home Broadlands in the New Forest. We all rushed to the window to wave.

All I could find was a tea towel, which I grabbed and shook furiously. At that moment Prince Charles and the new Princess of Wales looked up, saw me and returned my waves with their own.

That night I reflected on all that had happened, not just on 29 July 1981, but all the events, the laughter and the sadness that had taken me to Speaker's House at Westminster. And inevitably I came back to my family, the mother who had supported and loved me, the brother who had gone down the mines at thirteen so that I, the second son, as was the custom in the valleys of Wales, could be supported at school.

So much had happened since my grandfather had moved his family from Hampshire to Wales all those years ago.

CHAPTER TWO

The Beginning of the Road

My memory of my grandfather, John Tilbury, is still very clear. He had a cherubic, reddish face with a big white beard, and just before his last birthday, his seventy-ninth, a child asked him, "Are you Father Christmas?" He replied, "No, my son, but I belong to him."

A hero figure to me and my mother, he had come to the Rhondda Valley in 1872, when he was thirty-four years old. His family had lived for generations in Clanfield, Hampshire, where they had withstood the antagonism of the local vicar and founded the Clanfield Methodist Chapel. The local church establishment was so opposed to Nonconformity that John Tilbury had to run a small business buying and selling fruit to maintain his independence. It was while he was in Bristol selling his fruit that he met my grandmother, Elizabeth Loyns.

The granddaughter of a Frenchman who had fled to Somerset during the Revolution's Reign of Terror, grandmother grew up on a farm in West Buckland, near Wellington in Somerset. When my grandfather met her, Elizabeth was engaged in service as a lady's maid, but after their marriage they rented a drapery shop in Petersfield High Street.

My Aunt Lizzie and my Uncle Jack were born in the room above the shop but the family were soon on the move after hearing stories of the rapid industrial development in South Wales where new pits were being sunk every month.

The scars of the coal industry were yet to appear and the Rhondda Valley was thickly wooded with birch, mountain ash, elm trees and oak. My grandfather used to enjoy telling me how a squirrel could jump from one tree to another, from the top of the valley to the bottom.

Showing a shrewd business instinct, my grandfather, who began his new life in Wales as a greengrocer, switched to work as a building contractor. The fast-growing coal industry sucked in its manpower from England as well as from rural Wales, and grandfather set about building long rows of houses for the immigrant labour, soon establishing a highly profitable business.

So my mother, Emma Jane, was born into a comfortable Tonypandy home on 12 January 1881, the sixth of seven children, with Annie, George, Arthur and Ada being the other four born in Wales. They were a happy and closely knit family whose life centred around the English Methodist chapel established by John Tilbury and another English immigrant John Hearn. The need for a separate English chapel became apparent as soon as my grandfather discovered that only Welsh was used in the Welsh chapels. There was one other change he had to make to his churchgoing in Wales.

On his very first Sunday in Tonypandy, he dressed to go to the local church as he would have for chapel in Petersfield. When he arrived back home, he announced to my grandmother, "I'll not wear my frock coat and top hat to go to church again, Elizabeth. People were turning to stare at me as we passed."

I don't remember my grandmother, who died aged sixty-three in 1910, the year after I was born, but from all accounts family life was happy and comparatively comfortable. The only serious argument arose when my mother told her parents that she had decided to marry a young miner called Zachariah Thomas. They were both nineteen years old, and he was the first boy she had been out with. She often said later, "I probably would not have gone with him, except that I wanted to show off to Lizzie." My Aunt Lizzie had once seen them talking together and said to my mother, "Go home! Leave him," which had upset my mother's pride and made her more determined than ever.

So they married in 1900 and their family quickly grew: Ada May was born in 1902, Dolly in 1904 and Emrys in 1906. My brother Ivor and I were both born in 1909: I in January and Ivor in December. My mother used to enjoy telling the fact that when I was born I already had two teeth cut. Ivor and I were often mistaken for twins, and my mother relished telling the story of how she used to nurse us both at the same time. When she thought we were asleep, she would put us down on the bed. Ivor would dutifully sleep, but I would invariably open my eyes and yell for attention!

My father's family came to the Rhondda from Carmarthen, leaving farmwork for the attractions of a miner's wage. They were thoroughly Welsh, worshipping at the Welsh Congregational Church in Penygraig and speaking only in Welsh to each other. If only he had known it my father could have saved me considerable difficulties in my later political life when the militants in Wales were forever criticising my spoken Welsh. My mother was quick to recognise the advantages in being bilingual but no matter how often she asked him to speak to us in Welsh he always refused.

He would always say, "What's the use of me talking Welsh to the children if you don't understand it?" My mother's constant plea that she would learn it with us was brushed aside. I believe now that he was so anxious to improve his English that he could not spare a thought for the advantage we would have gained by being bilingual. One of my regrets is that my spoken Welsh is faulty because I never used it at home. I had to manage as best I could when speaking to my father's mother, who knew only one word of English: "damn".

It was around 1908 that my parents moved from Trealaw in the Rhondda, where their marriage and family had begun with such hope, to Port Talbot, where they stayed for two years and where family life started to crumble.

I am not sure why the move was made but I do know that those two years were critical for the family. It was then that my father began to drink. He would not have known the taste of alcohol in the Rhondda, but with no chapel, relatives or friends to keep an eye on him, he must have been persuaded to drink by somebody from the pit where he worked. Poor fellow, he couldn't take it. It ruined him and while he lived with us made my mother's life intolerable.

By the time we left Port Talbot and returned to Penygraig, there were constant bouts of heavy drinking. Even now my stomach sinks when I remember the scenes when he came back to our home in Hughes Street, Penygraig, after a drinking session. His alcoholic rages made him irresponsible and cruel. He smashed furniture and would hit out indiscriminately at my mother and we children. Saturday nights, when he had money to spend, were a nightmare.

I suppose he felt angry because we were all hanging round his coat-tails, stopping his freedom; he was still under thirty by the time we were all born, and no doubt resented his responsibilities. And there was so much ignorance then. There was no birth control and even after my mother married she still did not know how children were born. She had to ask the lady who did the washing for her mother how it would happen.

Even then we were fortunate in the friends we had around us. Across the road from our home was an infants' school and one of the teachers,

Miss Gould, a member of Tonypandy Methodist Chapel, took pity on my mother's struggle to care for Ivor and myself all day.

When I was two and a half, she suggested that I should begin school, and so, by the time I was three, I was learning to count with beads. All I remember of the school is that I pushed one of the beads right up my nose, where it stuck. Miss Gould and another teacher spent ages struggling with a hairpin trying to get it out, with me sneezing every time they touched me. Eventually I sneezed the bead free.

Ivor and I were always very close, and one day, when Mam wasn't looking, we went off hand-in-hand to explore. We were finally found in the grounds of the Naval Colliery, Penygraig, and taken to the police station. I clearly remember a huge policeman – or so he seemed to me – hoisting us on to a table and giving us chocolate as he tried to find out where we lived. We couldn't tell him!

Another memory of that time casts a much darker shadow. We had a neighbour, an old man called Mr Morgan, of whom I was very fond, and when he died I was lifted up to see him in his coffin and told to touch him. It was a terrible shock, and for over thirty years I was very frightened of death. All through my teens, whenever I drew near to a home where there had been a death, I would cross the road, rather than walk by on the pavement past the front room where the body would be lying.

I was five when the First World War broke out, and I can remember my father carrying me on his shoulders right down the main street of Penygraig. Everyone seemed to be going in the same direction, and they were all talking excitedly, saying that war had been declared and we were going to put the Germans in their place.

My father joined up at once, and at first it was heaven to be without him. There were no scenes, no troubles, and my mother seemed happy. But then one day she went to claim her allowance as a soldier's wife and discovered that someone in Kent, where my father had been stationed before being posted to Salonika, had already been granted his allowance. She had to go to court and show her marriage certificate before the allowance could revert to her, and the other poor woman could not claim anything. We never saw my father again. He went back to Kent after the war, and in 1925 died of tuberculosis.

Many years later, when I was driving with my mother to a National Union of Teachers' conference in Margate, we passed a signpost to the village where my father had lived. On the spur of the moment we decided to visit it and that was the closest we ever came to him or his new family after he had left us.

After my father's departure we were very poor, even with the army allowance, and we had to leave our home in Hughes Street to live in an underhouse at 139, Miskin Road, Trealaw. The word is hardly known now but an underhouse is a basement little better than a cellar.

There was a small living-room with one window and a door that opened on to the pavement, and two poky bedrooms with no windows at all. They were dark all day. We shared an outside lavatory – always referred to as "the dub" – with three other families, and my mother did her washing on the pavement in a wooden tub balanced on two chairs. Both my sisters went into service when they left school at thirteen, so after the age of eight I grew up with just Emrys and Ivor.

In those days there was a certain disgrace about receiving public help, and people would do any work to keep their families going. Mam used to do sewing or take in washing. Often, despite her worries, I would hear her sing as she rubbed the clothes on the scrubbing-board.

I remember waking one night and seeing the light reflected on the landing wall. I crept quietly out of bed so that I would not disturb my brothers, who shared the same bed, and as noiselessly as I could, tiptoed to the stairs to look over the banister into our living-room below. There was Mam, in the light of our oil-lamp on the table, busily sewing a dress she was making for one of the neighbours. Some instinct told her she was being watched, and she looked straight up at me and whispered, "George, what are you doing there?" I whispered to her, "What time is it, Mam?" She replied very softly, "It's two o'clock. Go back to bed and don't wake the others."

My young mind was in a whirl. I knew that Mam took in other people's sewing to earn enough to feed and clothe us. Young as I was, I wondered why other families should have a father who went out to work to keep the family. I lay awake in bed promising myself that one day my mother would not have to stay up working until two in the morning in order to look after us.

Our sparsely furnished living-room had a stone floor which was scrubbed with a hard brush every day, and was dominated by a splendid overmantel above the fireplace. It had a large centre mirror and three smaller ones, each with a shelf in front, decorated with twelve large brass candlesticks, which my brother and I cleaned every Saturday morning. There was also a mounted picture of the Wellington Monument near my grandmother's old home in Somerset. In front of the fire we had a home-made rag mat, and whenever it wore out, Emrys, Ivor and I made a new one.

Friday night was bath night. We put a large tin bath in front of the fire and filled it with water that had been heated in saucepans on the open coal fire. After taking our turn to bath, we would gather round Mam's rocking-chair, where she sat wearing her black sheen apron, and kneel to say our prayers. She would finish our prayers by asking God to help us to grow into good men and to bless our home.

The final act every night was for Mam to light the candles for us to take to our bedrooms before she lowered the wick of the oil-lamp and blew it out. Then my brothers and I jumped into the same bed, which we shared until we moved in 1925, when I was fifteen.

On Halloween night, the tin bath had quite a different function. Emrys, Ivor and I would fill it three-quarters full with cold water, strip to the waist, and then bob for the apples Mam always had for us on that day. It was great fun, putting our heads right down in the water to bite an apple.

During the war, nearly everything was in short supply. We queued for tea and butter, and once Mam walked three miles to Porth and queued for hours to buy some pork. We even queued for buckets when we heard that a shop in Penygraig had some in stock. When peace was declared, a crowd of boys in the village got together and kicked a large empty tomato tin all the way up the main road in Tonypandy, shouting: "The war is over! The war is over!"

There were many things we could not afford and had to do without, but Emrys, Ivor and I always had Sunday suits. We were allowed to wear them only to chapel, and had to take them off as soon as we got home. In chapel, we always sat behind Grandpa in his front pew seat made for two.

One Sunday, when he was coming home to our house afterwards, I started to whistle a hymn tune. "George," he said, "do you know what day it is?" "Sunday, Grandpa." "Well, it's the Lord's day. You don't whistle on the Lord's day." We had to be so careful in observing Sunday and that thought stays with me even now, yet I can never remember not enjoying chapel or Sunday School.

The Nonconformist chapels in those days were the citadels of reform and I grew up hearing stories of how the Church of England bishops were in favour of hanging and flogging and keeping the workers in their proper station, and how they had blessed the guns at the beginning of the war.

Most chapel members were Liberals, and when, in 1915, my mother joined the Labour Party, somebody told her she ought to be ashamed of herself when her father was such a good Liberal. She went straight to him and said, "Father, are you feeling upset because I have joined the Labour Party? Somebody told me I ought to be ashamed; that I am bringing disgrace to you." He smiled, and said, "No, Emma – the Liberals were the radicals when I was young. If I was your age, I'd probably be joining the Labour Party."

By now I was at the Trealaw Boys' School, where there was a teacher called Mr Thomas, who had an index finger that was stiff, like a piece of wood. He used to come and sit by us and dig it in our ribs to make us jump. It was at that school that I unsuccessfully first tried to shed one of my names.

My full name is Thomas George Thomas, and in Wales such duplication invariably leads to the nickname Tommy Twice. At the beginning of term my form teacher asked me my name, and I whispered, "Thomas," and then added much more loudly, "George Thomas." I was brusquely told to speak up, and had to repeat all three names clearly.

Like other children of our time we had to make our own amusement without the facilities of today, so when we wanted to play football, we either had to play in the street with a boy on the lookout for the policeman, or else climb up the mountain to where there was a plateau. There were no public playing fields and certainly no swimming pools.

The River Rhondda was out of bounds because it was so dirty. I went in just once, and it was no good trying to pretend to my mother that I had not, for I was absolutely black, like a miner. I got a beating on my backside for that.

In the summers just after the war, my mother managed to save to take us for a week's holiday in Swansea. We used to take all our own food, and booked just one room with a lovely lady called Mrs Leonard. She was poor too, but she always gave us a great welcome. We used to spend all day every day playing on the beach.

Most of my classmates at Trealaw expected to leave school at thirteen, and many would go straight down the pit. It sounds incredible today, yet because of the manly image of the work, we used to listen to those stories about life underground and feel quite envious of those who had already started.

I first realised the cruel side of mining when I was ten. Going home from school one day, I saw a grisly procession of miners carrying home the body of one of their mates who had been killed at work. Like everyone else, I stopped and doffed my school cap to pay a silent tribute, and then I made myself look at the body as it was carried past. It was covered with some dirty sacking and I remember thinking: "It's like carrying a dead dog."

It was the first strong stirring in me of resentment against social injustice, the beginning of dreams of reform. But, as Mam knew, dreams were not enough. Education mattered too, and she used to tell me about one of her friends whose son had letters after his name. The mere telling of that story was intended to inspire me to the same.

In the year that I witnessed the grim procession of miners, I sat the scholarship examination for Tonypandy Higher Grade School. When my teacher came to tell me I had passed, I raced out of school and ran the half mile home. Mam was out on the pavement doing some washing, and I could hardly speak for excitement as I panted out the news.

She was obviously delighted but I had to ask the urgent question. Could we afford for me to go? I knew that although the Labour Council had recently abolished secondary-school fees, we would have to pay for a school uniform. Still smiling, she replied, "We'll manage somehow."

As I approached the school gates on my first day, I was surprised to see all the bigger boys doffing their school caps to the road sweeper who was busy brushing the pavement and gutter. I duly copied them, but asked one big boy, "Why do we take off our caps for him? He's the road sweeper." It was a snobbish attitude to take, but I had a lot to learn. When I was told, "He won the Chair for Poetry at the National Eisteddfod. He is a great man," I felt ashamed of myself.

It did not take the school bullies long to realise that not only was I the youngest and shortest boy there, but I was not much good at fighting either. Every playtime I had to run like a hare escaping from hounds as the bigger boys chased after me and bullied me unmercifully. This torture went on until one of the other boys was so horrified by my misery that he told a teacher, Miss Firstbrook, what was happening. The headmaster summoned the whole school and, without mentioning my name, threatened to expel any boy caught bullying in future. After that, I was very happy there.

During my time the school was promoted from Tonypandy Higher Grade to Tonypandy Secondary Grammar School. We had some brilliant teachers, particularly Miss Llewellyn, the English mistress, and we used to think Miss Firstbrook was marvellous because she came up from Cardiff on a noisy old motorbike!

But I am afraid that the history mistress was not the cause of my deep interest in history; that developed later. She would come into the room and at once start dictating a lecture. It just poured out. She would say, "Full stop," and rush on to the next sentence: we were supposed to take it all down. She was a fine person, who later became a friend of Mam's, but her method was enough to kill any love of history.

Six months after I started at that school, Emrys left Trealaw Boys' School and went down the pit. Three years later, when he too was thirteen, Ivor started work in a shop. They were both very proud of me, and I felt I had to study hard because of them. Thankfully there was no gap between grammar-school boys and others in our valley – if there had been, I doubt if I would have stayed at school.

I owe my brothers a lot. When Emrys received his pay envelope at the end of the week, he never opened it. He would take it home and give it to Mam, who would hand him back two shillings. Even this he used to put on the overmantel and tell Mam it was there if she needed some more money before Saturday.

During his first week down the pit he cut his leg, but he just said he was grateful it was his leg and not his face: his trousers could hide the blue mark that the hardened coal dust always left in the flesh wounds miners got underground. There weren't any pithead baths, and when Emrys used to come home in the afternoons, we would leave the living-room while he had his bath in front of the fire. Miners resisted the idea of pithead baths at first because bathing in public was not their tradition. They were also afraid of fleas jumping from one person's pile of clothes to another. When baths were finally installed, the coal owners had to guarantee that the space between one clothes peg and another was further than a flea could jump!

Thanks to Mam's encouragement we all enjoyed reading. Our books were nearly all borrowed from the library, but once, when I was about fourteen, someone published a history of the Co-operative Women's Guild and our local Guild branch decided to club together to buy a copy. Since she was their president, Mam had it to read first. At the time, we had a dog called Fido, and one morning when we got up for breakfast we discovered Fido had made a meal of the book – there it was in tatters. I asked, "What ever will you do, Mam?" She saw the funny side of it and just laughed and said, "We'll have to save up and buy another one."

The Methodist Church, which my grandfather had helped to establish on the corner of Tonypandy main street, grew too small for all the town activities, and it was decided to pull it down and build a Central Hall. The old church had continued to be the pivot of our lives, and besides religious services we attended dramas, concerts, discussion groups and lectures there. The new Central Hall was to seat a thousand people, and Grandpa would take his camp-stool and sit on the pavement to watch the builders at work. It was an imposing structure which he called "The Greater Temple".

He was a little uneasy, though, about the billiard room that was to be included. I used to love to stand beside his stool and listen to his comments, and I remember him saying, "George, I am too old, and I like things to be as I have been accustomed to them. But I must not stand in the way of change: if the chapel thinks a billiard room is right, then I will not say anything against it."

My grandfather was invited to perform the opening ceremony of Tonypandy Methodist Central Hall but he died in 1923 shortly before the opening. All the community turned out for his funeral, and in the fashion of the day, his coffin was carried by friends the two or three miles to the cemetery. It would have been considered a disgrace if we had employed a hearse, because neighbours wanted to pay their last tribute by carrying the body to the graveside.

Before the procession left the house, a large number of men dressed in black assembled and sang the first and last verses of a hymn. Then they set off, stopping every few hundred yards to change coffin bearers and sing another hymn.

It was only a few months later with memories of grandfather very much in our minds that Emrys, Ivor and I put on our Boys' Brigade uniforms and marched through the streets of Tonypandy in the opening procession for Grandpa's "Greater Temple".

Even then I was becoming used to taking part in public services and that afternoon read the first lesson in the new Central Hall, having read the last lesson at Sunday School in the old church before it was demolished. Sadly, I was also to preach the last sermon in the Central Hall, before it was closed for lack of support in 1981.

CHAPTER THREE

To the Barricades

Life changed dramatically for us all in 1925 when I was sixteen. Among Mam's friends from childhood was a miner called Tom Davies, and early that year they told us they had decided to marry. It was an anxious time for me, as I felt we had been quite happy without him, so to begin with there was a coolness between us. But he was a generous and helpful stepfather, treating the three of us as if we were his own boys and I soon learned to respect him. I called him Dad Tom, and grew never to be afraid to ask him for anything. He had worked for several years underground, but in 1925 he was a winding engineer, lowering and raising the cage carrying the miners or trucks of coal, one of the best-paid jobs at the pit.

Mam's marriage meant that we could leave Miskin Road and move to a three-storey house at 201, Trealaw Road, one of a block built by my grandfather. For the first time in my life I had a bedroom of my own and somewhere to study without interruption – but not before we had got rid of the black beetles. Hordes of them infested the house, making some of the floors look as if they were moving. The remedy was to put pieces of cucumber skin all round the skirting boards: evidently beetles cannot bear either the smell or the taste. It worked – but to this day if I am presented with cucumber I push it firmly to the edge of my plate.

Two other decisions were made that year that were to determine the course of the rest of my life. The first was to join the Labour Party.

As well as being president of the local Co-operative Women's Guild, Mam was elected chairman of the Tonypandy Labour Ward, and I used to go to meetings with her. She was a very eloquent speaker, even though she had once been tremendously shy, so much so that when there were visitors at her parents' house, she would sometimes wait outside to avoid meeting them. She and I both believed that having to fight to bring up her children changed her, so by the time

I remember her, she could stand and face large crowds calmly, even when her speeches were interrupted by noisy Communist hecklers. Even then the Labour Party had difficulties with the hard left.

I made another decision that year one Sunday at a special youth service when the minister, the Reverend W. G. Hughes, appealed to all of us there to commit our lives to Christ. Those who were prepared to accept the call were asked to give public proof of their commitment by walking up to the platform where he stood. I felt myself go hot and cold. The challenge seemed directed straight at me. I said a silent prayer, and stepped forward. It was the watershed of my life and ever since then I have started each day with a moment of silent prayer.

So the pattern of my life began to form. At the same time the pattern for the country began to change. The reforms many of us were dreaming about were not so far away but first we had to suffer the agony of the General Strike.

Shortly before it began the Reverend R. J. Barker was appointed minister of Tonypandy Central Hall. His sermons were never less than forty-five minutes long, yet people would queue for an hour before the service to get in and there were seldom less than a thousand to listen to him. He was typical of those English middle class who are in a state of rebellion against the conditions of the poor compared with the comfort of their own people, and he was an essential part of the very radical atmosphere in which I grew up, when we all talked of revolution and of changing the system.

He was also an ardent fighter against Communism and taught me the importance of the individual and individual conscience, the basis of our democracy, which guarantees the rights of the individual at the same time as it depends on individual responsibility being accepted.

Tonypandy was already famous for its radical tradition. The year after I was born the pits had combined to strike against their owners and the Tonypandy riots followed. Troops were sent to subdue the rioters, and although Winston Churchill later denied giving the order to send them, he took the responsibility as Home Secretary. I was always told that the rioters came from over the mountains, but that it was our people who went to jail. The police behaved savagely; they brought in reinforcements from outside who could not even understand the Welsh accent, let alone Welsh ways. I used to hear stories of how they beat up people in their own homes, behaviour which caused a deep hostility and lack of trust that lasted throughout my childhood.

The people of Tonypandy retaliated as the Celts had against the

Romans: they went up the mountains to find the huge stones left behind by the Ice Age and rolled them down the slopes to keep the police away. By the time I was seventeen, the men who had rolled the stones were in their forties and were leaders on the Council and in the community. All of them had gone down the pit when only ten.

All these memories were revived when on 1 May 1926, the miners were locked out for refusing to accept a reduction in wages. There followed an agreement between the TUC and the Cabinet for ending the lock-out. But as soon as Churchill, then Chancellor of the Exchequer, heard that the compositors on the *Daily Mail* had refused to set an article condemning the miners, he tore up the agreement. The TUC then called a General Strike.

At first there was an almost carnival atmosphere in Tonypandy as the striking miners packed the main street, with every one of us expecting success. When the news came through nine days later that the TUC had capitulated, exhilaration changed at once to despair. I remember walking home fearful of what would happen to us. My fears were well-founded. Nine months of the miners' strike without income resulted in hardship beyond description.

Mam took a leading part in the setting up of local soup kitchens run by women volunteers on rota to provide one good meal a day for the children of the unemployed. The children liked the times when fish and chips or boiled eggs were served. I badly wanted to join my school friends for their communal meals in a chapel vestry, but as a safety man my stepfather was still at work so I did not qualify. But I do remember one day when the other women helpers persuaded Mam to let me enjoy fish and chips with the others because I had acted as errand boy for the organisers.

I also remember the terrible story of a former president of the Tonypandy Co-operative Women's Guild, who was sent to London to raise money for our soup kitchens. She was a natural orator and a formidable fighter, but when she returned after several months her story and appearance shattered us.

She had been given lodgings in a home where they could not afford to feed her. Day after day she had been out at street corners speaking to working people and collecting their coppers. They had also given her cups of tea and buns, which was all she had to live on for more than three months. Eventually she was completely worn out and came home to die. For years after that it was common for me to hear speakers at Labour meetings say, "Remember Joanna James." This was both a call to look after each other and a bitter reminder of the suffering endured by miners' families during the strike.

While the strike continued, we were kept going by a sense of loyalty and the faith that better days would be here soon. That was not to be: the aftermath of the industrial battle hit our community with savage cruelty. Long queues of unemployed workers snaked their way to the labour exchange, and men were forced to tell lies in order to get the fifteen shillings dole money.

The law meant that dole was paid only to those who could prove they were "genuinely seeking work", but since the only source of possible employment was the silent pits, miners were forced to compile fictitious lists of pits they had visited to ask for work. It was a charade, and the community felt degraded.

One way to fight back was to make sour jokes about the system. Mark Harcombe, a tremendously gifted leader of the Mid-Rhondda miners, used to tell of a man who called at the Naval Colliery, Penygraig, to look for work. The manager spoke sharply: "You know there's no work here, Dai. Come back in the spring." Instantly the reply came: "What do you think I am? A bloody cuckoo?" I can still hear the laughs of a cinema full of unemployed miners as they heard Mark Harcombe's story mirror their own experience.

The plight of those who failed to qualify for unemployment pay was the worst of all. They were driven to seek help from the relief officers, usually brutal men whose insensitivity made them loathed. Before they gave any assistance, these officers undertook a rigorous scrutiny into the income being received by other members of the family. This family means test undermined closely knit families, where perhaps a sister worked for pence doing washing and cleaning, driving young people to leave the community in a frantic search for work.

On my way to school every Monday morning during that great exodus I would see little family groups on the platform of Tonypandy railway station saying tearful farewells to somebody who had found work in Slough or Birmingham or Coventry or Nuneaton. In those days that was like going to China, because they did not know when they would be able to save enough to pay for a visit home.

There was not a family in South Wales untouched by such misery: it was like a terrible war taking our people from us. My mother helped to clothe three hundred Valley girls who found jobs as domestic servants in English houses. Their clothes and railway fares were provided by the Distress Fund set up by the Lord Mayor of London, and deep bitterness filled us as one by one they left their homes. Far from being grateful, the cry on everybody's lips was: "Our daughters are cheap skivvies for well-off people."

Mark Harcombe headed the committee that distributed aid from the fund in the Mid-Rhondda, and Mam was put in charge of relief for the women of Tonypandy and Trealaw. She used to visit families to give them a credit note to buy food and other essentials.

I vividly recall going with her to one home where, for the first time in my life, I was conscious that a pregnant woman looked different from others. This woman broke down and cried as she said, "I never thought that I would come to this." My mother's eyes welled with tears and I gripped her hand as tears ran down my own face.

Often homes were without food on the days just before payment of the dole. Faced with the nightmare of feeding their children and their men, mothers would often go without meals themselves and many suffered anaemia as a result. Small shopkeepers did their best to help by allowing debts to accumulate.

In the Mid-Rhondda Co-operative Society in particular, massive debts piled up and the society was in dire straits. The general manager, Phil Rowlands, showed enormous faith in the integrity of the mining community, and his trust was not misplaced. When better times returned, very few people failed to meet their debts but many of the small shopkeepers were forced to go bankrupt. As one after the other closed down, Tonypandy's main street had as many empty shops as those still doing business.

People could no longer afford to keep a best suit for Sundays, and chapel attendance began to fall as more and more people felt too shabby to worship in public. More than eighty per cent of the congregation were unemployed, so the pennies clattering on collection plates were truly sacrificial offerings.

A poverty-stricken community does not lose its sense of dignity, and when Lady Astor referred in the House of Commons to "the ragged army of the unemployed" she provoked a storm of fury. Such was the reaction that she decided to come to Tonypandy to talk with the unemployed.

I listened to angry conversations among our local councillors as they prepared to meet her. But when the day arrived, she scored a triumph. No doubt she had dressed modestly by her standards, but by ours she looked beautiful. I watched her smile without a trace of nervousness, and in reply to inquisitive stares she gave a friendly nod.

The people accepted that the remark had been made with sympathy, and she left the unemployed miners believing they had found an ally.

During this time Mam became a South Wales district speaker for the Co-operative movement, and she travelled the area speaking on such issues as "The Need for a National Health Service", "The Case for Free School Milk", and "The Case for Tin Helmets for Miners". As with pithead baths, miners were not at first enthusiastic about helmets. There was also a reason.

Throughout the miners' strike, all our young men used to climb the mountain and dig "a level", a long cave reaching far into the mountain where there were rich seams of coal. I used to accompany my brother Emrys, who had dug a level about twenty-five feet deep, and my job was to hold the sack while he packed the coal ready for us to carry down to Tonypandy.

One day he was digging by candlelight when he gave me a terrific shove and an enormous stone, weighing several hundredweight, thundered down on to the very spot where I had been. I was thoroughly shaken and asked him how he knew the stone was going to fall. He replied: "By the sound." This was at the time when miners were reluctant to wear helmets in case it stopped them hearing warning signs of danger.

I realise now that to have grown up in the Rhondda Valley during the harsh years of the Depression was a good training for life. We were too poor to be subjected to most of the temptations that assail the present generation, and without the distraction of television we learned to rely on our own resources, to love good books and to make our own pleasures in singing and dancing.

But then my boyhood came to an end. I had to decide what to do with the rest of my life. Gradually the idea formed that I should become a school teacher, although I was grappling with the overwhelming feeling that I was being called to the life of an ordained Methodist minister.

But as the uncertainty remained, I became a pupil teacher in Trealaw and then in 1928 with my classmate Trevor Bennett took a job as an uncertified teacher in Essex, leaving my Mam and home in Tonypandy for lodgings in Chadwell Heath, near Dagenham.

CHAPTER FOUR

A Taste of Westminster

Today the journey from Wales to Essex would seem routine, but that first time was an adventure, particularly travelling across London Underground to my lodgings run by a delightful Scottish widow. She was a good landlady, and it was a comfortable house, but that didn't prevent the agonies of homesickness. Families like ours did not have telephones then so the only means of communication was by letter. It would have made such a difference had I been able to talk to them at home.

Two girls from Tonypandy Secondary School, Griselda Lewis and Margaret Howell, were also working as teachers in the area, and Trevor Bennett and I used to meet them every Tuesday night, exchanging news, and then listening to Trevor play Welsh folk tunes on his violin. After a while I would invariably say, "Give us 'The Picture of my Mother on the Wall'." Every time he played it we would have tears in our eyes and we would insist that he must never play it again. The following Tuesday he was always asked for it.

I walked the three miles to work at the newly opened Fanshawe Crescent School in Dagenham to save the bus fare. My salary was twenty-five shillings (£1.25) a week, and my lodgings cost £1. I kept two shillings and sixpence (12½p) for myself, and sent the remaining 2/6d home. I enjoyed my year there, teaching all subjects to a class of sixty-three boys and girls of around eight years old. It was in fact illegal to have more than sixty children in a class, and I was given a special second register for three of my pupils which I had to hide when the school inspector called.

During my year in Essex I applied to colleges that ran two-year teacher-training courses, as I knew we could not afford the full three-year degree course offered in Cardiff. As it was, the British Legion gave me a grant of £50, but I had to rely on home for the rest of the funds to see me through my course at University College,

Southampton. I was deeply conscious of the sacrifices Mam and Dad Tom were making for me.

Two of my oldest and dearest friends in Tonypandy were Trevor Powell and Annie Thomas. The three of us had been inseparable in chapel activities but now I was becoming very fond of Annie. So before I left home the second time, I asked Trevor to look after her until I returned to Wales.

I was unhappy to leave the Rhondda but I soon began to enjoy college life. It was a different world from the one I was used to: the sheer beauty of the grounds alone mesmerised me – even the tennis courts were grass, not concrete as in Tonypandy Grammar School. I used to lie on the grass with my books on a Saturday evening, when the others had gone out, as I had not enough money to go into town. But I did not mind that at all. There was a magnificent library and on Saturdays I had it all to myself. It was there that my love of history developed. I had a photographic memory, and when I was writing an essay, I could visualise the pages of the books I had read.

In one of my early twice-weekly letters home, I mentioned that all the other male students wore plus-fours. Rather sententiously I added, "Of course, I know we cannot afford them." I should not have done it because I knew what their reaction would be. As I had anticipated, money for plus-fours duly arrived.

My big mistake was to wear them when I went home to Tonypandy. As I walked down Trealaw Road, I passed a group of miners squatting low on the ground, talking. As I passed them, one miner spat about three yards, looked up and said, "What's the matter, George? Are you working in water?" The group collapsed in laughter. They knew that miners who had to work in water invariably tied their trousers below the knee. I coloured, and hurried home to change. Those plus-fours never saw the light of day in Tonypandy again. It reminded me of my grandfather's story of the day he wore his top hat and frock coat to chapel for the first and only time.

It was not long after I had joined the college that I had an experience that was to stay with me all my life. The Professor of Education, Joe Cock, was a deeply committed Christian with a keen social conscience, and one day he asked for volunteers to accompany him to a local school for mentally handicapped children.

I volunteered, but when I got to the school and saw in the classroom, for the first time, the twisted bodies and over-large heads, I went outside and vomited. I was so deeply distressed that I did not go back to the class but returned to college. The next day Professor Cock asked to see me and said, "Mr Thomas, you volunteered to come to the school for mentally handicapped children, yet you walked out. What is the explanation?" I told him the truth: "Sir, I am sorry, but it made me sick. I couldn't bear it."

He looked at me dispassionately and said quietly, "And what if it was one of your own family?" I was ashamed, but I tried to explain that I had never seen anyone like that before. He just said, "Are you going back? If everyone behaved as you did, think how hard life would be for people born with handicaps from which you do not suffer." I returned to do my voluntary stint in that school, and continued it as long as I was in Southampton.

Professor Cock realised, too, how much my mind was in need of broadening in other ways. One day he told me he was going to the New Forest to give a lecture to the Workers' Educational Association and asked if I would go with him. It was the equivalent of a Royal Command. In the car on the way, he asked me what newspapers I read. When I told him the *Daily Herald*, he wanted to know which others I read. "I'm Labour. Just the *Daily Herald*, sir," was my somewhat sharp reply, but I shrivelled as he said, "Are you so narrow-minded that you cannot even read another point of view?" He had scored a bull's-eye and ever since then I have taken care to read as many points of view as possible.

I always went home during college vacations, and one winter's night, Emrys, Ivor and I were sitting around our kitchen table when there was a tremendous roar and rumble beneath us. The oil-lamp on the table shook. We were scared. Mam uttered two words: "The pit!" and we dashed for the door. As we opened it, we saw that every family in the long street was doing the same. A stream of light shone out from every house as men and women ran without speaking to the pithead half a mile away.

It was heartbreaking to be one of many hundreds standing helplessly as the rescuers went down to try to save the men. We all knew someone down the pit. Each rescue worker carried a canary in a cage which they would hold out well in front of them underground to test the air for poisonous gases, for such an explosion could only have been caused by gas.

Dad Tom was the winder on duty that night. He had lowered the cage when the men had gone down to work; now it was his task to lower the rescuers and then raise the bodies of the dead and injured.

In the long vigil, the only sound was an occasional sob from the shawl-covered women waiting to discover the fate of their husband, brother or son. That night brought home to me just how great the debt was that I owed my family and the people of the Valley.

Towards the end of my course in Southampton, Professor Cock offered me an exhibition to stay on there to take an honours degree in history. I am afraid my answer pained him: "I have to get out and start earning money." He agreed to help me find a teaching job in London and to arrange an appointment with a friend, the Professor of History at London University, who would help me enrol for an extra-mural diploma in history.

It was shortly before I left college that I received news from home that hurt me deeply at the time. Trevor had more than fulfilled my request to look after Annie and they were planning to marry. They were obviously in love and it was right for them to marry. Happily they remained, and still are, very dear friends of mine.

There have been other women friends who have played an important part in my life but somehow marriage never seemed quite right and it remains my single greatest regret that I never had children of my own.

So it was that I found myself alone again in London teaching at Rockingham Street School near the Elephant and Castle. I lodged in Coldharbour Lane, Brixton, and from there used to walk all around London, but most particularly to Westminster where the two threads of my future life came together. On Sundays, I would attend services at the Central Hall and on Tuesdays I would go to their weekly Methodist fellowship meetings.

During the rest of the week I would often walk over to Westminster after school to join the queue for the Strangers' Gallery in the House of Commons. I never cared what the debates were: the sheer drama of the place thrilled me and I began to notice how MPs behaved and how the business proceeded. Once, when Will John, the MP for Rhondda West, spoke, all the Tories burst out laughing. I thought they were extremely rude but they have their successors today on both sides of the House. I also noticed the Speaker, Mr E. A. FitzRoy, the Conservative member for Daventry, who mumbled the names of the members he called to speak. Unless I recognised them I had no idea who they were and I have never forgotten how infuriating it was for me to listen to a member without knowing either his constituency or his name. I remembered the frustration clearly when I sat in the

Speaker's Chair and was determined not to make the same mistake.

During the autumn of 1931, Labour Party supporters were still furious with Ramsay MacDonald, who had formed a National Government with the Tories, Liberals and a few Labour defectors. One night I came out of a meeting in the Central Hall to be immediately caught up in a demonstration of chanting protestors. I began to make my way through the crowds, but as they pressed forward mounted police forced them back. Thoroughly frightened by the surging violence, I jumped clean over the railings which then surrounded Parliament Square. I was safe on the green, but had great difficulties in getting back on the pavement as the spiked railings were more than four feet high. I was lucky to get home without being arrested, for that night the police were in a mood to push anybody into the van.

I never did contact the Professor of History at London University, for no sooner had I settled in London, than I saw an advertisement for a job at Marlborough Road School in Cardiff. The chance to return to Wales was irresistible.

My brother Ivor had just bought a splendid new belted overcoat, which I borrowed in order to make a good impression at the interviews in Cardiff City Hall. I waited with about twenty other applicants in the corridor leading to the interview room. It seems bizarre to me that the corridor now contains bronze busts of Jim Callaghan and me as Cardiff MPs. When I learned that the committee had decided to appoint me, I could not have begun to guess what a difference their decision was going to make to the rest of my life. It meant that I never fulfilled Professor Cock's ambition for me, but many other doors opened within months of my return to Wales.

At that moment I just felt satisfied to be coming home: that I would be able at last to contribute my full share to the family income. I returned to London to complete the school term, and came back to the Rhondda for Christmas.

CHAPTER FIVE

A Few First Lessons

My first morning at Marlborough Road Elementary School for Boys was not auspicious. The headmaster, Mr Francis, greeted me by saying that I would be taking Standard One, the youngest children just up from the infants' school, and that my first lesson would be reading. I protested that not only had I been taught to teach senior children but that I had not been taught how to teach reading.

Mr Francis, a kindly man, solved the problem by taking the first few lessons with me. I taught hundreds of boys to read after that shaky beginning. But before we embarked on my first reading class, I noticed that the timetable also contained singing. By now on the edge of panic, I had to tell the headmaster that I had not been taught to teach singing either and that the children would run out of the class if I started singing. "In that case," he said, "you'd better lock the door."

In the end, I became very fond of music lessons where I taught the Welsh airs and hymns I liked myself. One day, as I was in full cry, I saw Mr Francis glance into my classroom window. I could see that he was smiling. He had noticed that the door was not locked, and that the children were not running out.

In those days teachers sat with a cane on their desk but I preferred to remember that I had been trained that the teacher's own behaviour would have the most influence on the children. One small incident was proof of this. I used to keep a handkerchief tucked in my sleeve ready to wipe the chalk off my hands. It was not long before every boy in the class had a handkerchief showing from inside his cuff.

Marlborough Road was quite a small school and there was no danger of any pupil being lost in the crowd. Many of them suffered the effects of the Depression, and I particularly remember a boy called George Edgebrook.

One morning in the middle of class he suddenly fainted and collapsed on the floor. When he had come round, I asked if he had eaten something at breakfast that morning, which had upset him. "I didn't eat anything, Sir," he replied. "I never have breakfast, we can't afford it." Schoolchildren were entitled then to buy little bottles of milk at a halfpenny each, but they had to be paid for a week in advance and Mrs Edgebrook could not afford the weekly 2½d. I saw that the money was paid and George had his milk.

Within weeks of my starting teaching in Cardiff, our family moved from Trealaw Road to 62, Ely Street, Tonypandy, which was to be my home for the next twenty years. There were three rooms downstairs, one with a big bay window, and three upstairs; but above all, there was electric light. There was neither bathroom nor hot-water supply, and the toilet was at the bottom of the garden, but the excitement of having electric light for the first time in our own home is something I shall never forget.

Another memory I have of Ely Street is Friday nights. Dad Tom enjoyed his grog and on Friday, pay day, he would arrive home merry and bright. He always had two things to say to me: "Be sincere – and always pay your turn." Even in his cups he was concerned to see I had the right values.

Once back in Wales my life was soon very busy. I had joined the National Union of Teachers as a student and became press and parliamentary secretary of the Cardiff Association of Teachers. I came to know the South Wales press and BBC very well, and in due course realised the advantage people in public life have if they are used to working closely with the media.

In Tonypandy I used particularly to enjoy the Mock Parliament which the new minister, the Reverend Cyril Gwyther, had organised. We debated such issues as "The Abolition of the Death Penalty", "Prison Reform", "Should We have A National Health Service?" and "The Right to Work". As many as two hundred young men at a time would take part – we were not so advanced as to think it was something for women as well.

Cyril Gwyther himself always took the role of Speaker, and when he entered the hall, wearing his gown, we would stand and bow to him. I served in various offices, including Prime Minister and Leader of the Opposition. Debates were always vigorous, with examples of oratory which seems part of the heritage of Valley people. We examined every subject from a Christian viewpoint, and I quickly learned the invaluable lesson that different Christian believers may draw diametrically opposite conclusions from the same set of facts.

Life in the Rhondda gradually became a little easier as more pits resumed work, but unemployment continued to be the crucial issue of the day throughout Britain, and plans were made for a great national march to London. News of the arrangements being made in the North and North-East, Lancashire and the Midlands, reached us in Wales, and I was given joint responsibility for the organisation of the Tony-pandy contingent of unemployed workers.

The night before the march, Inspector Gwilym Williams, Chief of the Mid-Rhondda Police, came to tell me that if any marchers were seen collecting money the organisers would be prosecuted for begging. This was grim news, for it was the custom at such demonstrations for buckets to be carried so that sympathetic onlookers could contribute by throwing in their coins. Inspector Williams knew this as well as I did, and he followed up his threat by saying, "I thought I would give you fair warning, and you can also tell the others." I spent two hours calling on the other organisers to alert them. Before the march set off, we told the collectors to be careful. "Leave it to us, George," said the chief steward, implying that defeating the police on such a simple issue was something at which Tonypandy men were expert. Later, one of the collectors gave me a broad wink as he moved surreptitiously among the crowd, carrying his cap.

During that period there were many other examples of police antagonism towards political organisers. We used to hold meetings and debates which were addressed by some of the finest orators of the day. The Communists were equally active and at one of their meetings the redoubtable Tom Mann came to speak. He had started work in the mines when he was ten, crawling on all fours harnessed to a coal box for twelve hours a day. Now he was nearing eighty and, together with Harry Pollitt, who accompanied him on to the platform, was a founder member of the British Communist Party. Arthur Horner, another Communist and the South Wales miners' leader, was also there. Plain-clothes detectives took notes of all the speeches made and later Tom Mann and Harry Pollitt were charged with sedition.

I was horrified because I had heard every word, and the remarks that formed the basis of the charge against Mann were in fact made by Pollitt. The police attitude seemed to be that since the words had been said, it did not much matter who had actually spoken them.

When the two men came to trial, a policeman claimed to have written a shorthand version of Mann's speech. An expert called by the defence said it was not shorthand at all. The policeman then said he had "only written down what was seditious", and when the defence counsel asked him, "Do you hold as seditious anything you disapprove of?", he replied firmly, "Yes!" That answer was enough to see that British justice prevailed. Both men were acquitted.

After the unemployment march, Sir Oswald Mosley announced that he was going to hold a meeting in Tonypandy, accompanied by his Blackshirt followers. I called a special meeting of the Labour Party which decided that our supporters should boycott the occasion. The overriding concern was to avoid the violence that had accompanied Mosley's meetings elsewhere.

When the evening arrived, I made sure that I would resist the temptation to heckle the speakers, by going to our main local cinema. The manager, Dick Lewis, used to stand at the entrance to the Empire, resplendent in his dinner jacket and bow tie. Before I went in to the film, we had a chat about my fears that the Blackshirts would try to stir up violence. When I came out at the end of the show, I almost bumped into Police Sergeant James, who stopped me on the steps and said, "I want you. You tore my cape when you attacked me at Mosley's meeting tonight."

I was highly indignant, protesting that this was the first I had heard of any violence. Fortunately, Dick Lewis was still on the cinema steps and heard our conversation. He said he could swear that I had been in the cinema all the evening. Sergeant James decided to let me go with a warning! I was angry and frightened. I knew only too well what a narrow escape I had had, and realised that any left-wing sympathiser, no matter how non-violent, was at the mercy of trumped-up police evidence.

One of my friends was less fortunate. Police officers swore they had seen him climb on to the lorry where Mosley, surrounded by his Blackshirts, was haranguing an angry crowd. My friend weighed over twenty stone and had great difficulty in climbing even on to the step of a bus, but the police evidence was sufficient to get him three months in prison. The whole community was seething with indignation because we knew that lies had been told on oath in court.

The memory of those days came to me strongly when I visited the Duke of Devonshire's home, Chatsworth in Derbyshire, in 1981 when I was Speaker and sat next to the Duchess's sister, Lady Mosley, who turned out to be a warm, compassionate woman. If anybody had told me in the 1930s that I would thoroughly enjoy being with Lady Mosley, I would have been furious.

In the atmosphere of international violence in the 1930s, it was only natural to have sympathy with organisations working for peace. One of these was the International War Resistance Movement, and it was with a group of its members that I travelled abroad for the first time, to Denmark. We sailed from Harwich to Esbjerg and I was miserably seasick. I stayed in the home of a couple who were members of the War Resistance Movement, and they were particularly kind, taking me to see the sights and insisting they were glad of a chance to practise their English when I said I wished I could speak Danish.

For the first time I realised that, although people all over the world have much in common, their differences are extremely important too. At the end of the visit I was buoyed up by the excitement of so many new experiences, and felt certain I would be all right on the voyage home. But as soon as I put my foot on that boat the smell of the oil upset me. And before we had even sailed out of harbour, I knew I was a confirmed poor sailor!

At this time, I also became secretary of the Workers' Temperance League, within the Labour Party, to encourage all members of the Party to avoid the evils of alcohol. In particular, it required Labour Members of Parliament to promise that they would not drink while they were in the House of Commons.

On one occasion Dr Salter, the member for Bermondsey, came to address a conference and to preach in Tonypandy Central Hall. When he arrived at our home to stay overnight, he said very loudly to Mam: "I am a vegetarian." "Oh, yes," she replied. As soon as we had shown him to his room, she took me to one side and whispered, "George, what *is* a vegetarian?" I explained that I thought it meant that he did not eat meat. She looked at me with a mixture of consternation and astonishment. "He doesn't eat meat! Well, what does he eat?" "I think he only eats vegetables." She had never heard of such a thing.

We gave him the middle room, between the parlour and the kitchen, and while he was working at the table in there, with his window open, we were talking quietly in the kitchen. Suddenly there was a loud roar, and he shouted, "Will you stop talking, please. I am working." Dad Tom looked at Mam, and I could tell he was about to explode. But both she and I put our fingers to our lips, and after giving us an angry look he just got up and went out.

Many radical people in the Thirties joined the Communist Party, and for a time Stafford Cripps was expelled from the Labour Party for working too closely with the Communists. He came to Tonypandy to address a big rally in support of a united front between the two parties, and the following week I presided over an opposing rally which we called "Answer to Cripps". The hall, which seated a thousand people, was packed, but things did not go as smoothly as we expected, for among the crowd was a contingent of Communist hecklers.

At a meeting in the Empire cinema a few days previously, Will Mainwaring, the MP for Rhondda East, had been heckled by young people and had shouted, "Take no notice – they're a lot of sheep sent here by the Communist Party." When I stood to open our meeting, I was greeted with a loud "Baaaa!" We all laughed, but then came a sustained chorus of "Baas", some high, some low, but all very loud. It was typical of Rhondda humour, but it completely destroyed our meeting.

One of those who left the chapel and the Labour Party to become a Communist because she felt we were not moving fast enough, was Annie Thomas – by then Annie Powell. Her general spirit of revulsion against the social cruelties of the time made her impatient for change, and she stood as a Communist candidate in the local elections. It was a long time before she was finally elected, but she then went on to become the first Communist mayor in Britain. She has remained a Communist, of the old-fashioned radical kind, ever since.

The most able Communist orator in the Rhondda then was Lewis Jones, from Clydach Vale, who had studied at Ruskin College. He could always command a large audience with a devastating wit which he used to great effect against those of us who were Labour. We were implacably opposed to each other, but he taught me one of the best lessons I have ever learned.

It was at a time when Mam was desperately ill with uraemia, a kidney complaint from which few people then recovered, and the doctor had told me it would be a terminal illness. One day, in the main street of Tonypandy, I saw Lewis Jones and hoped I would be able to avoid him, but he asked, "How is Mam?" My eyes filled with tears, and I saw his eyes were also full. His compassionate spirit shamed me. It was the Communist Lewis Jones who taught me to respect political opponents just as much as political friends.

Mam's illness worsened and the day came when two doctors called to see her, and asked to speak to me privately. We went into our parlour, and they told me that Mam only had an hour to live. I can still see the senior doctor standing by the table and plucking a black grape off a bunch which lay on a silver dish. I don't think he really knew what he was doing as he brought himself to say, "Your mother's life is now in the hands of her Maker. We've done everything we can." Then they both left the house.

Half an hour later, the younger doctor returned. He had remembered a formula he had been taught as a student, and had looked it up in his college notes. I took the prescription he held out, and ran like the wind to the chemist. All I remember of that medicine is that it looked like a bottle of water, but the very first dose of it calmed my mother. From then on she started to recover. It was like a miracle. She lived for nearly another forty years, long enough to see me attend the funeral of both doctors.

Mam had no sooner recovered from her kidney illness than an open wound broke out on her leg. She was taken by ambulance to Cardiff Royal Infirmary to see a skin specialist, and on the way back the driver, Mr Thomas – known to everybody as Mr Thomas the Ambulance – said, "You're very quiet. Didn't you have good news?" At which she burst into tears, which was most unlike her. Finally she managed to answer him, and said that she had been told she would never walk again.

That skin consultant might have been good at his work, but he was not very good at human relationships, or at gauging people's powers of recovery. We knew it would be bad for Mam to be stuck at home all day, and Ivor and I decided to find the deposit to buy a Morris 8 on hire-purchase. We took her to Llantwit Major, a lovely little seaside village in the Vale of Glamorgan and after several visits persuaded her to get out of the car. Within a year she was walking again, having proved the doctors wrong for the second time.

CHAPTER SIX

War and Victory

The declaration of the Second World War marked the end of an era characterised by long-term unemployment and brought a personal crisis for me. For some time my pacifist views had been badly shaken by Hitler's concentration camps and by Mussolini's incursion into Ethiopia. I went through an agonising period of self-examination, and decided not to go to a tribunal as a pacifist but to join one of the armed forces. I duly appeared before a medical board who declared me Grade C, meaning that I was not considered fit for military service – although they did not tell me why.

I felt I had to make some contribution to the war effort and joined the special police in Tonypandy, a decision my Labour friends found hard to understand. Their qualms were based not only on past suspicion of police attitudes, but also on the fact that the head of the Glamorgan police force, Chief Constable Lindsay, was openly hostile to Labour representatives and had reduced public confidence in the police to zero. For my part, I thought it no bad thing for the Mid-Rhondda community to see the chairman of the local Labour Party wearing a police uniform, though I certainly had not forgotten all the past clashes. On the whole, the work was pleasant but among the four regular officers was one who proved all was still not well within the force.

One night, Ron, one of the War Reserve police officers, a boy of nineteen, came to see me in deep distress. He had been on duty with the regular sergeant and they had been patrolling outside a blacked-out fair marquee. They had waited in the dark outside the tent until eventually a young lad came out to urinate. As soon as the boy stepped out of the tent, the sergeant had barked at Ron that he must book him. The boy started to cry, rightly saying that he had done nothing wrong. Ron took his side, but the enraged sergeant insisted that a charge be made. Ron told me that he knew he should not have complied, but that he felt he had had no choice. I advised him to go to the sergeant, tell him that I knew what had happened, and that I – by now a sergeant myself – was very angry. That way, although the sergeant would undoubtedly give him a hard time, Ron would at least be able to face himself without feeling ashamed. He took my advice, which was not easy for him, and the blustering sergeant decided to drop the case. I soon learned that the other officers had doubts about his fairness. None of us came out of it very well because none of us reported it to a senior officer.

Our only excuse was that life was far from normal then. All of us had good friends or relatives who were killed or wounded, either in bombing raids or on active service. From Tonypandy we could hear the bombs thumping down on Cardiff and see the anti-aircraft guns exploding in the night sky, always wondering who was being hit. Knowing the terrible things that were happening did nothing to alter the shock when I arrived at Marlborough Road one morning to find that the school had been flattened. Our building had been empty but many people had been killed in the surrounding houses.

I was transferred to Roath Park School where I particularly enjoyed taking scripture for the whole school, a task I believe should never be done by anybody who is not a Christian. I believe equally strongly that we should never stop teaching Christian knowledge in our schools, a stance that was later to be attacked in the first few weeks of my Speakership.

By this time I was president of the Cardiff Teachers' Association, and in 1942 I was elected to the national executive of the National Union of Teachers (NUT), which was to prove rather like a second university for me. Still raw and inexperienced, I began to meet men from all walks of life – some of them tough customers – who taught me how to deal with people with strong opposing views.

One of the first things I did was to propose a resolution that the NUT should affiliate with the TUC. What a row that caused! It was considered most unprofessional that teachers should be expected to mix with workers, and Sir Frederick Mander, the general secretary, made the mistake of saying, "I'll get you off this executive because of that." When the next election came, I had the highest vote in Wales, but Fred Mander soon got over it and we became firm friends.

Those days were for me the developing years. I was not really aware of it at the time, but looking back I can see that I really changed. One man who was unlike anyone I had met before was G. C. T. Giles, the first Communist president of the NUT, and the only Old Etonian ever to be president. I had been on the executive only a year when he and his Communist supporters asked me to stand for the presidency. I told them it was far too soon but that I would fight the following year.

They put great pressure on me, and then Giles told me that if I refused to stand, they would support Ralph Morley, a Labour member from Southampton, and they would oppose me the following year. Morley was duly elected, helped by the fact that his supporters were riding a wave of popularity throughout the country because of the tremendously brave stand the Red Army had made at Stalingrad. And when I stood the following year, they opposed me, as Giles had said they would, labelling me "a careerist".

The meetings of the national executive were held in London during the war and once when I was returning home I went into the grill room at Cardiff station while waiting for my train to Tonypandy. Before the war nobody would sit at a restaurant table with a total stranger, but in the war years all this changed, and a young airman came and asked if he could share the table. We started to talk and he told me he was going to make his very first broadcast that night in a BBC production of *How Green is My Valley*, playing David, the leading part. I told him I would listen with great care and then write to tell him what I thought, adding only half seriously, "Do you want me to be honest, or just kind?" The poor fellow had no choice but fortunately his performance was brilliant. He told me that although his real name was Jenkins, he had taken his schoolmaster's surname, and acted under the name of Richard Burton.

It was not long after this brief encounter that in 1944 Mrs Elizabeth Andrews, the women's organiser for the Welsh Labour Party and the first woman Justice of the Peace in Wales, asked me if she could submit my name to Transport House for the list of prospective parliamentary candidates. In due course, I received a letter from Mr Shepherd, the national agent of the Labour Party, inviting me to go to Transport House to be interviewed. My name was put on the list and to my surprise I received several enquiries, including one from Blackburn in Lancashire, which at the time had two members for the same constituency.

The other candidate, who was interviewed on the same day, was a *Daily Mirror* journalist called Barbara Betts, who later became Barbara Castle. We were both adopted with great enthusiasm by the Blackburn Labour Party, and I felt very excited as I travelled home. But as soon as I arrived back in Wales, I began to have doubts about whether I could afford to go to Blackburn often enough to nurse the constituency until the general election came. A week later, I was invited to be a candidate for Cardiff South so I wrote to Blackburn to tell them with great reluctance I must withdraw, as I did not think I would be able to nurse the seat from Cardiff.

When I went down to the selection committee in Cardiff South, there were several other candidates there, but I only remember the man who won – James Callaghan – dressed in his naval lieutenant's gold-braided uniform. He beat me by one vote, and I always tell him that in the wartime atmosphere his uniform was worth more than just one vote. When he expressed his thanks to the selection panel for the confidence they had placed in him, he suddenly referred to me. Tapping me on the back, he said, "I am sure that this young man will get adopted by another constituency." We both laughed when we discovered that he was younger than I was.

At that time, I knew him only as Lieutenant Callaghan, and when we met again at the Labour central committee room in Cardiff, I asked him what his Christian name was. "My family call me Leonard, but for politics I'm going to use my second name, James," he replied, adding, "Jim is a much better name for politics." Both his wife Audrey and I continued to call him Leonard until the late Sixties, but then we had to give in, acknowledging that to the rest of the world he was Jim.

I was teaching at Roath Park School one day, when an old miners' leader known as Meth Jones – his real name was Methuselah – came to ask me if I would let my name go forward for the Cardiff Central constituency. I did not give him an immediate answer, but said I would like to have time to think about it. I went home that night and talked it over with Mam and Dad Tom, who both said I should seek selection. They were right. This time I was chosen and became prospective Labour candidate for Cardiff Central. This meant that I attended the Labour Party conference held in Blackpool in May 1945, just ten days after fighting had ceased in Europe. It was a heady, exciting time.

Clem Attlee and his team in the National Government were given their marching orders and told they must be prepared to leave the Government and insist on a general election. Ernest Bevin made a tremendous speech on international co-operation which was later to earn him the Foreign Secretaryship, and we all voiced our determination to build a better Britain and prevent the unemployment of the pre-war years. Parliamentary candidates who were in the Forces were given leave to come to the conference, and I remember sitting next to Major Denis Healey. We were all trying to catch the chairman's eye, and he succeeded, making a trenchant speech that caught the mood of the conference. When he returned to his seat, I told him: "Major Healey, you have a great gift for vituperation." He has often reminded me of that, and I think it must have been in his mind when I reprimanded him from the Speaker's Chair thirty-eight years later for calling somebody a hypocrite.

The election was held on 5 July, almost six weeks before the atom bomb forced Japan to surrender. We had a month for the campaign, fought in almost perfect summer weather. I was not to know it then, but it was to be the happiest campaign of my career. There were two other candidates in Cardiff Central, and none of us had fought a parliamentary election before. Charles Hallinan, a much liked local solicitor, was the Conservative candidate; and Peter Hopkin Morgan, a delightful twenty-three-year-old, the Liberal. The three of us became firm friends. The sitting MP, Sir Ernest Bennett, who had abandoned Labour to support Ramsay MacDonald in 1931, was not seeking re-election.

I had leave of absence from my job, and accompanied by my supporters patrolled the streets of my prospective constituency with a loudspeaker. Together with the Labour candidates for the other two Cardiff constituencies, we held tremendous meetings which leading politicians such as Attlee and Herbert Morrison came to address. Harold Laski, who was then chairman of the Labour Party, and a strong supporter of Jim Callaghan, spoke at one of these meetings, and struck me as being a very arrogant fellow.

An old lady who was obviously a Labour sympathiser asked a simple question after he had spoken, and in front of the huge crowd, he said, "Madam, you need to buy a sixpenny book on logic." I felt the coldness sweep through the meeting. It was my turn to speak: "With every respect, it's not that lady who needs a sixpenny book on logic, but some people who need a warmer heart." The meeting applauded loudly. I never liked Laski after that and Attlee was quite right later in the campaign to tell him: "A period of silence on your part would now be welcome."

At the very first general election meeting I addressed in Cardiff, a young man stood up and announced: "I want to say something." The chairman told him firmly that he could either ask a question or be quiet. "But I want to say something," he repeated. I did not recognise him, but something about him was vaguely familiar and I suggested he be allowed to say whatever it was, rather than risk an incident at the meeting.

As soon as he started to speak, I realised it was George Edgebrook, and he told the story about fainting in my class at Marlborough Road School and being given his free milk. If ever a man had cast his bread on the waters for it to return in the form of cake! I was grateful to George, but I was very moved too. Poor fellow, he did not live a great deal longer. The seeds of malnutrition in those early years took their toll.

The cornerstone of my campaign was a determination that the poverty of the Thirties should never return. My slogan was: "I will fight to ensure that no mother suffers as mine has done." I never failed to get frantic applause by a declaration that private enterprise would never again be allowed to put profit before people. I wanted to use politics as a means of translating Christian values into practice, for I believed then, as I do now, that Parliament is one of the means for Christian people to make the world look like God's world – though I do not believe it is ever right for the Church to tell people how to vote. I used to look with dismay at the door of the local Roman Catholic church in Cardiff Central where they had pinned a notice saying it was a mortal sin to vote for George Thomas. That went on for three or four general elections, until Archbishop Murphy came to Cardiff and forbade such practices.

My only real moment of concern in the campaign was when it was announced that Winston Churchill was coming to speak in Cardiff. Everyone was deeply grateful for his courage during the war, and my supporters feared that his personality would cause a landslide of support for Charles Hallinan. In retrospect, it is astonishing how we misread the signs and refused to accept the evidence staring us in the face. Churchill was due to travel along Ninian Park Road to his meeting at the football ground. My supporters had knocked on every door along that route and asked people to put my election poster in their window for Winston to see. Nearly every house displayed my picture, but we still could not believe that we were going to win.

Once, when I was addressing an open-air street meeting, a sailor in uniform came and asked to use my megaphone. I handed it to him with some trepidation, for I had no idea what he was going to say.

There was no need for alarm; he simply told the crowd: "All the Forces want you to vote Labour." He returned the megaphone, smiled, and wished me luck. We had to wait three weeks after polling day to see if the sailor had been right, the length of time it took to collect the Forces' votes from camps and battlefields around the world.

Eventually the day of the official count came, and the boxes from overseas joined the boxes of local votes. I stayed for several hours to watch the counting, and every time I made myself glance at a ballot paper it seemed to have a cross at the top where Hallinan's name was printed, rather than at the bottom next to mine. My supporters kept telling me that it was looking good, but I just could not believe them. The result was not due to be announced until the next day, so finally I went home to Tonypandy.

The following morning was wet and grey, and Mam went to Cardiff with me to hear the result. I met Charles Hallinan going in to the City Hall, and together we walked amicably up the wide staircase. I was still convinced he had won, and congratulated him. But when we arrived at the count, I soon realised that the votes were going my way. I was elected on an overall minority vote, but had a clear lead of around 4,000 over the Conservative.

We assembled in our raincoats outside the City Hall for the Lord Mayor to read out the results:

Hallinan, Charles	11,982	Conservative
Hopkin Morgan, Peter	5,121	Liberal
Thomas, George	16,506	Labour

The crowd of people standing before us in the pouring rain shouted and cheered. Shortly after that we heard that Hilary Marquand had won Cardiff East and Jim Callaghan, Cardiff South. A clean sweep for Labour.

I stayed in Cardiff that night, celebrating with the local Party. When I went home next day, climbing up the familiar slope to our house, I saw to my surprise that every house in Ely Street had a flag hanging from the window. Outside our house someone had chalked on the pavement: "Congratulations George on your good work in Parliament." At that time I had only been in the public gallery, but that pride in my election to Parliament was typical of the Rhondda.

Labour had won a landslide victory and in great cities across the Commonwealth cheering crowds demonstrated their approval. In

India, fervour ran particularly high because the return of a Labour Government raised strong hopes of independence. Britain's standing as a parliamentary democracy was never higher abroad than it was when Clem Attlee drove to Buckingham Palace to be sworn in as Prime Minister. The world marvelled that the British nation could proclaim its pride in Churchill's superb wartime leadership and yet withhold from him the reward of leading the first post-war Government.

During the interval between the election and taking our seats in Parliament, I invited Jim Callaghan to come and stay for a week in my home so that we could get to know one another better. One day, we decided to go to Cardiff to introduce ourselves to officials of the City Council. As we walked in St John's Square, Cardiff, Jim suddenly turned to me and asked, "What are you going to do in this Parliament?" I was puzzled by the question and hardly knew how to reply. Eventually I said, "Well, I shall do my best to look after my constituency." In retrospect, I realise he must have thought me very naive, for he said, "Before the end of this Parliament, I shall be in the Government." I asked Woodrow Wyatt what he would do, and he replied, 'Make money!'"

That conversation upset and surprised me but time was to prove Jim and Woodrow Wyatt both right.

CHAPTER SEVEN

George Thomas MP

I felt eight feet tall when I walked through the great Carriage Gates into Palace Yard, Westminster, for the first time as a newly elected Member of Parliament. I thought of Palmerston and Pitt, of Gladstone and Disraeli, and all the other giants of our parliamentary history. I never lost that deep sense of the privilege of being an MP.

During the war, the Chamber of the House of Commons had been completely destroyed by a bomb, but because the damage was invisible from the road, it was a well-kept secret. The rebuilding and repairs went on for several years, and it was actually in the House of Lords – arranged to look like the Commons – that I took my seat for the first time.

The Chamber was absolutely packed. Members were standing below the Bar, around the Speaker's Chair, and sitting in the aisles. I sat next to Jim Callaghan and a man with a streaming cold, which I was afraid I would catch. He turned out to be Michael Foot. I was a great admirer of his radical father, Isaac, and remarked, "Your father is a great Methodist – and a teetotaller." Michael smiled and replied, "My father is a good man; but I don't share all his views."

During parliamentary sessions, I used to lodge throughout the week at a friendly little Welsh hotel called the Harlingford, near Russell Square. It suited me because it was completely temperance, and other members from the same sort of background stayed there too.

I went to the House of Commons first thing in the morning to collect my mail, and take it to the library. Sometimes I received between thirty and forty letters in one day, and had to write all my replies in longhand as I could not afford a secretary. In those days members had no allowance for expenses, and all office and accommodation bills had to come out of our low salaries. We had no special room to work in, and if the library was full, members had to sit in the corridors. So we did get to know each other quite well.

I particularly remember the always courteous Anthony Eden, who called me "Tommy", which I rather liked. Once when we met just outside the library, he said, "Hello, Tommy. Have you settled down yet?" When I replied, "This is a wonderful place, Mr Eden, and there are some wonderful people here," he laughed outright. Then he said, "You are quite right, Tommy. There are wonderful people here, but there are also some of the other sort. The good thing is that we can choose our own friends. You be careful in your choice."

On the Labour benches Clem Attlee was an unusual leader for the Party. He had the reserve of an English squire and it was torture to get him to unbend. No political leader ever had fewer tricks about him. His speeches rarely lasted longer than twenty minutes, but he had a sharp tongue and in half a dozen words could puncture the pride of the loudest opponent. It was his obvious sincerity and patriotism that gave him the authority to control a parliamentary team drunk with its sudden access to power.

This modest demeanour camouflaged a shrewd brain and whenever the Parliamentary Party was torn in raging conflict, he allowed others to make the running. His views were kept to himself. Then, when the dust finally settled, he was in his place, sitting like a Buddha, undisturbed and alert. He was very shy and reticent when conversations turned to religion, but he held deep Christian convictions.

In 1946, Winston Churchill was invited to Cardiff to receive the Freedom of the City. I was desperately anxious that the great man should not fail to recognise me in front of the Cardiff hierarchy, so I sought him out in the Commons smoking-room where I knew he liked to meet his colleagues.

Feeling rather nervous, I approached him to say, "Mr Churchill, you are coming to Cardiff tomorrow to receive the Freedom of the City and we are looking forward to welcoming you." His face creased as he smiled: "You are doing me a great honour. I look forward to the ceremony." Knowing he had no idea who I was, I added, "My name is George Thomas. I am the Member for Cardiff Central." He replied, "I look forward to seeing you in your own city."

The next day thousands of people poured into Cardiff and lined the streets to give Churchill an enthusiastic welcome. I was among a small group invited to have tea with him in the Lord Mayor's Parlour at City Hall. Suddenly he looked across at me and, turning to the Lord Mayor, asked in a loud whisper: "Who is that?" I have never been able to resolve whether it was his sense of humour or whether I really had made no impression on him at all.

I had no difficulty in deciding the subject of my maiden speech in Parliament. It was something which was to preoccupy me for more than twenty years: reform of the property leasehold system. At first this might not seem the kind of subject to be of burning interest to a young idealist but I had learned otherwise during my general election campaign. It was of particularly urgent concern to thousands of people in South Wales.

The system of leasehold, whereby the freehold reverted to the owner once the leases ran out, was creating widespread misery. During the industrial expansion of the nineteenth century, property in South Wales had largely been developed on the basis of 100-year leases, so by the mid-twentieth century, roughly a million people were in fear of being made homeless. Old people used to come to me frantic with worry. Not only were they losing their homes, but they were also faced with repair bills for hundreds of pounds which they could not possibly afford to pay.

Time and again I went to the offices of the major ground landlords in Cardiff and pleaded with them to reduce their demands. Sometimes I was successful: usually I failed to elicit even a glimmer of compassion. In Parliament, I pursued the campaign for leasehold reform in every way I could. By my questions and speeches, the House learned that this subject would not be allowed to drop.

The Government pushed ahead vigorously with other social and economic reforms. There was a feeling of crusade as we took into public ownership the essential industries of coal, gas and electricity. Each night as we trooped through the division lobbies* someone would call out, "Come on, George. Strike up!" and I would start to sing "Guide me, O thou Great Jehovah." Instantly there would be a mighty choir singing its way through the lobby.

Nothing caused greater delight than the legislation setting up the National Health Service. Like other MPs, I detested having to approach hospital almoners to try to get some old person's hospital charges reduced. The largest building in my constituency at that time was the workhouse. I loathed the place and longed to see it abolished. It may seem incredible now but the superintendent insisted on being called Master by both inmates and visitors alike.

---

*Members divide to pass through one lobby or another according to whether they are voting for or against the motion.

Once, when I called at tea-time, I saw the inmates get just one thick piece of bread and a bit of cheese. I complained to the Master, who snapped, "They are paupers. They should have taken greater care not to come here." My sharp response that they had never had sufficient income to save for old age was shrugged away. Another day I went to visit the workhouse when it was raining. An old couple I knew were sitting on a bench outside. I told them they should go inside. They would catch pneumonia sitting in the drizzle. The old lady replied, "George, they separate us when we are in there." The image of that couple remained in my mind throughout the health service debates.

Newly elected MPs are exposed to all sorts of pressures and temptations, and it is easy for a novice to get into trouble – as I did. An invitation to a World Peace Conference of Young People to be held in Warsaw came to me out of the blue in the autumn of 1945. Since Denmark was still the only foreign country I had visited, the invitation seemed too good to refuse. I really was an innocent abroad, for I had failed to appreciate that the Soviet Union was using this international youth conference as a front organisation for its political manoeuvres. Yet perhaps it is just as well that I was so naive, or I would not have undergone, and been everlastingly influenced by, one of the most harrowing experiences of my life.

In the former ghetto of Warsaw, I stood on piles of rubble that stretched out for miles. The air was foul from decaying bodies which still lay beneath the rubble. My eyes filled with tears and I turned my head away to prevent my Polish guide from seeing my emotion. But he was too quick for me: "You needn't be ashamed to cry. General Montgomery shed tears when he stood here."

I sat one day with a circle of young people and noticed a six-figure number tattooed on the arm of one of the girls. Innocently, I asked why she had it. I knew at once that I had made a ghastly mistake. The whole group stared at me in silence until one of them switched the conversation back to the youth conference. Later I was told that the tattoo had been done when the girl was imprisoned in Auschwitz concentration camp. She still woke screaming after nightmares and was fighting to get back to normality. I still cringe when I remember my ignorance.

At the same conference, I asked a young Pole what he wanted to do in life. With emphasis on every word he said that he wanted to go to the United States to live. I was surprised, remarking on the fact that he was a Communist and the USA the most capitalist country.

Instantly he replied, "I am a Jew. If you look at Polish history you will see that we have a pogrom every fifty years or so. I want to get out."

Before I left Poland I joined the other delegates in a visit to Auschwitz. We were taken on a conducted tour by a former inmate. We saw the ovens that had been used as human incinerators, with the charred bones still inside. One large room was filled with the hair that had been shorn from victims' heads on their way to the gas chambers. Another room was piled with sandals and shoes – children's as well as adults'. I dared not speak. The experience was too horrifying. When I entered the gas chamber where so many had been murdered, I silently prayed that such evil should never happen again.

Later that year, when I attended the Nuremberg trials of the Nazi leaders for a few days as an observer, my mind kept going back to Auschwitz. I stared down at Goering with the horror I would have felt at seeing a python lying in my path. When I saw an American military policeman push a truncheon in his side to make him stand to attention when addressed by the judge, I felt no sympathy for him.

In a room outside the court, the French prosecuting counsel showed me some of the evidence he was going to submit. There was the shrunken head of a Polish boy whose crime was to have fallen in love with a German girl. His head, mounted on a plaque and used as an ornament, had been found in a German official's house. Another exhibit was a jar of soap, just like a jar in a village store window, except that it contained the fat of human beings. A third exhibit was a lampshade made of human skin torn from the chest of a Polish prisoner while he was still alive. It had been discovered in the house of an Auschwitz camp guard.

I left Nuremberg reinforced in my belief that Britain had no choice but to use force against the Nazis. I had not forgotten my pacifist ideals though, and when Attlee's Cabinet decided to bring in peacetime conscription, I rebelled. We had had enough of war.

There was a three-line whip when the bill to introduce national service came before the House.* But I had already said that even if there were a forty-three-line whip, I would not vote for it. After the

*A whip is a notice to members from their party's organisers in the House stating the business of the House and requesting their attendance; if it is underlined three times, it is a summons to attend the debate and vote with the party.

division (or vote), I was summoned to appear before Willie Whiteley, the Chief Whip, and Herbert Morrison, Leader of the House. Morrison was a man I both liked and admired, but this did not prevent us from having occasional disagreements. He always gave short shrift to any Labour backbencher who failed to support the Government and immediately accused me of disloyalty. I turned to the Chief Whip, whom I knew to be a fellow Methodist, and challenged him to deny that there are times when a man must follow his conscience, even though it might lead him to vote against his party, as I did. Wearily, Whiteley said, "You can go, George. But remember that you were sent here to support the Labour Government." Morrison was furious. He turned angrily to Whiteley: "You haven't got a promise out of him that he will not do it again." Whiteley ignored him and with a red face repeated, "George, you can go. Your interview is over."

The most unpleasant encounter I had with a member of that Government was with Chuter Ede, who as Home Secretary had to decide whether or not the Royal prerogative of clemency should be exercised in cases where the death penalty had been ordered by a High Court judge. I have bitter memories of how he fulfilled this solemn duty.

Two murders were committed on the same night in the Aberavon constituency. In the first case, a young girl had been sent by her mother to a friend's house to repay ten shillings borrowed earlier in the week. When she arrived, only the twenty-year-old son was at home, and he brutally assaulted the girl before murdering her. Her body was recovered from a nearby rubbish tip.

In the second case, a young courting couple missed the last bus to the girl's village in the next valley. As they set off to walk over the mountain to the village, they met the young man's brother on his way home. The young man asked his brother to explain to their parents why he would be late getting back. Just forty minutes later the young man ran down the mountainside and used a public telephone to tell the police that he had accidentally killed his girlfriend. His story had the ring of truth about it. He said they had been having intercourse and that he had exerted such pressure on the girl's throat she had died. He was frantic with grief and freely recounted the story to the police.

Both the young men were sentenced to death. I became involved in the second case when the father and brother of the condemned man came to the Commons with a petition asking for clemency. W. G.

Cove, the member for Aberavon, was not available when they arrived, so one of the attendants in the House asked whether I would see the visitors instead.

I went to the central lobby where the father and the brother, the latter with the petition clutched in his right hand, were waiting. They asked me how they could get the petition to the Home Secretary. I immediately said I would take them to the Home Office, but I warned that although we would go to the Home Secretary's Private Office, they would not be able to see Chuter Ede as he had to be as remote and impartial as a judge. They fully understood.

I walked over to the Home Office with the anxious father and brother. My mind was in a whirl as I pictured the young man in the condemned cell, knowing that his hope of life depended on the success of the petition. I arranged an appointment later in the day with the Home Secretary for W. G. Cove and myself.

At four o'clock, Cove and I went to Chuter Ede's room in the Commons. We were given a frigid reception. The Home Secretary wasted no time in telling us that he would not recommend the exercise of the Royal prerogative of mercy. He suddenly said, "You know there were two murders in the Aberavon constituency that night, and in each case a young man has been sentenced to hang. The young man you have come about is a Protestant, and the other is a Roman Catholic." Bitterly, I asked, "What on earth has that got to do with your decision?" His reply shattered me: "I am not going to offend my Catholics in South Shields [his constituency] by reprieving a Protestant and allowing a Catholic to hang." Cove and I protested vigorously, but Chuter Ede would not budge. The three of us were angry as we broke up the meeting.

In due course, both the young men were hanged. Mam and I went to call at the home of the one for whom I had intervened. His mother showed me the last letter her son had sent her from the condemned cell. The young man, who was twenty-three years old and had served in the army in Malaya, told his mother that he was at peace with God: that he repented of his wrongdoing and that he was prepared to meet his Maker.

As I read the letter, my blood chilled. The clergyman who attended that condemned man must have striven hard to get a twenty-three-year-old to think along those lines. The weeping mother described to me how, on the morning of the execution, she had been given a sedative to make her sleep, but it had not worked. All the clocks in the house had been stopped so that she would not know exactly when it was nine o'clock, the moment of the execution. Together, she and I looked at the picture of her dead son in silence.

When Chuter Ede left the Home Office he told the Commons that he had changed his mind about capital punishment. As I listened to him say that the case of Timothy Evans, whose innocence was proved after he had been hanged, had made him opposed to the death penalty, I recalled my own unhappy dealing with him and wondered if the boy from Aberavon was also on his conscience.

CHAPTER EIGHT

A Lesson in Greek

I really should have learned from the Polish experience just how vulnerable newly elected MPs were to outside political exploitation. I finally learned the lesson in January 1948, when I became caught up in a very dangerous episode in Greece. I was asked by the National Union of Students to investigate the conflict between the Greek Government and the students at Athens University.

I set out on the journey full of excitement at the prospect of seeing Greece for the first time. By the time I reached Athens, the Government had closed down the University, and I was met at the airport by Professor Georgiou, who took me to his home. I did not know it but I was already in the hands of a group determined to indoctrinate me with anti-Greek-Government propaganda.

The following day my interpreter Christos took me to visit a so-called relative in prison in Piraeus. My instructions were to remain silent and to let Christos explain that we were taking food to his cousin. We were admitted into the prison where I saw about twenty men held in dreadful conditions in one room. One man who was obviously very ill lay on the floor. I left the prison burning with anger but my anti-Government indoctrination was not complete. It was next put to me that I might like to visit Macedonia before returning to England. When I think back at what happened, I am ashamed at my gullibility.

At the suggestion of my Greek hosts I asked the British Ambassador in Athens to arrange transport to Larissa. He was most co-operative, giving me an army jeep complete with a cockney driver called George and fitting me out with a heavy white duffle coat and army boots.

On the way I stayed overnight with the local mayor of Larissa. In the morning Christos, George and I set out to visit a mountain village that was believed to support the Government forces by day, and switch allegiance to the guerrillas led by General Marcos by night. Christos was sitting in the back of the jeep. I was in the front with George.

We were about an hour's drive from Larissa, when without warning we ran into a gun battle. Bullets fired from a monastery high on a hill whistled past us. George stopped the jeep, jumped out and rolled under it for shelter. I did not wait for an invitation. Christos joined us.

Using extreme cockney terms, George told me he would not drive any further. He insisted that the only sensible course was to return to Larissa as fast as possible. This made sense, but Christos persuaded me that he and I should go on foot to a village which we could see and which did not seem so very far away. George, very sensibly, returned to Larissa in the jeep. Christos and I rolled into a ditch by the side of the road while bullets whistled above us. I was frightened and knew that death could be very near. As we lay in that ditch, I said my prayers.

The shooting stopped after about an hour and we began the walk to the village. The clear mountain air had made it look much nearer than it really was, and as we walked across heavy ploughed fields, my rough army boots rubbed the skin off my heel and I began to limp. Every step was painful, so it was a relief to see Greek soldiers approaching wearing British army uniforms, as was their custom immediately after the war. When they pointed their weapons at us, I contented myself with telling Christos to explain that I was a visiting British Member of Parliament. In Athens, such identification had worked marvels – here it was different.

Christos told me that the troops were guerrillas, and that they were demanding my passport. A nasty atmosphere developed when I declined to part with my only real proof of identity. Christos succeeded in getting the troops to relax, but they made us walk in front of them to the village. By this time, I should have realised that Christos was a Communist. The gun battle we had run into had been between guerrillas in the monastery, and some nearby Government loyalists.

The villagers received us enthusiastically and told us that soldiers would escort us to the mountain headquarters of General Marcos, the rebel leader. The journey up Mount Olympus by mule took two and a half days. On the second day, a giant eagle swooped down and the captain of the troops fired his pistol. He missed the bird and I burst out laughing. He was furious. Christos explained that the captain had fired only to frighten the eagle away. It had been big enough, he said, to pick up a man and take him right up to its nest. He added that they often lifted sheep that way.

General Marcos, a man of about thirty with considerable presence, explained through Christos why his guerrilla army had been formed, and welcomed me as the first parliamentarian from the West he had met. He asked me to take a letter to the United Nations, which was then meeting in Athens, inviting the world's press to send representatives to talk to him and to report on guerrilla activities. The General assured them of safe conduct. In return for my promise to deliver his letter, I was given a guide to take us back down the mountain.

The two-day return journey felt even more like an episode from a wartime adventure than the outward one. Our guide, a small man with a mean look, knew the paths on Mount Olympus as well as I knew the tracks on the Rhondda Valley mountains. When Christos and I finally left him, he told us to continue walking for one mile when we would come to a quarry. Every worker there was a supporter of the guerrillas, and one of them would get us back to Larissa. Christos soon found help, and we were given a lift in a lorry.

This was my time of greatest anxiety, for I knew that when we travelled on the no-man's land between guerrilla- and Government-controlled territory we were most exposed to attack. I had taken photographs of the guerrillas in the mountains, and when we were challenged by the sentries guarding Larissa, the rolls of film, together with Marcos's letter, seemed to burn in my pocket.

The British Army were angry, believing that I had deliberately planned to meet Marcos, an opinion that I quickly learned was widely shared. Another shock came when I was told that my absence in the mountains had made world news. It had been assumed that the guerrillas had killed me, and Jim Callaghan had pressed the Foreign Office to make a statement.

Because I had to stay overnight in Larissa, I returned to the mayor's house where I had earlier received such a warm welcome. This time there was a mood of sullen resentment, for the mayor also believed I had deliberately collaborated with the guerrillas. I felt guilty thinking of the letter in my pocket from Marcos to the United Nations. If the mayor learned of that, he would be bound to feel I had betrayed his people. Yet I had given my word to Marcos that in exchange for safe conduct back to Larissa I would deliver his message. I was determined to keep my word.

My night in the mayor's house is one I shall never forget. I sat in my bedroom in the dark wondering whether I should tell the army commander the whole story but finally decided it was wiser not to involve him. At that time I was a heavy smoker, and as I lit yet another cigarette I was suddenly conscious of a footstep outside the house. I froze, for I knew there was a strict curfew and that nobody was allowed on the street after dark. The hostility arising from the suspicion that I was helping the guerrillas meant my life was in danger, and I knew it. At the sound of the footstep, I hastily stubbed out my cigarette since it made me an easy target for anyone outside the window.

I waited for the slightest sound. Then I heard it again. It was unmistakably a footstep. Frightened, and moving as silently as possible, I hid behind my bedroom door and sat on the floor for the rest of the night. It seemed an eternity before dawn. I crept down the stairs and hurried to the British Army barracks where I poured out the story. When I had finished, the commanding officer said drily, "I didn't tell you, but I put a guard on the mayor's house last night. I was anxious about your security." It was a British soldier's footstep that had frightened me.

I took Marcos's letter to the United Nations and returned to London with great relief. No sooner had I done so, however, than the League for Democracy in Greece sprang into action, organising enormous rallies for me to address. I was particularly well received in the universities, but the ensuing publicity became an embarrassment for the Labour Government.

Ernest Bevin, the Foreign Secretary, finally sent for me, and in rough language explained that I was being used by the Communist Party. My pride was injured; no one enjoys being told that they have been manipulated. I did not want to believe that I was an innocent abroad, and I reacted sharply to Bevin's lecture. Nonetheless, I began to look with a more searching eye at the people who surrounded me at the rallies. Soon I realised that Bevin had indeed been right, and I resolved to leave foreign affairs to people with greater experience. The whole Greek episode was a major political blunder on my part, and I was fortunate that Clem Attlee understood that my behaviour was due to naivety rather than malice.

The strains of the adventure affected me badly soon after I returned home. Tony Greenwood, a future Housing Minister and then my closest friend in the Commons, insisted I should visit the Greenwood family doctor in Harley Street, who told me that all I needed was a rest.

I felt much better after this visit so that it was a surprise when Arthur Moyle, Parliamentary Private Secretary to the Prime Minister, told me that Attlee wished to see me. It was the first time that I had had a private interview with the Prime Minister and I naturally felt apprehensive.

Attlee could not have been kinder. He sat behind his desk with his pipe in his hand. A plain white saucer served as his ashtray. He had apparently received a letter from one of my constituents expressing anxiety about my health. I explained that I had just had a check-up but he told me crisply to be in Palace Yard the next morning at ten, when I would be taken in his car to be examined by his doctor.

He sent for me again a week later to say that the doctor had recommended I should go to Switzerland for six weeks' rest. When I said that I could not possibly afford the trip, Attlee replied, "You have friends in this House, George. The bills will be paid." I was deeply touched but went on to say that I could not leave my constituency for so long a period. Attlee explained that a neighbouring MP would look after it for me. This time I was emphatic that I would not go to Switzerland. We agreed that I would rest at home for six weeks.

Attlee's deep English reserve hid a profoundly compassionate nature: at the time he was so mindful of my welfare he was also grappling with enormous economic problems. Outside national politics he loved to talk about two other subjects – cricket and local government, being particularly proud of the fact that he was the first Mayor of Bethnal Green to refuse to wear robes. In the way he brushed aside my escapade in Greece when he learned I was unwell, he also taught me that political disagreements should never be allowed to cloud human relationships. He became, and remains, one of my folk heroes.

I did manage a short break in Canada during the spring and when I arrived back in Tonypandy I found that Dad Tom, who had been ill for some time, was in a very bad way. It was almost as though he was hanging on to life just long enough to see me home.

Somehow, news that my stepfather had died reached Anthony Eden and he sent me a handwritten two-page letter of sympathy. In it he referred to his feelings at his own father's death. I was very moved. As a backbencher from the opposite side of the House, I felt the letter confirmed my belief that Eden really cared about people. As long as he lived, I remained one of his admirers and I hope history will be kinder to him than his contemporaries were.

The Thomas family *Back row, l to r:* Ada, Mam, Dorothy (Dolly). *Front row, l to r:* George, Emrys, Ivor. All our clothes were made by Mam

Aunt Ada and Mam

Father, 1913

Brother Ivor (far right) was apprenticed to Masters in 1928 where he earned 7s 6d a week

Left: The "underhouse" where I spent my childhood. Only the bottom storey is shown in the photograph. The "gully" with stone steps leading up to Miskin Road is now incorporated into the house, but where it was can be clearly seen to the right of the small window

Below: Miskin Road, Trealaw

Left: Form 4, Tonypandy Grammar School, 1924–5
Back row, l to r: George Thomas, Thomas Kiff, Gordon Tanner. *Middle row, l to r:* Gwladys Jones, Edna Davies, Gwyneth Jones, Miriam Cory. *Front row, l to r:* Margaret Nash, Doris Elliot, Margaret Howells, Sadie Griffiths

Below: Councillor Owen Buckley, JP, photographed in Tonypandy in the 1920s— the man who did most to encourage me to become a Methodist preacher

Labour Party Summer School, 1932. Mam is in the centre of the back row with Self centre front row. Behind my left shoulder is Mrs Andrews, the first woman magistrate in Wales

Methodist Central Hall,
Tonypandy

On holiday with Ivor in
Brighton, 1932

Dad Tom and Mam, 1947

Sergeant Thomas 714, Glamorgan
Special Constabulary, 1943

Macedonia, 1947. I am standing next to the first Andarte (guerilla) whom I met
on my visit to Greece. Also in the picture are (far left) the schoolmaster with
whom I stayed and the shepherd who acted as our guide

Declaration of election result, 1945 *L to r:* Jim Callaghan, Hilary Marquand, Peter Hopkin Morgan (Lib.), the Lord Mayor, Tapper Jones (town clerk), Self, Sir Ernest Evans, Sir James Grigg, Charles Hallinan (Con.) and Emlyn Jones, the Liberal candidate for Cardiff North

Welsh parliamentary Labour Party, 1951 *Back row, l to r:* Walter Padley (Ogmore), Goronwy Roberts (Caernarvon Boroughs), Arthur Pearson (Pontypridd), Granville West (Pontypool), GT (Cardiff West), Desmond Donnelly (Pembrokeshire), Tudor Watkins (Brecon & Radnor), Percy Morris (Swansea West), Nye Bevan (Ebbw Vale), Jim Callaghan (Cardiff South East), Harold Finch (Bedwelty), Harry Mitchell (Secretary of the Welsh Labour Group), Ness Edwards (Caerphilly), Peter Freeman (Newport), Elwyn Jones (Bangor). *Front row, l to r:* Dorothy Rees (Barry), George Daggar (Abertillery), David Mort (Swansea East), Robert Richards (Wrexham), David Williams (Neath), Emlyn Thomas (Aberdare), Viscount Hall (former MP for Aberdare), David Grenfell (Gower), James Griffiths (Llanelli), S. O. Davies (Merthyr Tydfil), Eirene White (Flintshire)

Self and Mam with (left) Aunt Ada, paying her first visit home in 42 years, 1955

Campaigning in Grangetown, Cardiff, 1955

Above: Our peace march to protest against the United States exploding the first hydrogen bomb, 1954
L to r: George Craddock, Fenner Brockway, Sir Richard Acland, Tony Greenwood, Self and Tony Benn

Left: Getting signatures for the petition for Leasehold Reform outside Cardiff market

On arrival from Kenya at Chileka Airport in 1967, being presented to the
Malawians gathered to meet the President, His Excellency Dr H. Kamazu Banda

Self with Jomo Kenyatta and the Attorney-General during my visit to Kenya,
1967. Before the war Kenyatta had lived for a time down in Cardiff's docks when
only the Labour Party would have anything to do with him

As Minister of State in the Commonwealth Office I called on the late Mrs Indira Gandhi in New Delhi on 28 November 1967. The photograph shows me presenting a book, *Art Treasures of the World,* to Mrs Gandhi

Pembrey Sands, 9 September 1968. Visiting an airman blown up by one of the bombs exploded in Wales before the Investiture of Prince Charles

My mother presents me with a daffodil on the day I was appointed Secretary of State for Wales, 1968

Mr Kellett, Regional Chairman of the National Coal Board in Wales, and myself at Ogmore Valley pit in 1968 during my term as Secretary of State

Her Majesty the Queen, accompanied by HRH Prince Philip and HRH Prince Charles, visits the Welsh Office in 1969 — the Queen's first visit to a Government department. The Permanent Secretary, Sir Goronwy Daniels, is on the right of the picture

With HRH Prince Charles and Bernard, Duke of Norfolk, during the preparations for the Investiture, 1969

Driving to Caernarvon Castle with HRH Prince Charles in the open carriage. In Wales top hats are traditionally worn only by undertakers at funerals and I couldn't bring myself to put mine on!

The Labour Cabinet, 1969 *Back row, l to r:* Judith Hart, GT, Cledwyn Hughes, Richard Marsh, Ted Short, Willie Ross, George Thomson, Tony Benn, Anthony Greenwood, Edward Shackleton, Roy Mason, Jack Diamond and Burke Trend (Secretary to the Cabinet). *Front row, l to r:* Peter Shore, Denis Healey, Barbara Castle, Lord Gardiner, Michael Stewart, Harold Wilson, Roy Jenkins, Richard Crossman, James Callaghan, Fred Peart and Anthony Crosland

Parliamentary victims of cartoons in the House of Commons magazine. *L to r:* Jack Ashley, Self, Sir Keith Joseph and David Steel

On the way to Marmaris, Turkey, September 1973

Self and Jim Callaghan receiving the Freedom of the City of Cardiff in 1975

Self with Jim Callaghan and his wife Audrey greeting Henry Kissinger when he arrived in Cardiff for the Freedom Ceremony, 1975

During the long summer recess of 1948, Konni Zilliacus, a left-wing Labour MP, invited me to join a broadly based parliamentary delegation visiting Czechoslovakia, Yugoslavia, Poland and the Soviet Union.

First we went to Yugoslavia, where students from across the world were helping to rebuild the war-ravaged land. Tito received us in his magnificent home, resplendent in his field-marshal's uniform weighed down with the highest decorations he could bestow upon himself. His Alsatian dog was the one that had saved his life during the war by alerting him that enemy troops were approaching.

Tito's appearance was in sharp contrast to Stalin's when we met him at his residence in Sochi on the Black Sea. Stalin's plain drill suit bore no decorations, and he clearly felt no need to buttress himself with medals. It reminded me of how Churchill used to wear a boiler-suit during the war, and I noticed that Stalin, a pipe smoker, also used a plain white saucer as his ashtray. As he laughed and talked there was nothing to betray him as the ruthless murderer of his own people. He was clearly determined to leave us with the impression of a friendly man, but it struck me as odd that he sent greetings to neither Churchill nor Attlee.

Both in Poland and Czechoslovakia, I felt very uneasy. The Polish people were divided by their fear of Russia and their need to co-operate with her. Their premier, Gomulka, was expelled from the Communist Party that September and their Socialist and Communist Parties were merged. Czechoslovakia had undergone a Communist coup d'état that February, and their foreign minister, Jan Masaryk, had been found dead beneath his office window a month later. His successor, Clementis, with whom we talked at length, was forced to resign in 1950, and was tried and executed on charges of Titoist and Zionist conspiracy. I was relieved to get out of both countries.

CHAPTER NINE

Trouble for Labour

The boundary changes of 1950 merged three-fifths of my constituency of Cardiff Central into Cardiff West, making it a safer Labour seat. The general election held in February that year, however, was anything but safe for the Labour Party as a whole. The Government's economic policies were not succeeding, and a Conservative victory was feared. After the biggest turnout of voters the country had ever known, Labour did win, but by the desperately close overall majority of eight.

I was most anxious that some concrete progress should be made on leasehold reform, and before the House closed for the summer recess, I tabled a motion calling for an immediate standstill order intended to give temporary protection to those tenants whose leases were due to expire in the near future. It had become a matter of urgency, because the procedures necessary to effect the introduction of permanent legislation for leasehold reform were proving to be very long-drawn-out and complex.

I collected the signatures of 125 Labour MPs in support of my motion, but was not successful in forcing any immediate action. During that summer, I spoke to many constituents who were facing eviction orders, and when Parliament reopened in the autumn I waited anxiously to hear if one particular item had been included in the King's Speech. It seemed an age before King George VI finally reached the expected reference to leasehold reform. After that, the Government acted swiftly, and by Christmas the Leasehold Property (Temporary Provisions) Bill had been passed, ensuring a two-year protection period for tenants whose leases were due to expire.

Early in 1951, I had my first taste of what it might be like to be Speaker when Sir Charles MacAndrew, Chairman of Ways and Means (one of the Speaker's deputies), invited me to join the Speaker's Panel of Chairmen. This opened the door for me to preside over standing committees in the House, and even over the whole House when the committee stage (that is, the detailed examination) of a bill was taken on the floor of the House. I soon developed a taste for the work, and tried to model myself on Sir Charles.

Two secrets determined his success. The first was his complete impartiality: as a result, although he was a Conservative, the Labour Party also trusted and respected him. The second was that he never tried to make any member look small in front of his colleagues. Difficult members were treated with such courtesy they found it hard to resist his pleas for co-operation.

It was much the same with the Speaker, W. S. Morrison, also a Conservative, with whom Sir Charles worked in close harmony. Until Morrison became Speaker, I had gone to his constituency, Cirencester and Tewkesbury, to open the Labour Party summer fête each year. I decided not to go when he assumed the Chair because in doing so he gave up his Party allegiance. One day, as I passed his Chair, he commented that I had not been to the Labour fête. When I explained why, he replied, "It isn't fair. I gained a thousand votes every time you came!"

His commanding presence and resounding voice made him a great Speaker and, as I watched him in the House, I never dreamed that the wig which covered his head would one day cover mine, and that the silver buckles on his shoes would be fitted to mine.

At this time the newspapers were full of stories about divisions in the Cabinet over the question of charges for teeth and spectacles supplied by the National Health Service. One night early in April 1951, I was sitting alone in the members' tea-room when Nye Bevan came and sat by me. I told him that Labour's backbenchers were relying on him to prevent Hugh Gaitskell from forcing these health charges through the Cabinet. His response was immediate: "I will not remain a member of a Government that imposes health charges." He added that he was on his way to address a public meeting in the East End. Next morning, the national press carried screaming headlines reporting Nye's threat to resign if charges for teeth and spectacles became government policy.

The speech provoked a major political crisis. The tea-room and the smoking-room were crowded with members assessing possible consequences. I went into an almost deserted Chamber and saw Jennie Lee, Nye's wife, sitting alone on the third bench below the gangway. I sat beside her and whispered to her that she must persuade Nye not to resign as he was too useful inside the Cabinet.

Her angry reaction shook me. She could not have been more furious: "You yellow-livered cur. You're just like all the rest! You're another MacDonald or Snowden. Go away from me!" I could hardly believe my ears. I bowed to the Speaker and left the chamber. I was beginning to learn that the pursuit of power can be a very unpleasant business.

In his Budget speech a week later, Hugh Gaitskell announced that in future most people would have to pay half the cost of their dentures and spectacles under the National Health Service. Bevan stalked angrily out of the Chamber. Two weeks later he resigned from his post as Minister of Labour, and Harold Wilson resigned in sympathy from the presidency of the Board of Trade.

Attlee was in hospital suffering from a duodenal ulcer during this crisis. The strain of keeping together his Cabinet of strong men had clearly taken its toll. He had been Deputy Prime Minister throughout the war years, and had had six gruelling years as Prime Minister. The Parliamentary Labour Party was also showing signs of strain. Our main tasks seemed to have been accomplished. We had transferred all the basic industries to national ownership; we had established the National Health Service; and we had laid the foundations of the welfare state.

The bitter internal quarrels in the Parliamentary Party inevitably resulted in lack of support in the country. The pressure was increased by the Tories at Westminster who, sensing victory, made parliamentary life a misery. Night after night we were kept in the Commons until the small hours. The Opposition knew that the Government could survive only by bringing sick members from their hospital beds. With a majority now reduced to five, we were limping along. Robert Boothby revealed Conservative tactics when he publicly declared, "We will harry them to the death!" Finally, Attlee called a general election for 25 October.

Churchill won a small overall majority. One of his strengths was that, unlike Ted Heath later, he realised the supreme importance of gaining trades-union goodwill, by flattering TUC leaders with constant invitations to Number Ten and describing them as the Fourth Estate of the Realm. The old man's cunning political instincts enabled him to lay firm foundations for a long period of Tory rule.

One of the first things Churchill planned was to impose further charges on the health service and I organised a motion to the Parliamentary Labour Party that would commit the next Labour Government to the complete abolition of health charges. Many MPs who had supported Hugh Gaitskell over the original imposition of charges had lost their seats in the general election, and there was no difficulty in getting more than half the Parliamentary Party to sign the motion.

This turned out to be another occasion when I made Herbert Morrison angry. He told a crowded Parliamentary Party meeting that it was undemocratic for me to collect signatures before there had been any chance of a discussion. He strongly urged the meeting not to tie the hands of the Party leaders by supporting the proposal. After a stormy debate, the Parliamentary Party gave the motion a comfortable majority.

Shortly after this meeting, Elwyn Jones (the Labour member for West Ham South, and later Lord Chancellor) and I went on a visit to Israel, arranged by Ian Mikardo, whose brother-in-law was the Clerk of the Israeli Parliament. Leaks from the Party meeting had been reported in the British newspapers but I was surprised to find that the Labour leaders in Israel knew all about it. At the British Embassy residence in Tel Aviv I met Nye Bevan, who was on his way home from India, and he had heard about the meeting from Jennie Lee. He seemed to feel that the acceptance of the motion vindicated his resignation from Attlee's Cabinet. He laughed loudly as we talked of Herbert Morrison's discomfiture.

It was only four years since the modern state of Israel had been proclaimed, and the scars of her recent conflicts were raw. Tanks lay abandoned in the desert, and people used to gather in the King David Hotel to look towards Old Jerusalem in Jordan, and across the valley outside Jerusalem where the tombstones of Jewish people had been smashed by the Arabs.

That visit to Israel strengthened my horror of war and I was deeply shocked in 1954 when on 1 March, St David's Day, the United States detonated her first hydrogen bomb. It was that explosion which triggered off the Campaign for Nuclear Disarmament, which in a way I helped to form. When Fenner Brockway heard about the bomb, he called a meeting in a committee room in the Commons, which I attended with Tony Greenwood, Donald Soper, John Collins, Sydney Silverman, Lord Beveridge, Victor Yates, Tony Benn and a few others.

We decided to book the Albert Hall and hold a great peace rally against nuclear weapons. We had to select a chairman to preside at the rally and to my great surprise, Lord Beveridge, the father of the welfare state, announced, "My wife has said that in view of my status and position, I should be chairman of this meeting." I intervened to point out that we were not interested in Lady Beveridge's views on this particular matter. He went on to say that his wife had told him to withdraw if he was not going to be chairman. The meeting agreed with me, and Beveridge left to telephone her. When he returned, he said his wife had told him to withdraw and he left the meeting.

More was to follow. John Collins, then Canon of St Paul's, announced, "Well, now Lord Beveridge has gone, I think that I should be chairman." I could hardly believe my own ears: the sheer vanity of people who were professing to hold such high ideals. The rest of the meeting shared my view that we should not allow the Canon to nominate himself. Collins also left. When he had gone, my proposal that Donald Soper should be in the chair was agreed. Even in the peace movement, there are people who think of themselves first.

Later on, Fenner Brockway, Tony Greenwood, Tony Benn, Richard Acland, Victor Yates, George Craddock and I decided to advertise the Albert Hall rally and to express our horror at the hydrogen bomb by walking in sandwich boards from Victoria station up to Piccadilly via Westminster.

We gathered at Victoria, only to be told by the police, who were not very polite about it, that we would not be allowed to walk together. There had to be four hundred yards separating each of us. I soon discovered that walking on your own with a sandwich board can be a very embarrassing business. I will never forget the big fat clergyman crammed into a small car needling me all the time, saying things like "Go back to Russia, you Communist!"

I felt terribly awkward as I passed the Commons, and hoped no members would see me walking along with the board. Eventually I reached Horse Guards Parade, and the clergyman was still following, niggling and sneering all the time. At last I could bear it no longer, turned to him and said, "If you don't go away, I'll lift this board and bring it down on your head." That, of course, was what he wanted: "There! I knew you were all men of violence inside."

I did not join the CND movement, deciding that to belong to the Labour Party was enough for me, but I've always been proud that I took part in that walk.

My campaign for leasehold reform suffered a setback in 1954 when the Conservative Government passed their Landlord and Tenant Bill. The Home Secretary, Sir David Maxwell-Fyfe, claimed that to grant tenants the right to purchase the freehold of their own houses would pose too many practical difficulties, and an improved security of tenure

was as far as the bill could go. Coupled with that security, however, was the strengthened right for landlords to raise ground-
rents and charge for repairs considered necessary, when leases ran
out. When the bill was given its final reading, I ended a short
opposing speech by saying that it would not be the final word on the
subject.

A few months later, I was fortunate in the ballot which determines
those members who will be granted parliamentary time to introduce
a Private Member's Bill.* The bill to give leaseholders the right either
to renew their leases or to buy the freehold of their homes at a
reasonable price was presented for its second reading on a Friday in
March 1955.

Friday is the usual day for debating Private Members' Bills, perhaps
by design, as it is also the day when attendance in the House is low.
The debate went on for four and a half hours and at the division there
was a considerable majority in favour. It failed to carry, though, as
there were not enough members present to comply with Standing
Orders. It was a bitter blow and it was some time before I found
another way to resume the fight.

During that year, the leaders of both the main parties changed.
Eden succeeded Churchill in April, and at the general election in May,
the Conservatives were returned with an increased majority. Six
months later, Attlee announced his retirement. Some people thought
he might have gone earlier if he could have been sure that Herbert
Morrison would not succeed him.

His dislike of Morrison was part of parliamentary folklore, and I
had some first-hand evidence of it. When Attlee was suffering from
his ulcer, I went to visit him in St Mary's Hospital in Paddington.
The ward sister asked me to wait while she checked to see if he was
awake. She returned to say: "You are greatly honoured. The Prime
Minister will see you. Yesterday he told me to tell Mr Morrison he
was sleeping."

Morrison's standing in the Parliamentary Labour Party was very
low at that time. With shrewd calculation, Attlee had built up Gaitskell's reputation by appointing him to the key position of Chancellor
of the Exchequer, and he was the obvious front runner in the leadership
stakes. Nye Bevan was the third candidate. He was still a commanding
figure in the Party, but the violence of his personal attacks on colleagues

*A bill not sponsored by the Government.

with whom he disagreed had caused many wounds which were far from healing.

Despite an eleventh-hour attempt to prevent Gaitskell from getting the leadership by offering to stand down in Morrison's favour if Gaitskell would do the same, Nye was defeated. He got only 70 votes to Gaitskell's 157, while Morrison got just 40. The Party's right wing were jubilant, while the left were in near despair.

Morrison's defeat shattered him, and his cockney bounce disappeared. He never really recovered from the blow, feeling that he had been cheated by the Parliamentary Labour Party he had served so faithfully. I never told him that I had voted for Nye Bevan, although I think he guessed.

In 1956 I received an invitation from the State Department to tour the United States. It was still an adventure to travel to America in those days, and I decided to go for several months. As well as making visits in my capacity as a British MP, I ended up by preaching in every one of the states except Florida.

The presidential election, in which Eisenhower fought Adlai Stevenson, was taking place, and I was given tickets to attend both the Democratic convention in Chicago, and the Republican convention in San Francisco. It was fascinating to be able to look on from close quarters, yet not feel involved. I was amused by corpulent business men, with big cigars in their mouths, who wore boaters with the slogans "I like Ike", "Ike Likes Me", and – which I thought was the best election slogan of all – "Ike Likes Everybody".

I was in San Francisco when the news of the invasion of Suez was broken to the world.* I had met in San Francisco the Tory MP, Joe Godber, and we decided to follow the customary policy of British MPs who are abroad, always to defend our own country. Both of us took a very strong line in meetings that we addressed such as Rotary or the Lions' Club. Eisenhower made what I thought was a very cruel speech attacking the British. Because he was electioneering, principles did not appeal to him very much just then. My answer to Americans who were hostile to my speeches was, "If it were the Panama Canal that was to be closed, you would take a very different attitude

---

*President Nasser of Egypt had nationalised the Suez Canal Company, whose headquarters were in Paris and most of whose directors were French or British. The canal was of enormous international importance, and Britain and France took the controversial decision to land troops in Egypt to secure its free navigation.

indeed." Many years later they realised the full significance of that, when bargaining about Panama took place.

I arrived back in Britain to petrol-rationing and anger in the country and Parliament, where old friends were refusing to speak to one another after the passions that had been roused. The Tories felt that the Labour Party had behaved treacherously by supporting the exercise at first and then pulling back later, and accused Labour of letting down the troops – and Britain.

Harold Macmillan, who had originally been in favour of the invasion of Suez, showed his diplomatic skills in a remarkable way. I remember him, then Chancellor of the Exchequer, standing at the Bar of the House, looking round, and instead of going to his place on the front bench next to the Prime Minister, walking to a seat on a bench below the gangway to chat to Tory backbenchers, making it plain that he was distancing himself from Eden. He was a master politician at a time when his party was in terrible distress and dismay. It had led us into a war which we had not won and that is not typical of our history. And Macmillan pulled it back together. He had a way with people and a way with words which drew people to him.

On one occasion he stood up in the House and said, "Mr Speaker, Sir, I have the honour of having been awarded by His Majesty the King of Egypt (Farouk) with the Order of Chastity." There was a great roar of laughter which Macmillan allowed to die down before adding "Fourth Class". Of course that set MPs roaring louder than ever, and Macmillan quickly cashed in on the mood of the House to make his major points.

Looking back at Suez now, it is clear that if the exercise had been successful, the whole history of the Middle East would have been transformed. The Arabs learned that, although they were weak militarily, they had the strength to defeat big powers through the force of world opinion and the United Nations. Both America and the Soviet Union were determined to block us over Suez, and under those circumstances it was impossible to succeed. It was a watershed for us. I thought that the fear and bitterness would turn opinion against the Government, but not at all. People to whom I spoke were not blaming the Government that had gone into the crisis, but rather those who had withheld their support. The country was deeply wounded by the whole affair but even now, looking back from this distance, it is not easy to assess the merits or the demerits of the exercise.

Gradually parliamentary life assumed a more normal pattern, and in 1957 I experienced one of those fairly frequent occasions when the Commons expects members to be able to laugh at themselves. At that time, I used to sit in the Chamber next to Jo Grimond, the Liberal Party leader, and as I took my seat one day, I saw that the Tories were looking across and pointing at us. I asked Jo Grimond what was exciting them. He replied, "You, I think." I was puzzled. Still keeping a straight face, he said, "I think it's the way you are dressed." I looked down to see if I was buttoned correctly and everything seemed to be in order.

At that moment, Colonel Robin Chichester-Clark, an Ulster member who sat on the Government front bench as a Whip, nodded across to me to follow him to the Bar of the House, the white line that signifies the end of the Chamber for debating purposes. I followed suit, and when I reached him, the entire House erupted. I asked him to explain what was going on. He said, "Do you know that you are wearing an Old Etonian tie?" I answered him truthfully: "I bought it in the Co-operative store in Tonypandy. I liked the look of it." He grinned: "You're probably safe to wear it in Tonypandy, but not here – too many members are entitled to wear it." I gave the tie to an old age pensioner in my constituency.

When the Government established the Welsh Grand Committee in 1958, I was elected its first chairman. Several years before, I had tabled a motion to the Welsh Parliamentary Party to support an application from Cardiff to be the capital city of Wales. That caused a furore! Lady Megan Lloyd George, who had been MP for Anglesey and now represented Carmarthen, was fiercely opposed, and so was Percy Morris who represented Swansea. Nye Bevan did not normally come to our meetings – he could not be bothered with the nuts and bolts of government – but at the behest of Megan Lloyd George he came to this one. He was at his most abusive, aiming his attack directly at me. It was a very unpleasant meeting and the motion was defeated.

At the end of 1955, however, when the Government decided that it was politically wise to make Cardiff the capital, those who had been opposed before soon came into line. When they came to Cardiff on official visits, one could never have guessed at the hostility they had once shown the city. But by then, I was used to political expediency and many worse examples were to follow.

CHAPTER TEN

A Question of Colour

In 1959, I was selected by the Commonwealth Parliamentary Association to visit Kenya and the Seychelles in company with Paul Williams, who was on the extreme right of the Conservative Party. The views I held must have been a nightmare to him, but he was a charming companion and despite our political differences we worked together harmoniously from start to finish.

Before we left, Jim Callaghan, then Labour's Shadow Colonial Secretary, warned me not to ask to see the imprisoned Mau Mau leader Jomo Kenyatta. Callaghan told me that such a request would anger the entire white community as they held Kenyatta personally responsible for the Mau Mau killing and maiming of blacks and whites alike.

Paul Williams and I followed a set pattern in dealing with the many different political groups in Kenya. When we met the white people, Paul would take the lead. As a known right-wing Tory, he could speak in strong terms without them feeling he was biased against them. Equally, I could speak firmly to the black African groups because the Labour Party was considered to be their friend. The strategy worked admirably.

On one occasion, we went to a political meeting in the White Highlands where the chairman immediately launched into a personal attack on the Labour MP John Stonehouse, who had just been declared a prohibited visitor in neighbouring Uganda, where he had apparently upset the white community. As the chairman's abuse of Stonehouse proceeded, I stood up and told him that I was not going to sit there while he attacked one of my parliamentary colleagues.

As I stood up to walk out, Paul Williams also rose to leave, saying we would not tolerate discourtesy. We left in silence and walked to our car. Four sturdy young men ran across to us, and we thought we were going to be attacked. Paul said, "Stand with your back to the car, George, there's trouble coming." The young men merely wanted to argue their case against independence being granted to Kenya, but the incident underlined the tensions that prevailed as independence became inevitable.

While we were in Nairobi, we heard of the death of nine prisoners at Hola Camp and we insisted on flying down to see what conditions were like. We were led in front of cages in which Africans were locked like animals in a zoo. One of the prisoners was stark naked, and kept making faces at us, and I was told he was mad. When I said that if that was the case he should be in hospital not prison, the guard gave me a baleful stare but said nothing.

The atmosphere at Hola Camp was frightening. Hatred filled the air, and to add to everyone's agony, the temperature was 110°. It seemed crazy to have sited the prison in the hottest part of Kenya. I was shocked at how fear of a nationalist victory had led the British to such stupid brutalities and foolish decisions. Anxiety about our reaction to what we had seen made the prison authorities ultra cautious in the conference that followed our visit.

Before leaving Mombasa, I visited a Methodist missionary centre nearby, where the black superintendent minister told me that it was a Methodist missionary who had paid for his grandfather's freedom from slavery. He took me to a small graveyard where six missionaries were buried. He particularly pointed out the ages on the tombstones: they had all been men in their early twenties. Some had been murdered, and some had been stricken with tropical disease. The minister pointed to the dates: each missionary had died within months of arriving. When the news of each death reached London, another young man was ready to fill the place. In the judgement of some people, these young men were wasted; but the strong Church in Kenya is lasting evidence of their success.

Paul Williams and I made a three-day journey by boat from Mombasa to the Seychelles, the first parliamentary delegation ever to visit the islands. When we arrived at Mahe, the capital, we were rowed ashore in a small boat by the Seychellois men, with their friends swimming alongside, waiting to be thrown coins, which they caught most expertly.

On landing, we discovered that the islanders were more British than the British. They were descended from slaves landed by Royal Navy ships which had intercepted slave boats carrying Africans from Mombasa to America. The otherwise happy trip had two bad moments. The first was a visit to the local workhouse, where every inmate was dressed in a drab grey pauper's uniform. Tin plates were put in front of them, and their mish-mash of food dolloped on to their plates as if it was being given to dogs.

We were also taken out to a lonely island leper colony. There were three lepers, two women and one old man, being treated in their necessary isolation as if they were prisoners. The old man was an extrovert who seemed happy enough, but the two women sat in sullen silence just staring across the water in the direction of the mainland. My heart ached for them as I knew they were totally cut off from family and friends in the isolation caused by their leprosy. Medicine had not advanced far in 1959 with regard to curing or controlling the disease and it was almost as if the sufferers were treated as criminals. The old man had lost all his fingers and his toes, and had to be lifted from the bed to sit outside his cell-like room.

He gave me a toothless grin and indicated his hands and feet, and every time we looked again in his direction he laughed. The young male nurse who cared for him was a Christian and had been on the island for three years. His dedication and contentment was a marked contrast to the jealousies in Westminster.

The frustration of the long years in opposition was assuaged for me by the opportunity provided to play an increasing part in the Methodist Church, preaching in nearly every city in the country during the Fifties and early Sixties. Three days before one preaching engagement in York, I took part in a television discussion with Iorwerth Thomas, then the MP for Rhondda West. We had a sharp disagreement over the opening of public houses in Wales on a Sunday. My view was, and is, that anything that undermines respect for Sunday as our Sabbath Day undermines respect for Christian teaching.

I was no stranger to the controversy, having crossed swords with Herbert Morrison in 1951 over his plans to open Battersea Fun Fair, part of the Festival of Britain, on Sunday. People in Scotland, Wales, Northern Ireland and Cornwall were firmly opposed to Sunday opening – the fact that his major opposition came from the Celtic parts of Britain added spice to Herbert's fury. I was perhaps unkind to him when I said in the House of Commons, "My right honourable friend is sometimes described as a little Englander. He is not so, Mr Speaker, he is a little Londoner, who does not appreciate the convictions of those who live elsewhere." The following day I received a long, indignant letter from Herbert saying he would never come to speak in Cardiff again.

I now believe that the fight to preserve Sunday as a day set apart was more significant than we realised. It was the first major post-war attack on the place of religion in our national life. We lost that battle, and we have subsequently witnessed a substantial decline in the influence of the Nonconformist churches in Britain.

So I thought my views were fairly well known, but after the service in York a man asked me if he had seen me on television the week before. I said he had probably seen the discussion on Sunday opening of public houses in Wales. "That's right," he said. "It was two Thomases arguing about drink. Which one were you?" That taught me that television is better at giving impressions than details of arguments!

It was in July 1959 that the Methodist Conference did me the honour of nominating me vice-president, the first time the post had gone to an MP. My heart was full, thinking of my upbringing in Tonypandy chapel, when I was installed, together with the president, the Reverend Edward Rogers, at the conference at Liverpool in 1960.

As vice-president I went to Lake Junaluska, North Carolina, for the ninth conference of the World Methodist Church, and from there I went on a wide preaching tour. In Georgia, I met with difficulty.

My host had taken me on Saturday night to see the church in which I was due to preach the next day. It was an attractive white building, with colonial-style pillars and I said innocently, "What a beautiful white church." To my horror he replied, "Of course it's white, you don't understand our problems." My hackles rose and I asked as coldly as I could, "Are you telling me that black people are not allowed to worship here?" He was equally disturbed: "I told you, you do not understand our problems. Of course no Negroes worship there. They have their own church." With some trepidation, I said, "I do not pretend to understand your problems; I am only a visitor. My trouble is that you do not understand my problem. I cannot preach in a church where blacks are refused admission. I believe in the Brotherhood of Man."

I could not have caused greater offence. Soon the Bishop of Georgia was speaking to me on the telephone. His name was Moore, and I knew that he had Irish blood. He did not mince his words. He said he found it offensive that I should come to Georgia and create trouble. He wished he had never invited me. I listened to a lot more abusive references to people from the United Kingdom before I could get in a word by way of reply.

I finally managed to ask him if he could arrange for another preacher to take my place. He could not, but went on to ask that if he could make arrangements for me to preach in the "Nigra" church in the evening, would I preach in his church in the morning. I jumped at the lifeline for it would mean everyone in the community would know I did not support segregation.

Next morning I faced a crowded congregation in the white Methodist church. Not feeling that I had the right to use their own pulpit to attack them, I avoided any reference to segregation. Even so, a man said, "So you're another one-worlder!" I replied with a smile, "That's right, Sir. How many worlds do you believe in?" I received no reply.

In the evening, it was a totally different experience. I was the only white person in the church, and I felt that the congregation was rather embarrassed. But the welcome was warm and sincere. The minister said to everyone, "We are greatly honoured tonight to welcome Mr George Thomas, a British Member of Parliament, who is also a Methodist like us. His face is white, but his heart is as black as ours."

Since that memorable occasion, I have been privileged to preach in many other countries across the globe, but I have never forgotten the welcome of that congregation in Georgia.

CHAPTER ELEVEN

The Battle for Labour

The general election of 1959, which returned the Conservative Government with an increased majority, exacerbated the hostilities developing in the Parliamentary Labour Party. Nowadays, Hugh Gaitskell is being increasingly presented as a moderate man, but in fact he was anything but moderate. He stood way to the right of the Party, and could not be bothered with anyone who did not share his own views. In the members' tea-room he would sit only with his cronies, making it clear to everyone that he was content to lead a divided Party as long as his supporters were in the majority.

He came down to Cardiff on one occasion to speak for Jim Callaghan. He had not given me any indication that he was coming, but I had read about it in the Cardiff newspapers. On the Friday night I was at home watching the television news and saw Gaitskell being received at Cardiff station by Callaghan. I was just about to go out to a meeting, when the telephone rang.

It was Cliff Prothero, the Labour Party's regional organiser in Wales, who asked me to go to a Transport House press conference in the morning to meet Hugh Gaitskell. I refused, not just because Gaitskell had been discourteous in not telling me he was coming to Cardiff but because I felt strongly that he only wanted to lead half the Labour Party. And I had no intention of doing anything other than let it be seen that he was leading half a party. Prothero, an old friend, begged me to put in an appearance. I finally agreed that I would, after I had finished my constituency surgery.

As usual, the interviews took a long time, and when I reached Transport House the press conference was over. Hugh Gaitskell came up and put his arm around me and asked me to walk with him down Queen Street. I was still very angry: "I've seen you and Jim several times this week, and neither of you told me you were coming. If you want to lead half the Party, you lead it; but I'm not going to make it any easier for you."

The untimely death of Nye Bevan in July 1960 made Labour's chance of ever winning power under Gaitskell even more remote. The Party Conference in Scarborough was deeply divided. Gaitskell's official defence statement was narrowly defeated, while a resolution calling for unilateral disarmament was narrowly passed. It was after this that Gaitskell made his famous "We'll fight, fight and fight again" speech, defending his policy. That speech has contributed in recent years to the myth that he was a Party healer, but I do not believe that Labour would have got into power had he remained leader.

After the conference, Tony Greenwood resigned his Shadow Cabinet post and announced that he was prepared to stand against Gaitskell at the forthcoming leadership election. This put Harold Wilson in serious difficulty. Having emerged as the natural successor to Bevan, he could not afford to allow Greenwood to be the one to throw down the gauntlet. He therefore announced his own candidature, and Tony Greenwood at once withdrew. Although the result was a foregone conclusion, Wilson's supporters put up a good show. The great majority of Welsh MPs rallied to him, and the final vote was Gaitskell 166, Wilson 81.

Gaitskell kept Harold Wilson in the post of Shadow Chancellor for a further year, but then in a general switch appointed him Shadow Foreign Secretary. Wilson made no effort to disguise either his anger or his disappointment, but in the event it was the best thing that could have happened to him. Edward Heath was then conducting Britain's Common Market negotiations, and this gave Wilson plenty of opportunity to oppose him on the floor of the House. At that time, Labour still had grave reservations about joining the EEC, doubts which I wholeheartedly shared. I was always a great supporter of the Commonwealth, and believed the Common Market could do it nothing but harm.

I was a member of a delegation of forty Labour MPs which Wilson was asked to lead on a visit to Berlin. We were a motley crew, spanning the whole spectrum of the Parliamentary Labour Party, but we were unanimous in our condemnation of the Berlin Wall, which had just been built by the East Germans. Willi Brandt, who invited us all to his home, made it clear that Wilson was held in high esteem in West Germany. The tour enhanced Wilson's prestige, and gave him an opportunity to demonstrate his ability to get the right and the left to work together happily.

During this period I made another effort to further my campaign for leashold reform. First I appealed to the Welsh Parliamentary Party to support a petition that would force the Government to act. They bluntly refused to co-operate, so I decided to forge ahead on my own. As soon as the story written by my friend David Rosser – the political editor – about the All Wales Leasehold Reform Petition appeared in the *Western Mail*, I was deluged with letters of support. With the enthusiastic help of an all-party committee in Cardiff, petitions were sent to groups and individuals throughout Wales.

On five successive Saturdays, I stood with a table loaded with petition forms outside the St Mary Street entrance to the Cardiff City Market. The choice of site was inspired. Every person walking in Cardiff's main street had to pass, and people queued in their hundreds to sign. I made sure that publicity was given not only to our most prominent signatories, such as the Archbishop of the Church of Wales, but also to leaseholders who had a sad story to tell.

Within my target date of five weeks, more than 60,000 signatures had been obtained. I was jubilant. The support had crossed all party boundaries, as I had forecast to the Welsh Parliamentary Party that it would. The next step was to present the petition to Parliament. Cheers from my Welsh colleagues were music to my ears when I rose to my feet in the Commons. My hand was shaking as I read out the top copy. Then I bowed to the Speaker and made my way to deposit the petition in the big green bag behind his Chair. The whole House gave a generous cheer.

Within a few days, I received a message that Dr Charles Hill, Minister for Local Government and Welsh Affairs, wished to see me. I went over to his palatial Whitehall office, and he used his best bedside manner to greet me. "Well done, George. You have had a great triumph," was his opening gambit, spoken within the hearing of his secretaries.

Then he closed his office door, saying that he did not want any civil servants to listen to our conversation. He wanted to know what terms I would be prepared to agree. My reply was that I stood by the terms of the petition. I wanted full leasehold enfranchisement or nothing. This meant that I was insisting on the right of people to buy the freehold of their home, even if the ground landlord did not wish to sell. Charles exploded: "You know this Tory Government will never agree to that. Be reasonable, George, and settle for half a loaf now." He always liked to talk as though he was a National Liberal in a Tory Government.

We argued for about a quarter of an hour before we agreed that there was no common ground between us. I left knowing that the Government was worried by the success of the campaign, but I also knew that reform of the leasehold system would have to await the coming of a Labour Government.

After Hugh Gaitskell's sad and totally unexpected death in January 1963, things were very different at Westminster. Speculation about Gaitskell's successor led to political in-fighting with no holds barred. Harold Wilson was the candidate of the left, and I was one of his firmest supporters. Jim Callaghan and George Brown divided the vote of the right. The fact that Jim was my colleague as a Cardiff MP made my position embarrassing, yet I was in no doubt where my duty lay. Harold Wilson was the most likely man to bridge the chasm that divided the two sections of the Party.

Stories that were damaging to the respective candidates spread like bush fire. I never cease to marvel that whenever there is a major election amongst MPs, even the wildest rumours are repeated as though the gossips had proof of what they were saying. With their experience of the sorts of tales that are spread during dirty campaigns in general elections, it staggers me that MPs should either stoop to similar tactics themselves or take notice of the unscrupulous attempts at character assassination they hear. But they do.

One day Percy Holman, a much liked and respected member of the right wing of the Labour Party, joined me at a table in the members' tea-room. Naturally our conversation drifted to the election of the Party leader. Holman asked me if I had ever seen Wilson's wife, commenting that it was strange that she was never with him. Sensing hostility to Wilson, I said that I knew Mrs Wilson well and asked him what he was driving at. There was no reply. The truth was, I had never met Mary Wilson, but I felt angry at the low-level campaign of some of Wilson's opponents who were spreading rumours about his private secretary, Marcia Williams, now Lady Falkender.

When I recounted the tale to Wilson, he told me that Mary was very shy and did not like mixing in crowds. He asked me to go to his house that night and repeat the story to Mary. If he had handed me a thousand pounds he would not have pleased me more. He had given me the answer that I wanted. Harold's face was grim as he added, "When Mary hears this, she will come with me tomorrow to the Abbey for Hugh Gaitskell's memorial service." From that day on, Mary Wilson conquered her shyness and played a major part in Harold's public life.

During the campaign in the Parliamentary Party, there was deep bitterness between the Callaghan and the Brown supporters. Each felt that the other candidate should have stood down to ensure a straight fight between right and left.

One Friday night, Jim Callaghan telephoned me at home in Cardiff. He had promised to preach in Splott Baptist Church in his constituency and he wanted me to help him with his sermon. I was worried. He was not a preacher, and I was surprised that he had agreed to do it. He explained he had been pressed, and asked if I would meet him in the Royal Hotel, Cardiff, where he was staying.

He greeted me warmly, and for about ten minutes we talked about his proposed sermon. He had decided to take brotherhood as his theme, since he was the Shadow Colonial Secretary. When we had finished discussing the sermon, he suddenly asked whether I would say a prayer with him. This took me a little by surprise, but we knelt down in his bedroom and I prayed that we should both be given strength and guidance to be worthy of our calling as MPs.

When we rose from our knees, he said, "I hope I can rely on your support for the party leadership, George." I was embarrassed, and felt my colour drain away. I told him that he knew I was committed to support Wilson, but he persisted: "We have been colleagues for nearly twenty years, and I thought I could be sure of your vote." I did not want to quarrel, so in order to be able to leave, I said I would consider my position over the weekend.

In the Commons on the Monday morning, Harold Wilson drew my attention to a piece in *The Times* reporting that over the weekend George Thomas, one of Wilson's keenest supporters, had indicated that he was switching support to Callaghan. In genuine anger, I told him that Jim had jumped the gun and I had not promised to switch my vote. I told him to watch that evening's *South Wales Echo*. I then telephoned the *Echo*'s editor to make it clear that I was supporting Wilson. When the paper was published, it carried both Jim Callaghan's picture and mine, along with the heading "Cardiff MPs Divided".

It has always been my belief that the Callaghan–Brown split ensured Wilson's ultimate victory. When Callaghan dropped out and it became a straight fight between Wilson and Brown, a large number of Callaghan's supporters voted for Wilson more out of a desire to prevent George Brown getting the leadership than out of any wish to see Harold at the helm. But when the final result was announced to the Parliamentary Party, there was a tremendous ovation given to the new leader. Morale in the constituencies rocketed upwards, and we sensed a new era had begun.

A year before he became leader, Wilson had promised to speak at a public meeting in my constituency. When it became clear after the result of the first ballot that he was almost certain of success, I offered to release him from his commitment. His reply was characteristic: "Whether I am elected or not, George, I shall keep my promise to you." In all my dealings with Harold Wilson I have always found him to be a man of his word. It is rarely easy to get him to commit himself, but when he does so, his promise is binding.

Contrary to common belief, he also has a strong streak of modesty in him. When I told him that in view of his new position I had cancelled the school hall for his Cardiff West meeting because it had room only for five hundred people, and had booked the Sophia Gardens Pavilion because it holds three thousand, he was appalled. He was worried that the television cameras would concentrate on the empty seats, making a poor advertisement for his first meeting as leader.

Harold's reaction had undermined my own confidence and I spent an anxious week. I need not have worried. When the meeting was held, not only was the hall crowded, but there were three thousand people standing outside listening to the broadcast relay of the speeches. I presided over the meeting, and as we walked on to the platform, where twenty Welsh MPs were assembled, an enormous cheer filled the air and the crowd sang, "We'll keep a welcome in the hillside." Harold was visibly moved, and to my surprise was also nervous. He said, "I'm not an orator, George. I'm a House of Commons man." My reply was meant to be encouraging: "Nonsense. There's a lot of Nye Bevan in you."

Nye used to delight large audiences with his barbed humour, but Wilson was his equal that night. Outbursts of applause interrupted his sallies as he developed his theme. When he described the ageing Macmillan and his team as Steptoe & Son, he nearly brought the roof down. It was a firm conviction of mine that that tremendous public meeting gave Harold Wilson a new confidence in himself. No man could have asked for a more auspicious beginning to the Party leadership.

Wilson's first list of shadow ministers caused surprise in the Parliamentary Labour Party. As many devoted Gaitskell followers as left-wingers were given major portfolios. It was a courageous move, for

Wilson knew that the left were expecting him to place them in key positions just as Gaitskell had given all the plum appointments to his supporters. From that day it was clear that he was intent on having both wings of the Party sharing responsibility.

Macmillan's second Government had then been in power for three and a half years, and during 1963 it began to run into grave difficulties. The Vassall spy case, the row over the deportation of Chief Enaharo of Nigeria, and the scandals of the Profumo affair, all contributed to its embarrassment. Then on the eve of the Conservative Party conference, Macmillan was taken ill and had to resign. Alec Douglas-Home took over as Prime Minister, and by the time the general election was held a year later, Harold Wilson was well and truly established in the public mind.

Just before the election, Bert Bowden, our Chief Whip, summoned me to his room in the House to tell me that if Labour won I would be made Chairman of Ways and Means and Deputy Speaker. My delight was so obvious that Bowden decided he had better add a cautionary word: "Of course, if we have a majority of only half a dozen, we will have to give the job to a Tory, for we will need the vote."

The election result, showing that Labour had won by a majority of five, demolished my hopes of promotion and I told my Cardiff West supporters that I would be again sitting on the backbenches.

CHAPTER TWELVE

In Office at Last

On the Sunday morning after the election, when I returned home from chapel, I received a telephone call from Jim Callaghan. He had been with the Prime Minister, and he wanted me to know that I would be receiving a telephone call about being given a Government appointment. He would not tell me what the job was, that was the prerogative of the Prime Minister.

It was late afternoon before the telephone call came: "This is Number Ten Downing Street. The Prime Minister wonders whether it will be convenient for you to come to see him tomorrow morning?" The thrill of that first call from Number Ten will never leave me. In chapel that evening, my mind kept wandering from the sermon to speculate on the possible job I would be offered. I travelled overnight to London on the sleeper to wait in the Commons for my summons. It was 7 p.m. before the call came.

The Prime Minister was in the Cabinet Room with his jacket off and his sleeves rolled up. He greeted me with a smile: "We did it, George." As I sat down he went on, "The job intended for you has gone, as you know. We have had to give it to the Tories. Both Alec Home and Martin Redmayne [Conservative Chief Whip] have telephoned me to say they are quite prepared for Anstruther-Gray to carry on as Chairman of Ways and Means. They realise how difficult it is going to be for us with our small majority." I said I thought that the Tories had behaved well in their defeat, and Harold agreed.

Then came the teaser: "I have another job for you. It is one that calls for some humanity and compassion." I was intrigued: "Is it National Insurance?" Harold laughed. "No, that is largely a question of arithmetic." He responded to my guess that it was the National Health Service by saying, "No, though that is a job where there is need for compassion." Exasperated, I said, "If you don't tell me, Harold, I'll run up the wall." He laughed again: "You will be

Parliamentary Under-Secretary of State in the Home Office." This bowled me over. "It's a major department of state," was all I could muster. As I left Number Ten, I was walking on air.

I had been in the Home Office for four days, when I was puzzled to read in *The Times* that Major Anstruther-Gray had announced he did not intend to continue as Chairman of Ways and Means. I asked Michael Head, my Private Secretary, to get me the Prime Minister on the telephone. Incredulously, he repeated, "The Prime Minister?" "Yes," I replied, "yes, he's an old friend. He'll come to the telephone for me." As yet I had not become accustomed to Government protocol, and I saw nothing wrong in a Parliamentary Secretary ringing up the Prime Minister. My faith was justified. Harold was quickly on the telephone. He was patient with me for he knew he owed me an explanation. He assured me that he had not deliberately misled me. Home and Redmayne were happy for Anstruther-Gray to carry on, but they had not consulted him, having assumed that he would want to. But he was anxious about his parliamentary seat and was afraid of defeat at the next election if he continued as Deputy Speaker. Harold then added: "You can still have the job if you want it."

I had by now decided that I wanted to stay in the Home Office and in the event the job went to Horace King, who a year later succeeded to the Chair when the Speaker, Hylton-Foster, died suddenly. If it were not for the genuine misunderstanding about Anstruther-Gray, I would have missed six years' ministerial experience, but I might well have become Speaker ten years before I did.

Life as a junior minister was an eye-opener. It was weeks before I knew the names of all the civil servants with whom I had to deal. Even the hierarchical structure was new to me. My original impression that its various ranks were similar to those in the armed services proved to be very near the mark. It was even longer before I was able to make assessments of the civil servants who were giving me advice. I realised that whenever a change in ministers occurs, they are at their strongest. They know that a minister has to learn many lessons before he can fairly claim to be on top of his job.

Sir Charles Cunningham, a dour Scot, was Permanent Secretary throughout my service at the Home Office. His integrity soon earned my wholehearted respect, but his remoteness puzzled me. One day, after he had greeted me with an aloof "Good morning, Parliamentary Secretary," I said, "Sir Charles, I think I am a little afraid of you, and I don't like it. I'm the son of a miner, and I've never been afraid of people." His face crinkled into a bare hint of a smile, and he replied, "You're not afraid of me, Parliamentary Secretary." To my quick rejoinder: "Everyone is afraid of you," he said, "No, they are afraid of my expression. I cannot help it. I was born like it." From then on, I felt much closer to him.

Frank Soskice was Home Secretary, and he presided over the department with a lightness of touch. He trusted each junior minister, and in return received not only loyalty but also affection. We used to joke about his views on racial issues. The Parliamentary Labour Party put great pressure on him to introduce a bill making it an offence to discriminate against anyone on grounds of race. Many in the Party also wanted to ease the controls on immigration. At a conference in the Home Office, when these views were advanced, Frank erupted: "If we do not have strict immigration rules, our people will soon all be coffee-coloured." My protests were brushed aside. As for legislation against racial discrimination, Frank would have none of it. He thought such legislation would add to our problems, and in that I agreed with him.

My Private Secretary, Michael Head, was my mentor in the early days. When we had a meeting to share out the portfolios among the junior ministers, he advised me to try to get the general department because it involved a lot of House of Commons work. It was good advice, for the work gave me frequent occasions to speak. The two other portfolios for which I was responsible were police and immigration. The general department hid beneath its omnibus title responsibility for drink, gambling and Sunday observance. Throughout my parliamentary life I had played a prominent part in seeking strict control over gambling and the sale of alcohol. So far as Sunday observance was concerned, I was almost a Sabbatarian!

One day when I was having a snack in the members' tea-room, Harold Wilson came to my table and said, "Is it true that you are responsible for drink, gambling and Sunday observance?" When I smiled and said that was so, he raised both hands above his head and said, "Heaven help us! We face enough troubles without that." On a later occasion, when one of the train robbers had escaped, he came up to me in the tea-room again and said, "What's this about prisoners escaping? You need to pull your socks up in the Home Office." For once my reply floored him: "Prime Minister, I'm responsible for immigration; Alice Bacon is responsible for prisons. She can't keep them in, and I can't keep them out!"

In fact control of immigration caused me more heartache than anything else at the Home Office. I used to feel ill with worry when I had to order some poor man to be sent back to his own country. On one occasion, I had a telephone call from Eric Lubbock, the Liberal MP for Orpington, who protested that immigration officials at Heathrow were sending back to South Africa a teacher who had arrived that day. I asked what time the would-be immigrant was due to take off, and was told four o'clock. It was already 3.45, so I said I was probably too late but that I would try to get the man off the plane while I looked into his case. Michael Head instantly phoned Heathrow and asked for the man to be kept at the airport. But, after I had been told all the facts, I had to order that he be returned to his country.

Later that evening, I was in Frank Soskice's room when Michael unexpectedly and unusually came in. His face had a sickly pallor as he said, "Parliamentary Under Secretary, a man sent back to Africa from Heathrow today has committed suicide in flight over Rome. He cut his throat." I felt sick as I asked whether it was the man I had sent back. Head told me that it was not. That decision had been taken by an immigration officer. Relief that it had not been my decision blended with sympathy for the officer concerned. It was a wretched job trying to bring justice to immigration control.

Two cases in which I had been interested as a backbencher, typify the kind of minor problem that can turn into a labyrinthine nightmare for the Home Office. Before the election, my fellow Methodist, Ronald Lewis, MP for Carlisle, had unsuccessfully pursued the case of one of his constituents who had been dismissed by the Home Office from his post as publican in charge of one of our nationalised public houses (David Lloyd George had nationalised the brewing industry in Carlisle during the First World War, and for some reason it had never been restored to private ownership). The publican's dismissal took effect one month before he had been due to retire. Ron Lewis, a teetotaller himself, had sought my help on the grounds that it was unjust to sack a man only one month before retirement and thus deny him a pension.

I asked the Department for the file on the case and took it home to read. Soon it became clear that I had not been given all the papers, and I was indignant. When I returned to the Home Office, I insisted to the civil servant concerned that I must see everything connected with the case. He protested that there was half a ton of files, and that he had given me the ones that really counted. I was not satisfied, and said I would have the half ton.

Next day, to my dismay, two attendants took half an hour to carry in piles of files which they stacked around the floor of my room. I was aghast. If ever a minister was hoist with his own petard . . . I asked Michael Head to arrange for the files to be taken away and locked up without anybody knowing. The few that I did scrutinise confirmed that the Home Office had been correct to dismiss the publican, and I told Ronald Lewis that this was so.

After keeping the files for six weeks, I asked for them to be returned to the civil servant with my compliments. He came to see me and said, "You didn't read all the files, did you, Parliamentary Under Secretary?" I was obliged to admit that I had not. He had taught me the important lesson that trust is the only basis for co-operation between minister and civil servants.

The second case that caused me anxiety concerned one of my own constituents. A lady had been fined two pounds for a motoring offence in Cowbridge, in the Vale of Glamorgan. She maintained that she had been to Cowbridge to pay the fine, but two years later police had come to her home and arrested her for non-payment. The neighbours had watched her being taken away, and in the police station she had been treated as a common criminal. The registrar's book at Cowbridge had an entry in pencil indicating that she had indeed paid the fine as she claimed. However, since it was not written in ink, it was not valid. Unfortunately the man in charge of the book had died at about the date of the pencilled entry, so we could only guess why it had not been inked over.

Before the election, I had had great publicity when I unsuccessfully raised this case in a Commons adjournment debate. Now my constituent wrote and asked if I could reopen it as I was a Home Office minister. It was a humiliation for me finally to have to write to her and report that red tape had defeated us. I was convinced that an injustice had been done, but without more proof I could do nothing. That case will always rankle with me.

Ministers rarely discover much about the background of the civil servants with whom they rub shoulders every day, and it came as a pleasant surprise when I addressed a midday meeting for the Home Office Christian Fellowship, to find the large room absolutely crowded. Experience had led me to expect a dozen or so in attendance. I felt a little intimidated by Sir Charles Cunningham and several of his colleagues, but once I had made up my mind that the best thing I could do would be to give my personal testimony, my fears fell away.

My mind flew back to an occasion when I was preaching at Wesley Chapel, Oxford. As I left the vestry to go to the pulpit, the minister had told me the names of leading academics who would be in the congregation. I had immediately replied, "I am sorry I came. They are much too clever for me." My inner peace was soon restored when he said, "All they want is the simple Gospel message. Their needs are the same as yours and mine." I have never forgotten that, and it stood me in good stead, when I talked to the Home Office mandarins.

It was during my two years at the Home Office that I was one of the very few people allowed to visit Alcatraz, the dreaded prison based on an offshore rocky island near San Francisco. It had been arranged that I should call on the FBI, in Washington, while I was there on a visit to an International Christian Fellowship.

Edgar Hoover was not in town when I arrived, but I was fêted royally by his deputy. We discussed among other things the arming of police, and I recounted a story told me by an American who had heard shouting outside his block of flats. When he looked down, he saw a man running away from police, who were shouting that they would fire if he did not halt. The man continued to run, so he was shot dead. I said I thought that the constant carrying of guns perhaps made American policemen trigger-happy. "There's no danger of that," I was told. "We always shout, 'The FBI is here.' If they don't stop then, well of course we shoot to kill."

The consequence of this conversation was that arrangements were made for me to visit Alcatraz. It was as mysterious a place to me as the prison of the Count of Monte Cristo, so I was delighted that officialdom was prepared to let me see it. Police in San Francisco drove me down to a boat which ferried me across the strongly flowing water to the prison.

The head warden ensured that I passed through a metal detector before I entered the outer hall. Guns were locked in heavy glass cases ready for an emergency. Two great iron gates had to be unlocked before we reached the main prison workshop, where a large number of prisoners were sweeping and washing the floor. Some of the youngest had such baby faces they looked as though butter would not melt in their mouths, yet the warden told me that every man there had committed at least two murders. They were "lifers" in the sense that, as long as they lived, they would never be released. I spoke to the famous Birdman who, having accepted that the rest of his life would be on the rock, had reconciled himself to the study of birds.

When I commented on the absence of guns from the back pockets of warders, I was told, "We wouldn't dare carry a gun here. We would be overpowered by a group and then have the gun used against us." It did not come as a surprise when I was told that no one had ever escaped. The current of the surrounding water was too strong for either a swimmer or a raft. When a prisoner was taken to Alcatraz, he knew he could abandon all hope of ever seeing the outside world again. Alcatraz is shut now but it helped reinforce my belief that there have to be very pressing reasons indeed to keep men in such conditions for the rest of their lives.

After eighteen months in power, Harold Wilson called a general election for 31 March 1966. The Conservative Party was now led by Edward Heath, following Alec Douglas-Home's resignation, and it seemed a good time to seek a firmer mandate. Harold conducted a sparkling campaign, and towards the end of it came to Cardiff to speak at the election rally.

As was our custom, Jim Callaghan and I met for lunch on the eve of polling day and exchanged frank assessments of the likely results in our constituencies. During the meal, Jim remarked that if Labour won I would be promoted. This set me wondering, for Harold had mentioned nothing to me about promotion. Usually Jim and I guessed our constituency results fairly accurately, but this time the swing to Labour was far greater than either of us had forecast. When all the results were known for the country as a whole, Labour had won a sweeping victory with a majority over the Conservatives of 110.

As usual, Jim was well informed and I was appointed Minister of State at the Welsh Office, which had been set up just eighteen months before. It was strange to work in such a new department after being at a long-established one like the Home Office. Our main headquarters was in Cardiff, with just a handful of staff working in Whitehall. I soon discovered that the department's major preoccupation was to look for issues that we could say were specifically Welsh.

By setting up the office, the Labour Government had opened the floodgates for nationalism. Cledwyn Hughes was Secretary of State, and his nationalist fervour led to periodical tensions between us. Despite a genuine pride in my Welsh heritage, and my eagerness to advance Welsh culture, I have never believed in Welsh nationalism. My mother nurtured me with a deep affection for her parents' home counties, Somerset and Hampshire, and the anti-English sentiment always just beneath the surface in Welsh-speaking areas jars on me.

Anyone listening to my strong Welsh accent could be forgiven for assuming my attitudes would always reflect the views of the Welsh establishment. It was often resented when people discovered that this was not so.

At the time, the Welsh language was very much in decline. Industrial South Wales was almost entirely English-speaking, for in the counties of Glamorgan and Monmouthshire most people have English or Irish as well as Welsh blood in their veins. Three-quarters of the population of Wales live in these two counties and it is a fact of life that English is their first language. In reality, there are two separate populations in Wales: the vast majority in the English-speaking areas, and the small Welsh-speaking minority, who are widely scattered over the rural areas. Cledwyn Hughes had inherited from James Griffiths the Welsh Language Bill, which sought to give equal validity to both languages. Without opposition from any MP, this two-clause bill was enacted in 1966.

Lack of experience in promoting legislation had led the Welsh Office into the disastrous error of pressing forward a measure without adequate preparation for its operation. Normally any fundamental weakness would have been exposed in the Cabinet Legislation Committee, but when it came to the Welsh Language Bill, both English and Scottish ministers remained silent and gave it a clear run. They obviously felt that the Welsh Office must know what it was doing, but within months of the measure receiving the Royal Assent, its weakness was exposed.

The Welsh Language Society understandably seized with both hands the stick given to them to knock the Government. Every department in Whitehall was subjected to demands for bilingual publication of its documents. Local government came under the same pressure. Nothing had been done by the Welsh Office to pre-empt these demands, for the simple reason that no one had given any real thought to how the bill would work. Overnight, the Welsh language became a divisive issue.

There was one subject, however, on which I was one hundred per cent Welsh in my attitude. When employment in the Valleys was under discussion, memories of the cruel years of the Depression made me highly vocal. I was ready to work and to fight for the Welsh Valleys whatever the cost.

Glyncorrwg village is a lonely place, tucked away in the mountains at the top of a long valley leading down to Port Talbot. It was a single-industry area, completely dependent on its pit, and the National Coal Board had resolved to close the pit down. The Welsh Office exercised oversight on a broad field of Government activities, including industry, and although the actual power of decision about pit closures rested with the Department of Fuel and Power, we had the right to express views before decisions were taken.

Cledwyn Hughes was asked to go to Glyncorrwg to meet representatives of the community, who feared the social consequences for the village if the pit was closed. Cledwyn said he would not go as there was nothing he could do to help. My Valley blood was stirred, and I volunteered to take his place. John Morris, Parliamentary Secretary for Fuel and Power who was the local MP, came with me. In a crowded schoolroom we listened to local Church leaders, teachers and councillors – indeed everyone remotely concerned with keeping the village alive. Remembering my upbringing in Tonypandy enabled me to share the emotion of the audience, but there was no solid comfort I could give.

Nonetheless, we were thanked for going to meet them and for listening to the recital of their worries. I undertook to try to get alternative industry brought to the area, and the community leaders clutched at that straw. They knew that I was as worried as they were by the proposed closure.

Lord Robens, the former Labour MP Alf Robens, and the then chairman of the Coal Board, disappointed me deeply by his attitude when I appealed to him. Over the years we had worked closely together in the Commons, where he had proved to be a compassionate and kindly man, but at the Coal Board that side of his nature was not evident.

Glyncorrwg was a failure, but I did finally achieve success with leasehold reform, for which I had been campaigning throughout my twenty-one years in Parliament. The Leasehold Reform Bill, along the lines I had been advocating, was finally presented to the Commons by my friend Tony Greenwood in February 1967, and it was on the statute book by the autumn. My long campaign had at last borne fruit. Hundreds of thousands of householders could now buy the freehold of their homes, and the great petition which I had brought from Wales had not been in vain.

CHAPTER THIRTEEN

A Lost Generation

One Friday morning in October 1966, I set off for the Welsh Office in Cardiff as usual, commenting to Mam that autumn was really here. There was a bite in the air, mist clung to the ground and there was no warmth from the sun.

At about ten o'clock, the telephone rang in my office. The town clerk of Merthyr Tydfil was on the line: "We have suffered a major disaster at Aberfan where a coal tip has slid down the mountain and covered the school below. We may have lost over a hundred children and their teachers." I was at the school within the hour. Frantic efforts were being made by miners working shoulder to shoulder to get the bodies from under the rubble.

This was clearly a major emergency. The town clerk, the Chief Constable and I went to the Merthyr Town Hall to plan the relief work. Throughout the day, rescue efforts went on unceasingly and the mood became even grimmer. Every child brought out after the first hour had already died. Cledwyn Hughes, the Secretary of State, arrived by helicopter from North Wales at teatime. Later, Harold Wilson came to Merthyr Town Hall and put Cledwyn in charge of the rescue work, adding that he could call on all Government agencies and the armed forces if he felt their assistance was required.

When Cledwyn had completed all possible organisational steps to help the community through the crisis, he went to spend the night in the Llantwit Major home of Goronwy Daniels, Permanent Secretary to the Welsh Office. As a Valley man, I could not tear myself away, and I telephoned Mam, who like the rest of the country had been following the tragedy all day, to say I would not leave Aberfan that night.

No one went to bed. Every home was lit up, and the streets of the village were crowded with rescue workers travelling to and from the site. Journalists representing newspapers from across the world arrived in their droves. All I could tell them was that Aberfan had lost one generation of children beneath the rubble.

Each home I visited was in deep sorrow, but they accepted it as quite natural that I should have called on them. At two in the morning, I received a request to return to the police station at Merthyr Tydfil; the Chief Constable had received a message that Lord Snowdon would soon be arriving, and I was to look after him.

When Snowdon arrived, the Chief Constable gave him a situation report. More than eighty bodies had been recovered and were in Bethany Chapel awaiting identification by the parents. Three young teachers, who had been rescued, were putting a label on each child so that the parents could be taken immediately to their own child's body. Lord Snowdon asked who else was working in the chapel-cum-mortuary and was told that the Salvation Army and the Red Cross were there.

He immediately said, "If they can undertake that job, I can go in to thank them." The Chief Constable turned to make sure that I would go with him. We went to Bethany Chapel, where there was a little body stretched out on every seat. Suddenly I found myself standing by the body of the schoolmaster, whom I knew well. I stood staring at his brown shoes, which bore no trace of dust, although he too had been buried in the rubble.

Down at the site of the disaster, we moved between more bodies that had been brought out and were waiting to be identified by the teacher before being taken to the chapel for the helpers to wash their faces and hands. We were numb with horror.

Lord Snowdon decided he would join me in the visits to the homes of bereaved parents. At the first house, there was a young miner and his wife who was clearly expecting another child. The mother caught hold of me and sobbed. Her little girl was still under the rubble. She wanted me to say that there was still hope for her child, when clearly there was none. I could only talk about the wonderful way the miners had set about trying to rescue the children.

The father looked at me with agony in his eyes, and feeling the necessity to say and do something, he blurted out, "Will you have a cup of tea?" – the traditional Welsh way of expressing welcome. His wife still clung to me, so I shook my head. Lord Snowdon interrupted: "Yes, I would like a cup of tea, and the Minister can do with one also." When the young miner moved towards the kitchen in their two-down two-up cottage, Snowdon pushed forward. "Let me do it. I'm used to making tea."

In his absence I spoke gently to the weeping mother, telling her she must be brave for the sake of the baby waiting to be born. The father hovered around us, not knowing what to do. Snowdon re-emerged carrying a tin tray with roses printed on it, and I commented, "Here is the Queen's brother-in-law waiting on us." For a fraction of a second the darkness lifted from the father's face.

Suddenly the mother pulled herself away, and looking Snowdon straight in the face asked, "How would you feel if your child was under the tip?" Poor Snowdon, I felt for him as he replied, "That thought has been in my mind ever since I heard of the disaster. That is why I am here. I could not stay away."

In the next house we visited, the father of a little boy whose body had been recovered sat sobbing on a sofa as he clutched his son's school cap in his right hand. Without a word, Snowdon sat on the sofa and put his arm around the man's shoulders. We stayed there until the sobbing ceased.

When Snowdon eventually left Aberfan, he had carved for himself a special place in the affection and respect of that mining village. It took me three weeks after the funeral before I completed my visits to every house that had suffered bereavement. For weeks after that, whenever I closed my eyes to sleep, I saw the scene in Bethany Chapel that dreadful night.

The people of Aberfan were left not only with their unassuageable grief, but also with the threatening shadow of the remains of the tips that loomed above their village on the mountainside. Every time a shower of rain fell, their remaining children would be called indoors, or taken from their beds to huddle around the fire downstairs.

The fight to get the tip removed from the hillside above Aberfan continued bitterly and continuously for nearly three years and was to confront me very painfully when I became Secretary of State for Wales in 1968.

I was advised by all the experts – local authority engineers, Coal Board engineers and government engineers – that the tip was absolutely safe, and that it was therefore unjustified to ask the taxpayer to spend a million pounds on its removal. I went to the Treasury and had a tremendous argument, but failed to make them change their minds. I had to face the Aberfan people and tell them that they must not worry: the tip was safe because the experts said so. It was a dreadful experience.

I knew them all as they sat in front of me in the Welsh Office. An old man, Alderman Tom Lewis, their leader, stood up and said, "Secretary of State, I never thought to hear such words fall from George Thomas's lips. I thought you understood the problems of Aberfan. That tip is a nightmare for our people. You can say that it is safe, but we were told that before. Nothing could do as much for the peace of mind of Aberfan as moving that tip." Others there who were less polite in their language than Tom, but not as effective, were shouting and very angry. I promised to take the matter back to the Government in London, which I did at once.

I went straight to the station, and caught the first train. When I reached my flat, I rang Number Ten and was put through to Harold straight away. He said, "George, you've been having a rough time. I have just seen it on television." Unknown to me the television cameras had been inside the Welsh Office. I came to the point at once: "I am sorry, Prime Minister, but I can't do it. I just can't tell these people that the tip has to stay. They are afraid. Their protest has not been manufactured, it's a genuine fear from people who have been through a terrible experience."

Harold said he would help and asked me to go to Number Ten immediately. When I was with him, he picked up a white telephone and asked to be put through to Roy Jenkins, the Chancellor of the Exchequer. Within five minutes we had settled a formula whereby the Aberfan Fund and the Coal Board would each contribute a quarter of a million pounds and the Government would contribute half a million. The cost of moving the tip would be met.

My next task was to meet the Aberfan Fund Trustees. I thought that all would be well, but I had a rough ride from some of them. I made it clear that I was not asking for a penny of the fund that had been contributed by the public but only for the interest that had accumulated. I withdrew to allow them time to consider the offer.

As I stood in my office, my private secretary looked out of the window and told me that S. O. Davies, Aberfan's local MP, had walked out of the meeting. It was the best sign so far, as it meant that the committee was moving my way. Throughout the controversy, Davies was determined that no contribution should be made from the fund. Shortly after that, agreement was reached on the terms I had put forward. It was deeply satisfying for me when the Aberfan people held a dinner in celebration of the moving of the tip, and they made my mother and me the chief guests.

Like all of us involved in that terrible experience, the memory of Aberfan, and of its people who were so scarred by tragedy, stays with me always.

CHAPTER FOURTEEN

Adventures in Africa

Harold Wilson suddenly transferred me from the Welsh Office to the Commonwealth Office in June 1967. It was to prove to be the most exciting ministerial office that I held. The volatile state of some of the newly independent Commonwealth countries made me feel rather as though Pandora's box had been opened as I embarked on the extensive travels which my job involved.

I quickly found a greater sense of comradeship in the diplomatic departments than I had experienced elsewhere in the civil service. I was most fortunate to have Donald MacLeod as my Principal Private Secretary; his quiet courtesy matched a delightful, dry sense of humour and his combination of loyalty and ability helped not only to smooth my life considerably, but also to make it very enjoyable.

My chief was Bert Bowden, who closely resembled Frank Soskice in his dealings with junior ministers. Not afraid to devolve responsibility, he told me at our first ministerial meeting that I was free to take decisions as long as I kept him informed. This was just what I wanted. My mentors in the department were Sir Saville Garner, Permanent Under Secretary, and Sir Morrice James, the Deputy Secretary. Both had served as High Commissioners and were ideal advisers. Eric Norris, who later became High Commissioner in both Kenya and Malaysia, was another close confidant.

I had my first taste of negotiating on behalf of the Commonwealth Office in Ghana, a year after General Ankrah had deposed President Nkrumah. Ankrah was currently displeased by Britain's refusal to extradite a former Ghanaian High Commissioner charged with corruption. Roy Jenkins, the Home Secretary, maintained that political considerations prevented him from agreeing to an extradition order. Before I left for Accra, Harold Wilson advised me to tell the angry General that he could prosecute his former High Commissioner in our courts. There would be a fair trial and justice would be done.

I was not with Ankrah for more than a few minutes before I realised that it was not justice he was seeking. He received Eric Norris and me coldly and then embarked on a tirade of abuse intended to intimidate us. For half an hour, I listened to him spluttering out invective against the British Government in general and Roy Jenkins in particular. I marvelled at his vocabulary, and wondered who had been his teachers. He pulled no punches as he accused Jenkins of taking bribes to refuse the extradition order.

I had to interrupt: "Do you know Roy Jenkins? He is a pillar of rectitude." The General shouted, "No, I don't know him, and I don't want to know him." I remarked, "He doesn't particularly want to know you," but the General had resumed his abuse and did not hear. For the first time in my life I knew the truth of the saying that a man's eyes bulged with fury.

I began my reply in a low key. My job was not to irritate him further, but to secure his agreement to a London trial. In order to impress him with the sincerity of my offer, I said, "I am a Methodist, and I give you my word that the case will get a proper hearing in Britain." Ankrah's reaction amazed me. All animosity melted away as he exclaimed, "Are you a Methodist? Give me your hand. I am a Methodist too!" Suddenly I realised that it was Methodist missionaries who had taught the General his extensive vocabulary. In less than two minutes, he agreed to my proposal and we shook hands again.

"Now," Ankrah declared, "we will drink a glass of champagne to celebrate our agreement." I looked towards Eric Norris, expecting him to explain to the General that this Methodist was a strict tee-totaller. But to my dismay he nodded to me that I should humour Ankrah and seal the settlement in the manner proposed. When we descended the stairs from Ankrah's room afterwards, I complained of the strength of the champagne, but Norris said, "It was bloody awful. The worst I have ever tasted." Later that day, he sent home the customary telegram to report the result of our conversation, and I imagined that would be the end of the matter. I had not taken the precaution of reading the postscript to the telegram!

On my return, Harold Wilson asked me to go to Number Ten to report on my visit. I recounted the substance of my meeting with Ankrah, but when I had finished he said, "Go on, Minister of State. Complete your story. What about the champagne you drank?" Knowing my strong temperance views, the ministers present insisted on hearing the full story, which made me the butt of much teasing by Harold in the following months.

That was by no means the end of my African adventures, for at the time I joined the Commonwealth Office there were increasing fears about the possibility of civil war in Nigeria. Colonel Ojukwu had seceded from the Nigerian Federal Republic in May, declaring Biafra an independent state. It was decided that I should travel to Lagos to try to secure an agreement between him and General Gowon, head of the Nigerian Government. On my arrival, I was taken to the residency of the British High Commissioner, Sir David Hunt, who was later to win the BBC Television Mastermind trophy. Throughout my stay, he played recordings of classical music with the volume turned up very high so that the sound pervaded every nook and cranny of the house.

We met at tea to discuss the arrangements for my conference with Gowon planned for the next morning. Hardly had we sat down, when the telephone rang. David Hunt answered it himself, and after a few sentences, he called out to me, "The balloon's gone up." Ojukwu had struck the first blow of the war.

We decided that the wisest course was to go ahead with the conference. When we reached Gowon's headquarters, his Cabinet was assembled. Standing in front of them, he said, "Before we begin, let us have a reading from the Bible." I could see that my team were a little embarrassed, but the Nigerians did not blink an eyelid.

I immediately liked Jack Gowon, a slim, good-looking young man, whose single purpose was to end the civil war with maximum speed. To this end, he told me he needed planes and bombs. In addition, he sought a considerable increase in the small arms and ammunition traditionally supplied by Britain.

My immediate problem was that the London briefing had not taken into account the possibility that civil war might have started before I met Gowon. I had to act on my own initiative and try to assess what attitude the British Cabinet would adopt. Following my instinct, I advised Gowon's team that, although we would continue the supply of weapons and ammunition normally directed to Nigeria, we would not agree to provide planes and bombs to be used against Commonwealth citizens in a Commonwealth country.

Gowon's voice rose an octave to declare, "We will get all the aeroplanes and bombs we need, but you are driving us into the arms of the Communists. We do not want to buy from them, but if you refuse to supply us, then we shall have no option but to turn to them."

I remained firm. When I returned to London, the Cabinet confirmed that judgement.

In retrospect, however, I am convinced that decision was wrong. Nigeria had relied on the United Kingdom for her arms and ammunition, and there seems no difference in moral principle between supplying bombs and cannon. The war would have ended much sooner if we had met Gowon's demands. A side issue was that we allowed the French ammunition industry to exploit our decision. They had no scruples in supplying arms both to Biafrans and to the Nigerian Federal Government.

It was difficult for me to stay in the Government at this time. I agonised over whether I should resign office and return to the backbenches. My lifelong pacifist convictions made me feel a hypocrite in condoning the supply of arms of any sort to Nigeria. Two considerations prevented me. Ojukwu's propaganda machine was highly successful in the United Kingdom, and demonstrations against Britain's support for Gowon multiplied. My resignation would have strengthened the propaganda, and that was certainly not my wish.

But the main consideration was my staunch support for Harold Wilson. I rationalised my position by persuading myself that if I resigned I would be indicating that pacifists could only opt out of bearing responsibility. To this day, I still question my motives. Whether it was love of ministerial office or high principles that kept me in the Government, I will never be sure.

While Bert Bowden was away on holiday in August, and I was in charge of the Commonwealth Office, a crisis blew up in Uganda. Dr Milton Obote had been President for just a year, and our High Commissioner, Roland Hunt, had made repeated protests to him about his soldiers beating up white people as they travelled on a lonely road near the main military base. Obote appeared not only to have done nothing to prevent the assaults taking place, but actually to resent the diplomatic protests. Hunt's indignation overflowed when Ugandan soldiers made a white woman get out of her car and beat her with canes, and he decided to make a public protest. Obote was beside himself with rage, and a furious row developed between the High Commissioner and the Ugandan Government.

On the pressing advice of my senior advisers, I instructed Roland Hunt to return home for consultations to show Obote the full extent of Britain's anger. We could not have made a bigger mistake, for Obote interpreted the action as one of weakness. He added insult to injury by refusing to allow Hunt to return to take up his duties. This put the cat among the diplomatic pigeons. A petty dispute was suddenly transformed into a major inter-Government row.

It was decided that I should travel to Kampala to meet Obote and settle the dispute. Before I left London, I had a conference with the Prime Minister, who instructed me to try to get Hunt returned to Uganda for one month, on the assurance that we would then quietly transfer him to another post. Wilson thought that this face-saving formula would appeal to Obote.

When I called on the President, I was surprised to find him accompanied by his entire Cabinet. After conveying Harold Wilson's personal greetings and good wishes, I expressed regret that we had a dispute to settle. I defended our High Commissioner's conduct, and proposed that he should be allowed to return for two months after which we would quietly give him a new appointment. I deliberately inflated the period to allow room for negotiation. For two hours Obote and I argued, while nobody else said a word. Finally we agreed to adjourn to give time for further consideration.

Our second meeting was held in the garden of the President's residence. This time there were fewer ministers present, but Obote was as determined as ever. Again we argued for two hours, and throughout he kept making patterns in the earth with his walking stick.

I decided to play my last card: "Very well, Mr President, I will no longer try to reach agreement with you. I had hoped we could compromise on the formula I advanced to you, by which, although our High Commissioner has done no wrong, he would shortly be transferred. But you have refused to compromise. I will send the High Commissioner back to Kampala on Wednesday next. You have previously accepted his credentials so he is fully entitled to enter. If you block the admission of an accredited diplomat, you will cause a storm of protest in the House of Commons, and the dispute will be reported all across the world."

Obote stopped making patterns, and said sharply that I could do no such thing and certainly would not do it. My reply was emphatic: "Wait four days, and Roland Hunt will knock on your door." There was a pause before he said he would take the issue back to his full Cabinet. I said I intended to leave the next morning whether or not we had reached agreement. He simply said that his Cabinet would meet after the banquet that night and he would see me in the morning.

Despite our disagreements, he presided over a fantastic state banquet in my honour in the floodlit grounds of his residence, complete with a superb display of African dancing and beating drums. During the evening, a huge and highly decorated soldier approached as Obote whispered, "I want you to meet my Chief of the Army. He is after my job, but I keep one step ahead of him. He is thick." Idi Amin's massive handshake almost crushed my bones. It seemed unlikely that this smiling giant could have political ambitions.

The following morning I received a message that, since the President would be unaccompanied, he wished me to be alone for our final discussion. This was good news, for I realised that if he were to give ground, he would not want to do so before his colleagues. We met indoors, and this time the atmosphere was quite different. Obote took the initiative: "As you know, I have been anxious to help you, but my Cabinet has not agreed. I have now persuaded them to allow Hunt to return for six weeks." In the interest of goodwill between our two Governments, I said Britain would drop the request for a two-months' return. I sought, and was given, assurances that for his remaining six weeks Hunt would be treated courteously and fairly.

When Eric Norris and I visited Kenya, it was a very different situation from the one I had encountered in 1959. Jomo Kenyatta was now the President, and I was told that on no account should I say anything to upset him. He was annoyed with Britain over some financial matters, and the High Commissioner warned me that he would probably be quite rough in his dealings as he was old and irritable. My advisers were not to know that I had a trump card up my sleeve, for before the war, Kenyatta had lived down in Cardiff docks at a time when only the Labour Party would have anything to do with him.

When I was introduced to the old President, I said, "I bring you greetings from Cardiff, Wales, where you are remembered with much affection." Kenyatta's face creased into a huge smile. "Cardiff, Wales," he repeated softly, as though he were talking to himself. "Those choirs . . . and the cups of tea . . . and the Welsh cakes!" Turning with extreme cordiality, he asked me for news of the city and after a happy exchange of stories we soon settled the official business that had brought us together. Kenyatta insisted on coming out of the palace to have a photograph of us taken together.

I was then due to go to Malawi, whose President, Dr Hastings Banda, was just completing an official visit to Kenya. He invited me to travel with him in his aeroplane to give us an opportunity to get to know one another. He told me that whenever he went to England he always made an unofficial visit to Willesden, where he had once practised as a doctor, and where he still had strong links.

There was a mighty crowd waiting to greet him at the airport, and he was received in great state by members of his Cabinet, to whom he introduced me. They all referred to him as Kamazu. Holding my hand high in the air, Banda said, "This is Kamazu's friend. If you find him when his car has broken down, push the car, because he is Kamazu's friend. You must help him all the time that he is here."

Banda gave a state banquet in my honour, where he behaved with all the authority of a benevolent dictator. He was out of patience with most of his fellow African leaders, who put great emphasis on racial issues, and he told me that Britain was very foolish not to look after her own interests in Rhodesia and forget the clamour about racial discrimination. He also thought we ought to deal with South Africa as a friend rather than an enemy. A maverick among the African leaders, I liked him and respected his spectacular achievements in Malawi.

I could never, however, have shared Dr Banda's opinion that Britain worried too much about racial discrimination, and my experience of South Africa did nothing to make me change my mind. I touched down in Johannesburg on my way home, after a tour of Swaziland, Lesotho and Botswana. Our Ambassador, Sir John Nicholson, was holding his annual conference of the various Consuls and Consul-Generals scattered through South Africa and I had been invited to speak to them.

A story I had heard in Botswana had so angered me that I arrived in South Africa without any sympathy for her social policies. It concerned a black woman minister I had met while being entertained by Ruth and Seretse Khama. Her radiant personality and brilliance had quite captivated me, and when I discovered she was a doctor of philosophy, I was not at all surprised. She talked about some of the ways that apartheid was practised and, laughing at her own experience, said that because black people in South Africa were never allowed to try on shoes before they bought them, they often walked with a limp.

She told me of one occasion when she had seen a bright red hat in a shop window, and had said to herself, "That's for me!" She went in knowing that she would not be permitted to try it on, but once she had paid for it, took it to a mirror to see how it looked. The shop assistant became agitated and said, "You know you're not allowed to try it on in here." "But it's mine," she answered, "I've paid for it." The girl was not satisfied: "You'll get me the sack." She gave way and tried on the hat standing on the pavement.

Donald MacLeod and I were met at Johannesburg airport by a Third Secretary. I should have realised immediately that the Ambassador was giving me an unspoken message: it was his diplomatic way of putting his thumb to his nose. As we swung through the gates of the enormous mansion used as a residency by the British Ambassador, the driver gave a loud toot on the horn as a signal that we had arrived.

There was no sign of life, so we wandered through the thickly carpeted and expensively furnished lounge into the garden. Sir John and Lady Nicholson sat in the shade of a great tree drinking cocktails. The Ambassador did not bother to stand to shake hands. He nodded to a chair for me to sit. Donald was left to look around for another chair for himself. My Welsh temper was rising. I thought of the people in Tonypandy who could have given the Ambassador a lesson in good manners. More was to follow.

As we took our places for lunch, the Ambassador turned to me and said, "You know, Minister, apartheid is not as bad in practice as it is in theory." A picture of the smiling black lady who had not been allowed to try on her red hat flashed across my mind. With anger, I told him that if he really thought that, then our attitudes were poles apart. He was clearly out for a row, and repeated with emphasis, "Apartheid is not as bad in practice as it is in theory." A deep silence fell on the others as I told him that if he continued on that tack, I would leave his table. It was at that moment that Lady Nicholson tried to defuse the situation by asking, "From what part of England do you come, Minister?" The offensiveness of the Ambassador had made me so angry I contented myself with a brief "I do not come from England."

Donald, who had been looking at me anxiously throughout the exchanges, seized his chance to pour oil on troubled waters. In his delightful Scottish accent he explained, "The Minister comes from Wales, Lady Nicholson." Despite my anger I almost laughed when she received this piece of news by exclaiming, "Oh, Wales!" in a tone that implied it was a home for bad eggs and that explained everything.

Returning to London, I told George Brown, who was then Foreign Secretary, that I did not think Nicholson was a proper person to reflect the views of the British Government. I received an unqualified assurance from George Brown: "Leave it to me. I'll deal with him." Nicholson continued his tour of duty and entered into honourable retirement two years later.

Soon after this unhappy experience, I went on an official visit to India, Pakistan and Ceylon. Pakistan was under military rule, but General Ayub Khan was a cultured man with a keen sense of humour that appealed to me, and I found it hard to remember that I was in a country where there was no democracy. In every village I visited, I was garlanded with flowers, and I listened quite happily to stories of increased crops and improved drainage and water supply. Officials proudly showed me improvements made in agricultural techniques.

If I had not always been accompanied by a uniformed colonel, I could have overlooked the military discipline, which controlled all public activities. When the red carpet is laid down, and an enormous welcome arranged in each community with presents showered upon one, it is easy to swallow propaganda discreetly presented.

I left Pakistan with glowing memories of a friendly, hard-working people, and I quietly resolved not to mention my visit when I saw Prime Minister Indira Gandhi, but to speak warmly of my experience if anyone else referred to it. I had already met Mrs Gandhi at a Commonwealth Prime Ministers' Conference in London and had fallen under her spell. Her dark eyes seemed to carry the suffering of India's millions. Her femininity was expressed in her fantastic saris, and her passionate concern for the young. She looked frail, but she was actually one of the toughest people I ever knew. I was therefore very much on guard when we met in Delhi.

After an hour's talk, she suddenly asked with a smile how I had got on in Pakistan. I genuinely believed that I was answering with courage when I replied that I was much impressed, that the Pakistanis were lovely, hard-working people. Giving one of her warmest smiles, she said, "I know they are lovely people. They are our people. They should never have left us." When I ruefully explained that I thought I was being brave in saying what I did, Mrs Gandhi gave one of her more rare hearty laughs: "Now you know differently." In my last year as Speaker, Mrs Gandhi and her son, Rajiv, came to tea at Speaker's House. It was both a renewal of friendship with the Indian Prime Minister and an opportunity to talk to Rajiv. On the day of her assassination I felt, like so many others, that I had lost a friend and that the world had lost an outstanding leader.

From India I flew down to Colombo, where the infinite courtesy and charm of those inspired by faith in Buddha impressed me beyond measure. I visited a Buddhist Youth Rally and was touched by the warmth of the fellowship. The Buddhist priest's call to public service reminded me of my chapel days in the Rhondda. To my great joy, the Methodist Church in Colombo was absolutely crowded to the door when I preached on the text "Abide in me". The congregation sang Charles Wesley's hymns with the fervour of the Welsh.

During my period at the Commonwealth Office I met one of the ablest Commonwealth Prime Ministers, Lee Kuan Yew of Singapore, for the first time. Known in Britain as Harry Lee since his days at Oxford, he has a first-class brain, and does not suffer fools gladly. He avoids small talk, preferring to get straight to the point, and when I met him, he was infuriated by the British Government's decision to withdraw our forces from east of Suez. He came to London to fight the issue.

He lost that battle, and when he was about to return to Singapore, the Government made a diplomatic mistake. They asked me, a Minister of State, to be at the airport to do the courtesies and to see him away. A Prime Minister is entitled at least to a Secretary of State, and he could have reasonably expected the Prime Minister. When he came into the VIP lounge at Heathrow, he was clearly in a very angry mood. Each time I spoke to him, he snapped back the shortest of replies.

As we walked across the tarmac to the aeroplane there was a frigid silence, until I said, "Harry, you are being very rude to me. I have not done anything to offend you. I cannot influence Government policy. I'm Minister of State – I'm not in the Cabinet, and I do not think it's fair, since I've come out to Heathrow to see you away, that you should behave in this fashion to me." He stopped in his tracks, looked me full in the face and said, "George, you put me to shame. You are absolutely right. I am sorry. The quarrel is nothing to do with you, and I apologise." He was so contrite that I almost wanted to stop him. From that day, we have been firm friends.

I sat next to Harry when I represented the British Government at the coronation of the Sultan of Brunei. Tunku Abdul Rahman, Prime Minister of Malaya, was on my other side, and a good deal of banter took place about the occasion when the two men had quarrelled and Harry left the Malaysian Federation, opting for the independence of Singapore. Tunku Rahman told me that Harry had stalked out, and Harry cried, "No, no, no! You threw me out."

One of the perils of working in the Commonwealth Office was that every night, throughout the spring, autumn and winter seasons, there seemed to be a series of crowded cocktail parties at the various High Commissions. There was always a great deal of gossip, and people tried hard to find out one's unofficial opinions on the issues of the day.

I did not realise that Intelligence was at work at these gatherings, until one day Donald MacLeod put a note on my desk saying that Sir Saville Garner had asked him to show me a piece of information gathered at one of these parties. Apparently the Nigerian High Commissioner had said to someone, "George Thomas is only a jumped-up schoolmaster. He'll be out at the next election, so we needn't be worried about what he says." I read the note with interest.

I asked Sir Saville to come to my room to ask him why he had let me see the note. "I thought you might be interested," he replied. I laughed, and said, "Well, he is speaking the truth when he says I am a jumped-up schoolmaster. That's all I am. As for the next election, I hope he's wrong but we'll have to wait and see." I realised of course that Sir Saville was giving me a message, telling me to be careful at these High Commission drinking parties, and I asked if I had said anything that would put the Government in difficulty. "No, not yet," he replied with another smile.

The Nigerian High Commissioner turned out to be wrong in his forecast for my future, though I did not remain for very long at the Commonwealth Office; indeed, at one point, it looked as though I was going to be moved after only four months. One Friday afternoon in September 1967, when I was talking to one of the Deputy Secretaries, Donald handed me a message which he had been told was top secret. The Prime Minister wanted to see me on Sunday at 5.45 p.m. and I was to go in to Number Ten by the back entrance. The significance of that last instruction was not lost on me. Whenever Harold Wilson embarked on changes in his team, he was anxious to prevent media speculation, and instructed the ministers involved to use the back door and thus avoid a series of television pictures of ministers entering and leaving Number Ten.

Because Donald had become like a son to me, I discussed the matter with him, telling him that the summons meant I was going to leave the Commonwealth Office, either being moved sideways or into the Cabinet.

The next two days were agony. On the Saturday, I addressed a Commonwealth Conference at Edinburgh University, and I called at

Donald's home in Richmond for tea on my way home from the airport on Sunday. I had already telephoned Mam to tell her that I thought I might be going back to the Welsh Office. As I left the MacLeod home, a black cat ran across the road in front of my car. "A lucky omen, Minister," said Donald.

When I reached my flat, there was a note asking me to telephone Michael Hall, the Prime Minister's Principal Private Secretary. I knew this could only be bad news. And it was. I was told that the Prime Minister was deeply sorry, but he would not be wanting to see me after all. Something had happened that day that had changed his plans. In misery, I asked whether he was seeing many ministers, and was told that about twenty had been summoned. I felt absolutely downcast as I returned to Cardiff.

Believing that the Welsh Office had probably gone to Goronwy Roberts, who was my only possible rival if Cledwyn Hughes was moved, I telephoned Cledwyn's home. His wife Jean answered, and completed my despair when she said that Cledwyn was in London. After a pause, she asked me whether I had been called to Number Ten. I told her my story, and she then confided that Cledwyn had had exactly the same experience. He was not being moved. I could have danced with joy. I knew now that Harold Wilson's intention had been to send me to the Welsh Office in a reshuffle that for some reason or other never took place for Cledwyn or me.

CHAPTER FIFTEEN

To Wales with a Prince

The next Cabinet reshuffle took place nine months later in April 1968. This time I was not disappointed. I was told to go to the Prime Minister's room in the House of Commons at 5.45 p.m. and I was there by 5.30 p.m. As I sat in the anteroom waiting to be called, Patrick Gordon-Walker, Secretary of State for Education and Science, came out. His expression was always lugubrious, but on this occasion he looked positively funereal. I could see he was out of the Cabinet, and the awful thought flashed through my mind that I had been living in a fool's paradise. What if I too was going to be dropped?

Fred Peart saw the Prime Minister next, and he came out smiling. Then Harold's head came round the doorway and he invited me in. We had been friends since our first day in Parliament, but I was nervous as I entered his room that day. After all, a Prime Minister cannot afford to choose his Government on the basis of friendship.

He wasted no time in coming to the point. "You know why I asked to see you, George." My reply came from the heart: "I want to hear you say it, Harold." He smiled: "You are to be Secretary of State for Wales. You will be made a Privy Counsellor on Monday, and you will be a member of the Inner Cabinet." I left the room walking on air. I thanked God for the opportunity and for sparing my mother to share my happiness.

When I arrived at the Welsh Office in Whitehall the following Monday afternoon, the entire staff were assembled in the hall and greeted me with loud hand-clapping. A man would be a stone not to be moved by such a welcome home.

One of the first things Harold told me after I had taken office, was that I would be responsible for Prince Charles's Investiture as the Prince of Wales on 1 July 1969. This had become a highly controversial issue, and a minority of Welsh nationalists seemed to think that if they created enough noise and caused enough violence, we might be persuaded to drop the ceremony. An Investiture Committee had already been formed by Cledwyn Hughes, and in the early hours of one morning when he and Lord Snowdon, as Constable of Caernarfon Castle, had been due to attend one of its first meetings in the Temple of Peace, Cardiff, a bomb explosion had damaged the building. I was at a conference of the Welsh Council of Labour at the time, and when I heard about the sabotage, I made a speech charging the nationalists with having created a monster which they could no longer control.

There had been one uneasy meeting of the committee at St James's Palace before I took over. A Welsh minister of religion had insisted on speaking in Welsh, and Cledwyn acted as interpreter. I let it be known that if anyone wished to speak Welsh while I was there, they would be quite free to do so, but there would be no translations. In the event, that crisis never occurred again. It was agreed that the Duke of Norfolk would chair our meetings, since he was responsible for all state ceremonial involving the monarchy, and that I would serve as vice-chairman.

I liked the Duke from the start. His dry wit and Edwardian attitude fascinated me. The first time he came to see me in Whitehall, I asked him, as I had hundreds of other visitors, if he would like a cup of tea. To my surprise, he replied, "Never drink the stuff." When I offered him some alcoholic drink, he replied equally gruffly, "Wrong time of day." I clearly had a lot to learn about Bernard Duke of Norfolk.

Once, when he and I were chatting to Prince Charles, I commented that five of the Duke's predecessors had been beheaded by various monarchs. Quick as lightning, he corrected me: "Get your facts right, Secretary of State, the figure is six, not five."

At one of the three Investiture rehearsals we held in the grounds of Buckingham Palace, the Queen's place was taken by a most regal-looking person whom I did not recognise. I was told she was the daughter of the Duke. When the rehearsal was over, I told her how much I enjoyed working with her father. She smiled broadly: "Yes, I know, Secretary of State; but he is not my father, he is my husband!"

She introduced me to her three daughters and I asked them all not to tell anyone of my blunder. But the joke was too good for them to keep to themselves. My guess is that the story reached the Royal Household with imitations of my Welsh accent. At the next rehearsal, the Duke came up to say, "Have you seen my daughter?" and then roared with laughter.

It was inevitable that some tension should develop between us as the preparations went ahead. The Duke was responsible for all the ceremonial, and naturally enough put in a high bid for support from the Exchequer. He told me that he had his father's entire record of the previous Investiture of the Prince of Wales in 1911, and in great detail told me of the various military contingents that had taken part.

The Government had already decided that £200,000 was enough to spend but he insisted he must have an extra £50,000. To his angry declaration that the dignity of the occasion required more than could possibly be provided within the estimate of £200,000, I could only reply that I had every faith in his ability to ensure success. The Duke's face was set in cold anger. When it became clear that he was not going to get his way, he said he was not satisfied and asked to see the Prime Minister. He left the Welsh Office, courteously controlling his sense of outrage that I should have refused what he considered to be a reasonable request.

I was at Number Ten with Harold Wilson when the Duke's interview took place. He was taken aback when he saw me and his opening words were: "I asked to see you alone, Prime Minister." Harold was at his diplomatic best and said that he had invited me to be present because I was the minister responsible for the Investiture. There followed a highly civilised discussion, although the Duke pulled no punches. Harold was absolutely firm. In my experience, no one who served under him ever had cause to complain that he let them down when there was trouble. Loyalty to his colleagues was one of his strongest points. I found it strange that the Duke should not have realised this and thus have saved himself a second refusal.

It was our custom, when we had to meet for informal discussions, for the Duke and myself to take it in turns to go to each other's office. At the meeting after he had seen the Prime Minister, he kept me standing while he finished writing in a notebook. At the next meeting at the Welsh Office, I opened the file before me and kept my head down when I was conscious he was in the room. Eventually I looked up and said, "Hello, Earl Marshal, how are you?" He took the point very quickly and stalked across the room to my desk, pointed at me, and said, "I am going to call you George, and you will call me Bernard." It was a command, not a request, and I never found it so hard in my life to call any man Bernard.

Anyone with even a superficial knowledge of Wales could have advised Buckingham Palace that the build-up to the Investiture would not be easy. Labour Party activists disliked the idea of a Labour Government spending £200,000 on ceremonial, and in the Commons Emrys Hughes never gave up fighting the expense. He accused the Labour Government of getting its priorities wrong.

Throughout this period, I received almost weekly threats to my life. Once, when I was due to stand outside the Cardiff City Hall in support of the Lord Mayor who was taking the salute at a procession, I was sent an anonymous letter which said I would be able to walk to the City Hall, but would have to be carried away. I recall looking around the huge crowd and wondering if there was a would-be assassin among them. Often when I went to London, I would find Special Branch men guarding the entrance to my flat, and sometimes when I arrived at the Welsh Office in Parliament Street, there would be a constable by the door and I would know that the police had some particular cause for anxiety.

At home, my mother, who was eighty-eight in January 1969, was frequently awakened in the small hours of the morning by anonymous callers threatening my life. In the end, I had to take my telephone number out of the book and go ex-directory because I did not feel I had the right to expose Mam to the anxieties of this barrage from mindless extremists. Our bungalow, a few hundred yards from part of the Cardiff Teachers' Training College, was once plastered on the windows, walls and doors with Welsh-language literature and three girls in college scarves were seen running away by a passer-by.

The Welsh-language press was both bitter and malicious. Even the so-called religious newspapers became political, and included regular personal attacks on me. There was a period when Mam was included in the tirades, which I thought was reaching the lowest level of political activity. I was even attacked from the pulpit on occasion, and came to the conclusion that there were some people in Nonconformist Wales who had replaced the worship of God Almighty with the worship of the language. This was the kind of malevolence I was subjected to every week, without the great majority of people in Wales even knowing that the bullying was taking place.

I did not favour the idea of the Prince of Wales going to Aberystwyth College for a term before the Investiture; it seemed a bit patronising to Wales and unnecessarily provocative. Once the decision had been taken, however, I gave it my full public support. Shortly before his term there was due to start, I received a letter marked "Personal and

Private". I opened the envelope, and there was another envelope inside containing a handwritten letter from the Principal of Aberystwyth College, Dr Tom Parry.

In it he expressed grave fears about the current atmosphere in Aberystwyth, and indicated that he could not accept responsibility for the safety of the Prince. This was a major challenge. If the Prince could not go to Aberystwyth, we clearly could not hold the Investiture. I felt it would be a terrible thing if there was any part of the United Kingdom which had to be declared closed to a member of the Royal Family.

I called on Harold Wilson and showed him the letter. He agreed that it was very serious and said he would have to advise the Queen and asked for my advice. My personal view was that the Prince should still go but I called a conference with the Chief Constable of Dyfed and Dr Parry, to discuss the matter with them. In the event, the Chief Constable was quite confident that he could deal with the security and that the Prince would be safe. Nonetheless, the responsibility was mine.

As history shows, Prince Charles turned his stay in Aberystwyth into a personal triumph. The turning point came when he delivered a speech in excellent Welsh to the Urdd (Youth) Eisteddfod. Public opinion in Wales galloped to his side. He had undermined his fiercest opponents by tackling them with their own weapon. His growing popularity everywhere in Wales convinced me all would be well for the Investiture.

Special Branch police were at full stretch during the weekend before 1 July. The whole British establishment, including every member of the Royal family, was to be on parade in Caernarfon Castle, and it was well known that there were dangerous Welsh extremists at large. I received a telephone call from Scotland Yard to tell me that my objections to being accompanied by a detective must be set aside until the Investiture was over.

My reaction was instantaneous. "I have studied Special Branch for years. You cannot prevent a desperate man from shooting if he is determined to do so. All you can do is to catch the criminal after the deed is done." I am sure though that throughout that weekend I was rarely out of sight of at least one security officer.

On Sunday, 30 June, I went to Caernarfon Castle to see the preparations in progress. The square was so thronged with excited visitors that my car was slowed down to a snail's pace. Two tough-looking young men leaned in through my open window and spat "Bradwyr – Traitor!" at me.

I was in a tense mood when I set off early on Investiture Day to greet the Royal family at the specially built railway station two miles outside Caernarfon. Before I went on to the train to pay my respects to the Queen, I was told that they had been held up for two hours at Crewe because the signalling wires had been cut. The Queen asked if anything else had happened in the night and I had no option but to tell her that two men had blown themselves up trying to put a bomb on the railway line. I was sure though that she and the rest of the Royal family were going to get a great welcome and told her so.

The procession was headed by Prince Charles's coach, and David Checketts, his equerry, and I travelled with him. It was an uncomfortable coach with narrow seats, so I was quite unprepared when the Prince said, "This was Queen Victoria's coach, Mr Thomas. She rode in it herself." My answer came from the heart: "I hope she was more comfortable than I am."

About five minutes after we had left the station, a shattering roar came from an adjoining field. An extremist had exploded a bomb. People watching television saw the police run after and capture a suspect, but neither Prince Charles nor I knew what was happening. He turned to me: "What is that, Mr Thomas?" I improvised. "It's a royal salute, Prince Charles." When he said it was a peculiar royal salute, I could only reply, "There are peculiar people up here, Prince Charles."

As we drove through the narrow streets of Caernarfon, the crowds roared their welcome and pressed hard to reach the coach. I looked up at the people reaching out of the overhanging buildings. A determined killer could easily have thrown a bomb that would have wiped us out. It was a comforting moment for us all when we reached the security of Caernarfon Castle.

I led the Prince to the Chamberlain Tower, where he disappeared from the public view. Inside the Tower, I was pleasantly surprised to find two little children sitting in front of a television set. These were the children of Princess Margaret and Lord Snowdon, who rushed towards Prince Charles as soon as they saw him.

My greatest ordeal was to come. I had to read the Letters of Proclamation in Welsh – very old, stiff Welsh. I thought particularly then how I wished my father had taught me Welsh. From what I can gather, the Proclamation is something like Shakespearean English. I had worked very hard on this. My friend, the late Idwal Jones, the then MP for Wrexham, had recorded the whole text for me, and I had gone over it with him many times. A friend of my mother's from Holyhead had also helped and corrected me, and my great anxiety was that I might have too strong a North Wales accent at the end of the day. I was thrilled with the reception my recital received, and with the splendour of the ceremony as a whole. The Duke of Norfolk had done his work splendidly, and every detail of the complicated procedure went like clockwork.

The Queen was delighted and when she boarded the train to return to London I had never seen her so happy. It was clear that Prince Charles was going to be a popular Prince of Wales. Gwynfor Evans, the Welsh Nationalist leader, had been strongly opposed to the Investiture and had refused to attend the ceremony, which was followed by a triumphant tour through Wales. Gwynfor made the great mistake, at the behest of his agent, who panicked when he realised the popularity of the new Prince of Wales, of going to Carmarthen and standing in the queue to be presented to Prince Charles. I have always felt that the humbug of this upset the Welsh people. He lost his seat at the next election.

CHAPTER SIXTEEN

... Of Disappointments

The Investiture had been a crucial part of my time as Secretary of State for Wales but was by no means the only problem we faced in the Welsh Office. It had been finally agreed that the tip at Aberfan should be moved but the Coal Board presented us with a programme of pit closures that the Government had decided should go ahead on the understanding that uneconomic mines were to be closed.

The closure of a single pit meant that between five hundred and a thousand men could lose their jobs. New industries rarely employed more than a couple of hundred workers, so the task of solving the inevitable unemployment seemed insurmountable. Strong leadership by Glyn Williams, president, and Dai Francis, secretary, of the South Wales NUM was of enormous help at this time. They fiercely resisted some closures but ensured that law and order prevailed once a firm decision had been taken.

Generous Government grants, combined with the extraordinary adaptability of redundant miners, proved powerful weapons, and 195 new industries were established in Wales during my term in office. It seemed little short of miraculous that by June 1970 Welsh unemployment figures had fallen to 33,000 and the graph was still pointing downwards.

The good news in Wales coincided with a general improvement in the Government's fortunes. In April, after three years of trailing behind, the opinion polls showed a tremendous upsurge in the popularity of the Labour Government. Roy Jenkins, the Chancellor, was in a position to give generous concessions to the taxpayer, but introduced a neutral Budget as the Cabinet unanimously supported his argument that a "give away" Budget would be interpreted as an election bribe and rebound on us. Harold Wilson supported the strategy wholeheartedly.

Early in May, Harold told the Cabinet that he proposed to ask the

Queen for the dissolution of Parliament and then he went round the table, seeking the opinion of every minister in turn. We were all in favour of an early appeal to the country. As we ended the meeting, he said that he hoped we would all meet around the table after the election. We left in high spirits, expecting a great victory.

Throughout the campaign, the polls gave Labour a clear lead: we could not lose. On the eve of the election, I met Jim Callaghan for our traditional lunch. When I asked for his forecast, he said that he did not like the attitude of the young women voters, who seemed to be turning against Labour on the cost-of-living issue. He thought the election would be very close with a thirty majority either way. I still went to the Cardiff West count fully confident that Labour would win, so it was shattering to learn that the Government had been defeated. Jim's prediction of a thirty majority was right.

Harold Wilson called an early meeting of his old Cabinet to discuss the cause of our defeat. There was unanimous agreement that Harold had fought a great campaign and the reasons for defeat had to be found elsewhere. Many believed that resentment against scroungers who exploited the social services had worked savagely against us. The other major factor was Ted Heath's promise to reduce prices "at a stroke", which as Jim Callaghan had predicted had swung many young married women voters to the Tories.

When the inquest was over, Harold urged everyone to write down the state of things in their department when they left office, saying that it was easy to forget what was done. It was good advice. He also discussed the position of Horace King, the Speaker.

The Tories had told Horace that they would reappoint him as Speaker only if he promised to retire after six months. When the time came for me to be Speaker six years later, I remembered this incident only too clearly and was determined that I would retire before any hints were made.

Any outgoing minister is fascinated to see who takes his place and how his old job is valued by the Prime Minister, so I naturally agreed with those who thought that Ted Heath made a mistake in appointing Peter Thomas, MP for Hendon, chairman of the Conservative Party as well as Secretary of State for Wales. There was an immediate outcry in Wales and Anthony Barber's earlier statement that the chairmanship of the Conservative Party was a full-time job was recalled with anger. Poor Peter soon became labelled "the part-time Secretary for Wales".

The election brought considerable changes to the member-ship of the Welsh Parliamentary Labour group. Arthur Pearson, Harold Finch, Jim Griffiths, Eirene White, Cliff Williams, James Idwal Jones and Tudor Watkins had all decided to retire. They were people steeped in the traditions of the Labour Party and their de-parture heralded the end of an era. The new intake was very different.

They were the first generation to have grown up in the welfare state. They were the sons of manual workers, but they themselves had mostly moved into the professional class. Bryn John and Denzil Davies were solicitors; Jeffrey Thomas was a barrister; Neil Kinnock was a lecturer; Barry Jones and Caerwyn Roderick were teachers; and Tom Ellis was a colliery manager. For the first time, the group had only one former miner as an MP, Elfed Davies.

It was soon clear that the change in composition also meant a change in outlook. Two distinct and opposing schools of thought were represented. One, led by Cledwyn Hughes and Goronwy Roberts, provided strong supporters for devolution; the other, largely consisting of English-speaking MPs, was fiercely against it. I belonged to the latter group but saw it as my task to keep a united party.

As Shadow Secretary of State, I was forever seeking new ways to create at least a semblance of unity in Wales, for we were confronted by an increasingly vocal Welsh nationalist party. It was not difficult to get men like Cledwyn Hughes, Goronwy Roberts, John Morris and Elystan Morgan to make moderate speeches on devolution, even though they felt strongly on the issue; but Will Edwards and Tom Ellis were a different cup of tea. They went their own way and fanned the flames of nationalism at every opportunity. Fortunately, their influence in Wales and in Westminster was slight.

It did not take long for the new Welsh MPs to reveal their different gifts. Kinnock linked his star with Michael Foot and characterised his every speech by going far out on the left. Bryn John, Denzil Davies and Barry Jones soon showed that they were future ministers, and Alec Jones, who had succeeded the faithful Arthur Probert as secretary of the Welsh Labour group, grew in stature enormously. It became clear to everyone that he was bound to become a minister in the next Labour government. Ted Rowlands, who was returned at the Merthyr by-election, following the death of S. O. Davies, had already proved himself a successful junior minister. It was a privilege to be the spokesman for such an outstanding team – the best that Wales had ever sent to Westminster.

Cledwyn Hughes and I shared adjoining rooms in the House of Commons and naturally we spent a great deal of time discussing our own prospects if the Heath Government ran its full course. Cledwyn's constant theme was that I should not leave it too late to go to the Lords. If I went at the end of that Parliament, he consistently argued, I would still be able to serve as a minister in the Lords and gradually the idea began to appeal to me.

When my mother died on 21 April 1972, the thought of carrying on in the Commons suddenly held no attraction for me. It seemed that my ambition had died with Mam. She had been taken to hospital only a week before and her death came as a shattering blow. For a short time I even questioned my faith. The gloom was deepened by the death of the only remaining member of that happy Tonypandy family, my younger brother Ivor, only two months later. My faith was soon restored but this mood stayed with me for at least a year, and I discussed the matter with Jim Callaghan. His advice was unequivocal. I should tell Harold Wilson of my intention to retire at the next election. When I broke the news to Harold, he reacted sharply: "Why do you want to go? You'll be Secretary of State for Wales again." I told him I feared he would appoint me for a year, and then ask me to move over for a younger man, making it appear that I had been sacked for incompetence, and I wanted to go out with flying colours. Harold was very sympathetic. Despite his undoubted political toughness, he is soft-hearted in his personal relationships with those whom he trusts. Indeed I think it was that which led him into the misguided retirement honours list in 1976.

My own problems were resolved shortly after my meeting with Harold, when one of my parliamentary colleagues leaked the story to the *Western Mail*, which carried it on the front page. I was put on the spot. Either I had to deny the story, or my parliamentary influence as spokesman for the Welsh MPs would melt like snow on a spring day. It did not take me long to make up my mind. I issued an indignant denial, and reaffirmed my determination to contest the next election. In retrospect, the leak was an unmitigated blessing, for it resulted in a much longer House of Commons life for me.

The decision rekindled my ambition and at the 1974 election, I was looking forward to a return to the Welsh Office as Secretary of State for Wales if we won. The election was indecisive and Ted Heath tried desperately to arrange a deal with Jeremy Thorpe and the Liberals to keep him in Number Ten. I believed all along that he would fail and that Harold would be back in Downing Street.

The day Ted Heath eventually left Number Ten and Harold Wilson was called to the Palace, I had been with Harold all the afternoon in the House of Commons telling him he would be forming a government within the week. I was also confident that I would be in that government as Secretary of State for Wales.

I went back to my flat in Artillery Mansions and heard on the seven o'clock radio news that Mr Heath had resigned and that Harold Wilson was now the Prime Minister. I at once began thinking of things I would do in the Welsh Office and sat by the telephone waiting for the call from Harold. I waited and I waited, until at ten minutes to ten when I was just about to go to bed quite dispirited, the telephone rang and there was Harold himself asking me where I had been as he and his office had been trying to contact me, which was odd because as I told him I had been four inches from the telephone.

That delayed call should have alerted me to difficulties about my return to the Cabinet but I felt encouraged by the fact that he told me he was sorry he had not been able to contact me as he had wanted me to go to the Palace with him.

But now, with the benefit of that most precise science, hindsight, I know what happened. It had been decided long before that I was not going to be returning to the Cabinet and he was saying all the nice things he could, before breaking the news to me – probably the last person to know.

He then asked me to go to Number Ten and with great good fortune, I quickly caught a cab and was in fact with him in his room just as Big Ben was striking ten. Marcia Williams, Fred Peart, Gerald Kaufman and Peter Shore were already there and Harold suggested that we all watched "News at Ten" to see the events of the day before he and I went into the Cabinet Room, where he made all his appointments. He just watched himself waving outside Number Ten and then ushered me into the room. I winked at the others as I went in. He sat in the Prime Minister's chair in the middle of the table under the portrait of Robert Walpole, the first of the modern prime ministers, who introduced the Cabinet system of government.

Once settled in the room, I said that it was marvellous to be back where the power was. He couldn't bear it any longer because he knew what he was going to do and I did not. First of all he said, "George, you have been a good friend to me." I replied that we had been good friends to each other and what is more we had been loyal to each other.

And then he blurted out – and that is really the only way to put it – "How would you like to be Deputy Speaker and Chairman of Ways and Means?" I nearly fell out of my shoes: "What Deputy Speaker and not Secretary of State for Wales!" Harold knew me well and could see I was upset and immediately tried to reassure me: "Before you get agitated, remember how old Selwyn Lloyd is." This was an indication that Selwyn Lloyd would be going,* and I would have a chance to become Speaker.

It is hard to think straight when you are presented with a surprise like that and I was badly shaken and disappointed. I realise now of course that Harold did not have the Speakership in his gift. The House of Commons rightly insists on choosing its own Speaker and only a handful of Chairmen of Ways and Means have gone on to be Speaker. Finally I told him that if that was what he wanted me to do, I would. He tried to reassure me again: "You've always wanted to be Speaker." As a close friend, he knew that I was attracted to the post, although nobody is ever supposed to admit it. I would certainly not have done so in public.

Before I left, I asked who was going to get my job in Wales and he said he did not know yet. That is the only time he held anything back in all the time that I knew him, because he must have decided that the job was going to John Morris, MP for Port Talbot, and candidate of the Welsh-speaking people in the Welsh Labour group who, unlike me, shared their views on devolution.

I was the only former minister not to go back in the Cabinet and I realise now that my views on Welsh devolution, which the new Labour Government was determined to introduce in the new Parliament, had become an embarrassment to Harold. There is no doubt in my mind that many senior Labour politicians had impressed on Harold that devolution was unlikely if I was still in the Cabinet.

During the years of opposition, I had written a weekly column for the *Liverpool Daily Post* and I know that many times I had annoyed some Welsh Labour MPs by my strong resistance to Welsh nationalism. In retrospect, I think it was unwise to disregard their feelings and react the way I did. When Harold Wilson told me the names of a small

*Selwyn Lloyd had succeeded Horace King as Speaker in 1971.

group of Welsh MPs who had gone to him to protest about my views, I was even more outspoken. Harold made it clear that he had sent the delegation away with "a flea in their ear", but he advised me to be more on guard. This incident should have warned me that the road back to the Cabinet was not going to be easy, but I carried on as if nothing had happened.

Shortly after this, a journalist, who was writing for the *Western Mail*, told me that he had heard from a good source that John Morris would be the Secretary of State for Wales, not me, if Labour won the election. I dismissed this story, for I could not believe that Harold Wilson would lend himself to the intriguers. Common sense should have alerted me that the pressure on Harold would come from more influential sources than the little group who had protested about my journalistic activities.

When the February 1974 general election campaign began, Emrys Jones, regional officer for Labour in Wales, suggested that John Morris and I should share the Party television broadcast. Since I did not believe we were going to win the election, which Ted Heath had called in the hope of increasing his authority in dealing with the striking miners, I did not demur.

Incredible as it must seem to others, I was not at all bothered by appearing with John Morris. To the contrary, I accepted the story that it would be good to have a Welsh-speaking MP to share the programme. Throughout the campaign, I naturally saw my constituency neighbour Jim Callaghan on several occasions, but he gave no hint that he was aware of any threat to my position as Shadow Secretary of State for Wales.

News of John Morris's appointment was soon known and it was headline news in Wales. The morning after the announcement I went on the radio in Wales and was asked if I was disappointed. I thought it was rather a foolish question as everybody knew I was disappointed. I explained that John Morris had gifts that I did not possess and if I was to serve as Deputy Speaker, so be it.

Within a day or two I bumped into Jim Callaghan in the lobby behind the Speaker's Chair. There was not a flicker of sympathy in his attitude so I asked him if he knew before the election that I was not going back into the Cabinet. He gave me a brusque "Yes, I did," and we went our separate ways.

Politics can be a squalid business. I never have been able to understand the mentality of those power-seekers whose friendship is worthless when the going is hard. During all the intrigue that preceded the election, the participants maintained their pretence of friendship with me and never gave even a hint that danger signals surrounded me.

It is easy in retrospect to see how much my views on devolution were an embarrassment to people like Cledwyn Hughes, Elystan Morgan, John Morris and Tom Ellis, who lived in a world of their own cocooned by nationalist aspirations.

What is surprising is that Callaghan and Wilson should have miscalculated so badly the extent to which Wales wanted an Assembly of its own. I was thrown overboard because both of them fell into the trap of mistakenly believing noisy nationalist propaganda to represent the views of the majority in Wales. When the referendum they forced on Wales justified my attitude and helped to destroy the Labour Government, I had already been Speaker for two years.

This did not prevent me telephoning Cledwyn Hughes, a leading protagonist of devolution ever since his entry to Parliament, and expressing my delight at the resulting four-to-one rejection of a Welsh National Assembly. He angrily retorted that I was supposed to be neutral. It gave me enormous pleasure to say, "Oh yes. As Speaker I am entirely impartial: but on this issue I know on which side I am impartial!" I thought of the manoeuvres in which the pro-devolutionists had conspired to get me out of the way and I could not help but savour the final outcome.

It is strange how often an apparent setback proves to be a blessing in disguise. When the plotters quietly but insidiously destroyed my chance of returning into government, they were unintentionally doing me a great favour. My move into the office of Chairman of Ways and Means was a blessing in disguise.

It was a week after my interview with Harold that the motion went on the order paper for me to be elected Deputy Speaker and Chairman of Ways and Means. The House of Commons has had a Deputy Speaker since 1855 but the office of Chairman of Ways and Means goes back much longer because the House would not let the Speaker preside over them when they were talking about raising money – the ways and means of managing – because they were afraid that the Speaker would tell the monarch which MPs had spoken against raising the taxes that the King wanted. It is a very ancient and honourable office but the title is now held by the senior of the three Deputy Speakers who also works closely with the committees in the House and advises the Speaker on appointing members to the panel of chairmen to run the committees.

I resolved from the first day in my new role that party politics were ended so far as I was concerned. From then on I gave my wholehearted loyalty to the House of Commons and not to the Labour Party. It was not for me to allow the Labour Government to use me as a parliamentary pawn to get their own way.

I had seen some previous Chairmen of Ways and Means playing the party game to justify their appointment, and I remembered the resentment that had been aroused. Whatever happened to me, I was determined I would try to bring to my new office loyalty to the highest traditions of the Chair.

My first decision was that I would not attend any party political meetings in the House or in the country, except for the management committee of my constituency, because Deputy Speakers have to seek re-election on the party ticket. Every month, I gave a party speech in the privacy of the Cardiff West Labour Party management committee, but I never once made a party political speech in public.

Not everybody takes this view and the present Deputy Speaker, Harold Walker, has in fact canvassed for Tony Benn, saying it was unreasonable for people to expect him to be impartial. I think this is something that will have to be watched carefully if we are not to change the character of the office.

I began a new life then, the most obvious change being that I had to walk around the House wearing morning dress. It embarrassed me enormously at first, until I accepted it as a uniform to signal to everybody else that I was now linked with the Chair. I thought at first that I would miss the involvement with party politics that had been so much a part of my life but I found that I enjoyed my new freedom, sitting for the first time with the Tories, and Liberals, even the Nationalists – and that was something.

It was in 1975 during my period as Chairman of Ways and Means that Cardiff City Council gave Jim Callaghan and myself the Freedom of the City. This was a matter of enormous pride for me. I wished only that my mother had lived to witness the ceremony as I remembered how happy she had been when I had received the Freedom of my home borough of the Rhondda.

Callaghan was Foreign Secretary and he invited Henry Kissinger, then American Secretary of State, to Cardiff for the Freedom ceremony. Kissinger's presence changed the whole atmosphere of the day's celebrations. He was there for the sole purpose of paying tribute to the UK's Foreign Secretary and the media latched on to this very quickly. It was understandably seen as Jim Callaghan's exercise in oneupmanship.

I found it strangely moving to watch Kissinger's giant aircraft "The United States of America" make its landing at Cardiff airport. His bullet-proof car had been flown in to await his arrival and I rode in it with the two foreign secretaries to Cardiff City Hall, where we saw a demonstration with banners denouncing both Callaghan and Kissinger. Kissinger particularly enjoyed a banner boldly declaring "Callaghan out", and said, "That is not fair, Jim. I usually get top billing."

Callaghan had asked the City Council to allow Kissinger to make a speech at the dinner held in our honour in the City Banqueting Hall, so naturally he was there to praise Jim Callaghan's virtues, which he did superbly well. But both Kissinger and his wife showed a sensitivity about my position which touched me very much.

Meanwhile in the House of Commons I was settling into my new role, which was to prove a good apprenticeship for the Speakership, but very much easier. When backbenchers complained that I had not called them to speak, I could always point to the Speaker's list. That was an argument I could never use later on.

Selwyn Lloyd used to keep a pretty tight rein on his deputies but I used to tell mine that they should use their discretion if circumstances seemed to suggest that the list of MPs I had left them for debates was unfair in some way. But Selwyn made his promises and it was up to us to keep them.

Selwyn and I got on very well together, even though our backgrounds were totally opposite. He was Fettes School and I was Tonypandy Grammar. I thought he was a good Speaker. And I think he thought so too, as he kept on asking me who I thought was the greatest Speaker in my time in the House of Commons. I always used to tell him "Shakes" Morrison, who became Governor-General of Australia as Viscount Dunrossil. But then I would see Selwyn's face fall a little and I would go on to say, "Present company excepted, of course." Fortunately he had a very dry sense of humour.

I stayed with him twice at his home in the Wirral and preached in his local Methodist church. He was a genuine Methodist and very proud of it. When I went to the chapel, he showed me a pew with its own door, explaining that his father had it put there to stop him running up and down the aisles when he was a small and somewhat unruly boy. He then showed me two stained-glass windows, which he and his sister had put up in memory of their mother and father. His grandfather had once been a Welsh-speaking minister in Wales and Selwyn lent me a book on his life. One phrase, "I gave my heart to the Lord", was very heavily underscored. I asked Selwyn if his father had done this and was surprised when he told me he had done it himself.

I gave the address at his memorial service at Westminster Abbey and I could say with my hand on my heart that he was a man with strong Christian convictions. He was one of Harold Macmillan's victims in the night of the long knives when he was sacked as Chancellor of the Exchequer, and it hurt him to the very end. He could only do what the rest of us have to do, forget the disappointment and accept it. He made an astonishing comeback to be appointed Speaker following Horace King, by just being quiet on the backbenches.

My own chances of being Speaker could easily have been ruined during my time as Deputy – it would only have needed one good row and the House would soon have turned against me. In the event it did not happen and finally the day came when Selwyn Lloyd told me he was going to retire. For nearly a year before he retired, he kept telling me that he had had enough and intended to go. He was emphatic in June 1975 that he would retire after the Summer Recess. When we returned in October he told me he would retire at Christmas. In early December, he said he had changed his mind and would not retire after all. All these exchanges were on his initiative, and I always told him it was entirely a matter for him. Late in January 1976 he told me he would that day tell the Commons he would retire in ten days' time, on 3 February.

I cannot adequately describe my feelings that day. Common sense told me that I was a prime candidate, but I was not prepared to count my chickens before they were hatched. Members kept coming up to me to wish me well but all I could say was: "You are very kind." The ten days I had to wait were probably the longest ten days of my life.

Politics is a cruel business and to survive without bitterness one needs to be able to treat success and defeat alike. There could be no better example of this than Sir Alec Douglas-Home, one of the men for whom I have always had enormous respect and whom I would like to emulate in many ways. He was entitled to carry a great chip on his shoulder when his party dumped him straight after very narrowly losing the election to Harold Wilson, but he bears no malice and is at peace with the world.

I never went to Number Ten while Alec was Prime Minister, but I have become friendly with him since and he sits quite near me in the Lords. He has the rare gift of being on the best terms with all wings of the party and gets on as well with Ted Heath as he does with Margaret Thatcher just by being himself and having no personal ambition. His only loyalties are to the party and to the country. Everybody was surprised when he was chosen as Macmillan's successor – I think even he was. It was extraordinary to pick a man from the Lords, particularly as Alec had not played a prominent part in Government in the Commons, but his selection to follow Macmillan was largely to keep other people out of the job, like Lord Hailsham and Rab Butler whose long period in ministerial office had resulted in many enemies being made along the way. Rab Butler could be waspish but he was a superb operator in the House of Commons where, when he was making his most damaging remarks about the opposition, he would smile across to the Labour benches almost as if he was telling a joke. We would laugh back only to realise later just how cutting his remarks had been. Rab had a big following in the Tory party and Iain Macleod, who was a very shrewd man, wanted Butler to succeed Macmillan. Macleod resented the old magic circle and was never part of it.

It is the strangest thing that it was left to Alec Douglas-Home to devise a system for electing the Tory party leader which meant that his successor was the first one to be rejected. Alec Douglas-Home had the humility to take office under his successor and became Foreign Secretary in Ted Heath's Government. He has the personal happiness which has been denied to Mr Heath who, it seems, will never forgive the party for getting rid of him in favour of Mrs Thatcher.

Sir Alec realised that politics is a cruel game and that if a man does not bring the prize home, particularly for the Conservatives, then a price has to be paid. But the Tories made a mistake by acting too quickly after that election. If they had only given him time, they would have realised that the country had an underlying affection and respect for him. But in their anger at losing, the pressures were on; he was too much of a gentleman to say he was going to fight to stay there and he went quietly. I think the Tories had a jewel of rare price without realising it, and they acted for the short term rather than the long term. In the long term, his integrity, natural decency and undoubted ability would have proved an asset to the Party.

The truth is that he paid the price of not being good on television. It is tragic for our parliamentary democracy that the only way you can be a leader is by being good on the television screen. There is obviously much more to leading a country than that, but television performance is becoming a major factor in the minds of parties when they choose a leader.

Sir Alec's successor, Ted Heath, was also to learn how hard the Tories could be when they in turn dumped him after his election defeat. But he has reacted so differently from Alec. Ted seems to be forever on guard and to harbour a deep resentment. The wound from his defeat at the hands of one of his junior Cabinet ministers must have been very severe and may never heal. The irony is, of course, that it was he who decided that the Conservatives must have a woman in the Cabinet. He must have sensed her ability because even if you have decided that you need a woman in the Cabinet, you are not going to choose one who cannot do the job. Heath certainly did not make that mistake but I think he seriously underestimated her and never anticipated her strength.

He also behaved in such a way in office that he lost parliamentary friends wholesale. It may have been because of his deep reserve but many Conservatives felt as if he just ignored them, almost as if they were not alive.

Once you get over the reserve from which Heath suffers, you can find a different man altogether. He can be the most delightful company and yet in other circumstances he seems to go back into a hard and unyielding shell. I wrote to him when his father died and in reply he sent me a moving letter in which he poured his heart out – yet when I saw him afterwards and told him I would cherish that letter he gave me a very abrupt response. He could not bear to talk about anything so private. Sadly, I think he will never find the peace that Sir Alec so obviously enjoys.

He never dreamt he would have to face an election to stay on as leader of the Tory party; nobody else had. He was hoping that once being elected he would have been returned unopposed. But the Conservatives will not tolerate a loser. As Harold Wilson once told me, "Our boys talk a lot but they never do anything. The Tories say very little and the man is out before he knows he is under attack." The public schoolboys can be much rougher at the end of the day than the grammar schoolboys when it comes to guarding what they believe to be their own interests. If anybody is in their way they are not going to stay up all night feeling embarrassed that they will have to get rid of him. They did it to Anthony Eden, Alec Douglas-Home and Ted Heath. And they will not hesitate to do it again when they feel it is in their interests to do so.

CHAPTER SEVENTEEN

Mr Speaker, Sir

Once the news of Selwyn Lloyd's retirement was official, each of the separate parties in the House met to decide who they would propose as his successor. The first party to tell me of their decision was the Scottish Nationalist Party. Donald Stewart, their courteous and kindly leader, accompanied by Douglas Henderson, Chief Whip, came to say, "We have resolved unanimously and with affection that we want you to be the next Speaker." I was deeply moved by their confidence and said that whether I was elected or not, I would always be grateful to them.

The next day, Jeremy Thorpe and David Steel, both long-standing friends, came to my room in their official capacity as leader and Chief Whip of the Liberal Party. Also using the words "with affection", they told me that the Parliamentary Liberal Party had resolved unanimously to support my candidature. These two interviews set the pattern for the next few days. Humphrey Atkins, Conservative Chief Whip, told me his party had unanimously resolved to support me. James Molyneaux, leader of the Ulster Unionists, and Gwynfor Evans, leader of the Welsh Nationalists (who was returned to Parliament in October 1974), came with the same message. Before Cledwyn Hughes, chairman of the Parliamentary Labour Party, could reach me after their meeting, a group of my Labour friends had hurried down to tell me that the Party had supported my nomination with acclamation by banging on their desks.

On the day of the election I strictly followed the procedure that had been adopted down the centuries. Wearing a formal morning suit, I took a seat in the third row behind the Government front bench. Jim Callaghan left his seat on the Government front bench to sit alongside me. He said, "We sat next to each other on our first day in this House. This is your last day on these benches so I will sit next to you again." I was deeply touched by this gesture of friendship.

My election was proposed by George Strauss, Father of the House, and seconded by Sir Derek Walker-Smith, the senior Conservative backbencher. The House was absolutely crowded and I was on fire inside. When my proposer and seconder came to drag me to the Chair in the tradition of the House, Jim Callaghan threw his arm around me and prevented me going. I laughed: "I want to look reluctant, but not too reluctant." He let me go.

Conscious of my debt to the Cardiff West constituency for keeping me in Parliament for three decades, I had naturally invited the officers to London for the election. Selwyn Lloyd, who had invited his family and friends to see his departure, required all the tickets for seats in the Speaker's Gallery, and I was in a quandary about tickets for my guests. The Serjeant at Arms came to my rescue and gave me tickets for his box, right up at the far end of the Gallery. I was greatly relieved for it would have been a poor beginning if my Cardiff friends had been turned away.

The City of Cardiff had been represented in the Commons since 1542 but never in the following years had one of its representatives been elected as Speaker; indeed in the long history of the House, only once before had a Welsh constituency member been elected Speaker. That was in 1685 when Sir John Trevor, the member for Denbigh, was called to the Chair. The poor man suffered a squint in both eyes, which led to considerable confusion. For 300 years the Speaker had pointed to a member he had intended to call but Sir John's squint meant that members often thought they had been called when in fact he had meant to indicate the man sitting alongside. The Commons became so angry that they insisted "Mr Speaker do call us by name." I told the House that I hoped there would be no doubt as to whom I would call to speak in the future.

That day in February was also the first time the outgoing Speaker had been in the Chair for the election of the incoming Speaker. There were the tributes to both of us which made it a bit embarrassing as people did not like to be praising me too highly as Selwyn stayed in the Chair to declare me elected Speaker of the House.

I thoroughly enjoyed making my acceptance speech because I knew the House and I loved the House. We had shared a good many laughs there and the House was very kind to me. That night, I gave a private dinner party and Cledwyn Hughes was there with Jim Callaghan and John Morris, who had taken my job in Wales, but that night was a night for goodwill.

The House of Commons had now elected me Speaker but before I officially took over, I had to receive the approval of the Queen in the House of Lords. So the following day, I went to the Lords with Black Rod and the Serjeant at Arms carrying the mace (the symbol of the Speaker's authority) on his arm to indicate that I had not yet been approved as Speaker. Elwyn Jones was the Lord Chancellor then and it was all very courteous with plenty of bowing and doffing of hats, all the business the House of Lords seems to like.

After the necessary number of bows, I said, "My Lords, I have to inform your Lordships that Her Majesty's faithful Commons, in obedience to the Royal Command, and in the exercise of their un-doubted rights and privileges, have proceeded to the election of a Speaker, and that their choice has fallen on me. I therefore present myself at your Lordships' bar and submit myself with all humility for Her Majesty's gracious approbation."

To which the Lord Chancellor said, "Mr George Thomas, we have it in command from Her Majesty to declare her Majesty's entire confidence in your talents, diligence and sufficiency to fulfil the impor-tant duties of the high office of Speaker of the House of Commons to which you have been chosen by that House; and in obedience to the Commission which has been read, and by virtue of the authority therein contained, we do declare Her Majesty's Royal allowance and confirmation upon you, Sir, as Speaker of the House of Commons."

I replied, "My Lords, I submit myself with all humility to Her Majesty's Royal will and pleasure, and if, in the discharge of my duties and in the maintenance of the rights and privileges of the Commons House of Parliament, I should inadvertently fall into error, I pray that the blame may be imputed to me alone and not to Her Majesty's faithful Commons."

Now I was really Speaker in a tradition that goes back nearly 700 years, a thought that always makes my blood tingle. There are people who want to change the ways we do things in Britain and in the House, but very often change is just for change's sake. Traditions that have endured through the centuries must have something about them and you need a very good reason to tamper with them. If there were such a reason then they would probably not have survived as long as they have. And at the very least, they give a sense of continuity and security – not complacency – which so many other countries have good cause to envy.

The day after I had been to the Lords, I walked for the first time as Speaker in the procession from Speaker's House to the Chamber of the Commons. I was naturally apprehensive and went into my bedroom and knelt down to pray before leaving.

A great surprise awaited me when my procession to the House began, led by the Serjeant at Arms with the mace now on his shoulder. The entire library corridor leading from Speaker's House to the central lobby was lined on both sides with members who bowed as I passed for the first time in robes and full-bottomed wig. The first one I saw was Oscar Murton, Chairman of Ways and Means. My guess is that he had organised the whole exercise and I knew it was the members' way of wishing me good luck. When I arrived in the central lobby the usual large crowd of visitors and members was assembled. My legs felt as if they had turned to wood and I was terribly self-conscious. I do not think I will ever forget the moment I climbed those three or four steps up into the Chair and realised that the buck stopped there; that it is all right to have that ambition, to have that wig put on your head, but there are responsibilities that go with it.

I had been a Member of Parliament for thirty-one years but there had been no other moment like the first time I sat in the Chair as Speaker. My thoughts raced through past years. Above all, I thought of the days of poverty when I lived with my family in the underhouse in Miskin Road, Trealaw. Mam, my two sisters and two brothers had died, but I knew how proud they would have been at seeing me in the Speaker's Chair. I wondered, too, what Clem Attlee, Herbert Morrison and the others would have thought. Secretly I believed that they would have been happy to see how much I had mellowed, from the days when I was a rebellious backbencher.

I thought that I knew the House of Commons thoroughly when I became Speaker, but in my first few months in the Chair I learned otherwise. There was a side of the Commons that had remained hidden from me throughout my thirty-one years there. It was as dark as the other side of the moon, and it was unattractive. At first I was merely shocked by the things I was learning, but in a short while, shock changed to anger.

It has become customary for members to be called to ask a supplementary question on another member's question to a minister. Very frequently several members will stand up hoping to ask a supplementary question, but only one or two are called before the Speaker moves on to the next question. If every member who stood up was called, the House would never deal with more than half a dozen questions in the hour allotted for that purpose. After Question Time, ministers often make a statement on Government business, which leads to a further period of questioning by members.

I found in my first six weeks as Speaker that supplementary questions would go on and on, despite all I did to hurry things up. I would call about two supplementaries on each question from either side and move along. This was a very difficult time for the Government and there were Government statements nearly every day, which produced further flurries of questions and supplementaries. So every day there were the regulars who, no matter whether it was fish, unemployment, Cuba, the Middle East or the Penge sewage works, would jump up on everything. And were expert on nothing. To curb this, I got into the habit about half an hour after the start of the Government's statements of saying I would take three more questions on either side. That would avoid the terrible tension that built up with people waiting to be called and the awful rows that would follow if they were not. Selwyn Lloyd had them and I was determined that I would not.

In my first few months as Speaker, the pattern was always the same after Question Time and after Government statements. By the time I had returned to Speaker's House, there was a pile of letters waiting for me. The people who were disgruntled that I had not called them had already been in the library and written me an offensive letter complaining bitterly. It upset me at first and I used to send soothing replies but it did not take long for me to realise that the bully-boys were trying it on. The aggravation and complaints usually came from the same small group. I knew I had to stop it and one day I stood up in the House to say that I had been receiving letters from some members complaining that they were not being called. The House, of course, responded in the traditional way with cries of "Oh", indicating how deeply shocked they were at such behaviour.

But I think many members were genuinely appalled that people were trying to force me into calling them and there was general approval when I told the House that such action was counter-productive. Anybody writing a letter of that sort in the future would make it very difficult for me to call them. Most of the letters did stop, although there was a dribble all the way through my seven years. There is no doubt that the Speaker's most potent weapon is the right to decide who to call to take part in debates or to ask questions.

My instinct for survival drove me to deal with the back-stage operators with a toughness I hardly realised I possessed. I knew that to give in to intimidation of any sort would make my life a misery.

The other technique of parliamentary bully-boys is deliberately to create a scene if they have not been called, after they have stood up several times: the fact that other members are in the same position makes no difference to them. At first I used to believe that sheer vanity goaded them into making fools of themselves by making them raise false points of order as a protest at being overlooked.

Later I realised that their technique was coldly calculated. They would shout and rave like people possessed in the hope that next time I would call them rather than face a repeat performance. When they found themselves overlooked again, they began to realise that their public bullying was ineffective. Nonetheless, until they learned their lesson, it was a time of strain for me.

The control of questions is at the Speaker's discretion and I think the best interest of the House is served if there is a limit to questions and statements because you have to move on to the business of the day with a crowd of other members who want to speak. I made sure we finished Question Time on the stroke of 3.30 p.m. but I did try to be fair and once allowed it to go on beyond, because a member had objected that a question had affected his constituency and I had not called him. If I knew a question affected a particular member or his constituency I would call him.

Questions to the Prime Minister were changed for the worse when the Labour MP for Newcastle-under-Lyme, John Golding, devised "open questions" to the Prime Minister during the Labour administration. He asked the Prime Minister to list his engagements for the day, which meant that you could ask a supplementary question on virtually any subject by saying, "During the course of the day, will the Prime Minister be considering so and so?" or "I notice the Prime Minister is not visiting my constituency today. Can he please tell me when he will be coming to inspect the very real difficulties there?"

The House thought open questions were a marvellous idea and tried to put them to other ministers who did not have the Prime Minister's right to transfer questions to the relevant department. I felt I had to protect Question Time and made a statement to the House, which I had to repeat a few months later, that I would not allow any open questions to any other minister because it would alter completely the character of Question Time. I also believed the House had the right to know the real nature of the questions being asked; after all, that is what the notice on the order paper is all about. Without this ruling,

I am convinced that Question Time would have degenerated into an uncontrollable classroom brawl. It is bad enough as it is.

I kept a register of the number of times members were called for Prime Minister's questions, which came to prove very useful in the future. I remember the Labour MP for Walsall North, David Winnick, once getting up on a point of order to protest that he had not been called and he wanted to know the basis on which I called members to ask questions of the Prime Minister. This was a very impertinent question and I told him that I did not have to give reasons as to how I chose the people I called, but I was able to add, "Everyone who has been called this afternoon has not been called more than once before. The honourable member himself has been called four times. I keep a register." There was a great laugh: it demolished him, at any rate for the time being.

Another cause of discontent was my attitude to private notice questions, which did not have to go on the order paper and so could jump the queue. I would receive half a dozen of these a day for a long time and would turn them down, as I felt they had to be of real urgency. Most times they were not and, if they could wait, it was not fair to those who had put their questions on the order paper and had to wait their turn.

The House itself had earlier decided against having questions without notice on the order paper and yet this is what was happening. I felt then and I feel now that this has ruined Prime Minister's Question Time. Churchill and Attlee; Eden and Macmillan; Heath and Wilson all had in their time constructive questions in which they dealt with important matters.

There was the occasional uproar but it was not sustained all through Question Time as it is so often now. I think the House needs to take special care lest its cherished freedom of speech gets drowned in a torrent of abuse from a minority who do not want to allow people to put a point of view with which they disagree. The House of Commons is about debating, arguing, talking, expressing different views and, through speaking in the House, appealing to the nation.

Sustained barracking is a very ugly development, which I felt was organised, and it made me realise that whereas Selwyn Lloyd had boasted that he had not named or suspended anyone throughout his Speakership, that policy was no good for me. Selwyn's view of ignoring as much of the trouble in the House of Commons as possible was not always wise.

I spent many hours in my rooms trying to decide how to tackle the problem of dealing with members in the Chamber in the coming months. Finally I decided that I would have to take firm action very soon or the House could easily spin out of control and Parliamentary business become impossible. It was not long before I would have to suspend the House in order to save the dignity of Parliament. The time would also come when, unlike Selwyn, I would face the very unpleasant task of having members suspended from the House.

In those early months, I was also to face an even greater strain, when I discovered how the major parties were proposing to look after their party interests. Key people from the Opposition and the Government would come to sound out what my rulings were likely to be on certain issues and it was not unusual for me to be told that a poor view would be taken if I decided to rule in a particular way. I soon became convinced that both sides were engaged in an effort to gain the ascendancy over me. Polite but barely hidden menaces would be forthcoming in the privacy of a chat in my rooms. I decided that I must take action to assert both my independence and my impartiality. I knew I would not have long to wait for the opportunity.

It duly came when I was told in discreet terms what was expected of me in connection with a ruling on which I had reserved judgement. I listened courteously and carefully. My response was not what was expected for I turned sharply and pointed to my door: "See that door. I do not mind walking out through that door tomorrow, but I will go with my head high. I am not going to be pushed around. And as a backbencher I would tell the House why I had resigned." I was immediately assured in the most fulsome terms that the last thing anybody wished to do was to try to push me around. It was simply that they wished me to know the party viewpoint. There was no more trouble there.

Within two weeks I had the opportunity to use the same technique and identical language with the major party on the other side of the House. The result was the same. It is not easy for a Speaker to remain totally impartial and remote from any covert dealings, but if he fails on this, he might as well resign, for his life will not be his own. In my case, I found life much easier once I had my confidence and everybody in the House knew that I was determined to act strongly whenever I believed things were getting out of hand, and that, whatever happened, I was not going to be bullied.

CHAPTER EIGHTEEN

A Tory Sees Red

Just before I was elected Speaker, Harold Wilson had taken me into his confidence to say that he would be resigning as Prime Minister within a few weeks. It is true that we had been friends for thirty years and that we had always trusted each other but I believe that he was telling me then because he knew he could trust the Speaker. He was one of many members who trusted me with their problems both political and personal, knowing their secrets were safe with the Speaker. There were times, though, when I think many of them were coming to the preacher rather than the Speaker.

So I was prepared on 16 March 1976 for Harold's retirement announcement, which took nearly everybody by surprise and left them puzzled as to why he was leaving Number Ten. Jim Callaghan became Prime Minister and the difference in style was soon apparent. I had always found Harold to be open in his dealings, while Jim was much more guarded. It was also true that Jim had taken over at probably the most difficult time for the Labour Party, which had lost its overall majority in the House when John Stonehouse formed his own English National Party with a membership of one and Brian O'Malley, the member for Rotherham, died.

It was this that led to the new Prime Minister's first taste of an angry House at the end of April and he reacted quite differently from his predecessor who would play for time with long replies. The House had burst into fury over the decision of the Committee of Selection, whose task it was to appoint standing committees (with their membership reflecting the relative strengths of the parties in the House), to ignore the fact that the Government had lost its overall majority and still give them a majority on the committees. The matter came to a head when the Committee of Selection was appointing a committee to investigate the question of private medicine and pay-beds within the National Health Service. It also led to my first mistake in the Chair – or at least to the first of which I am conscious.

At the end of a stormy Question Time, Nigel Lawson, the Conservative member for Blaby, requested leave under Standing Order No. 9 (which deals with applications for emergency debates) to move the adjournment of the House to discuss a matter of urgent and specific importance, namely the action of the Selection Committee. I rejected the application because I believed it was dangerous for members to seek to involve the Chair in party fights of the kind we had just seen. I regretted my words within seconds for I realised that Lawson was well within his parliamentary rights.

In the evening I received a long letter from Patrick Jenkin, a front-bench Conservative spokesman, protesting against the words I had used, and on Friday morning I received a request from Nigel Lawson to come to see me. The interview convinced me that I should make a statement in the House. I therefore explained to the Commons that as the custodian of the unwritten Constitution I had made a mistake and that any honourable member under similar circumstances would be entitled to make an application under Standing Order No. 9 for the adjournment of the House. I believe the House appreciated the explanation but in any case I felt it would be unwise to leave uncorrected on the record words I myself regret having used.

The debate lived up to all expectations and opened to a crowded House. The chairman of the Selection Committee, Captain Hugh Delargy, the Labour MP for Thurrock, was one of the most respected members in the Commons and had entered Parliament in 1945. Irish to his finger tips and emotional, he rarely took a great part in debates.

That Monday, however, was different. His committee had been divided and the controversial decision was made on his casting vote. He made a moving speech, a fighting speech, and concluded with the words: "We are not dishonourable men." His face was flushed as he sat down and the House was in a very excitable mood.

John Peyton, the then Shadow Leader of the House, who led for the Opposition, can be cutting and wounding; his phrases are directed to create maximum hurt in those to whom he is opposed. But on this occasion, he began with a tribute to the personal integrity of Hugh Delargy and said that nobody questioned his honour, that this was a political argument.

The morning after the debate, Hugh Delargy collapsed and died, and emotion swept through the House still full of the debate the night before, a major parliamentary occasion. I told John Peyton that his guardian angel must have been with him, because if he had made one of his savage attacks – of which no one is more capable than he – he would have blamed himself for Hugh's heart attack. As it was, no one could say that John Peyton had behaved in any other than an impeccable manner. The storm between the parties relaxed because of Hugh Delargy's death and the parties agreed that the Government and Opposition should have 50–50 on standing committees.

Two other events occurred around this time to remind me that there was far more to being Speaker than presiding over the House of Commons. In the last week of April 1976, I read to the House of Commons the resignation letter of Sir David Lidderdale as Clerk of the House after forty-two years' service in the Commons, and immediately afterwards read the resignation letter from Mr D. C. L. Holland, the Chief Librarian since 1967, who had a total of thirty years' service.

To my astonishment Sir David came to see me to complain bitterly that I had read the letter from the librarian at the same time as his own. He felt that the Clerk of the House was in a very special position and asked that, when the time came for a motion of thanks to be put down in the House, his name would not be linked with that of anybody else. It never ceases to astonish me how men in high positions can be so touchy about little things. I remember clearly thinking then that I hoped that the experience of privilege and powerful office would never have the same effect on me.

Then on Monday, 10 May, David Steel, the Liberal Chief Whip, asked to see me urgently. When he came into my room I thought he was going to burst into tears. He was clearly upset and I knew before he said a word that Jeremy Thorpe had at last given in to the cruel campaign that had been conducted against him after his name had been linked with an alleged murder attempt. It was 2.15 p.m. The announcement of Jeremy Thorpe's resignation as Liberal leader would be made at four o'clock that afternoon. David said that as Speaker I had the right to know, but he asked me to keep it secret because as yet not all Liberal Members of Parliament had been told. I expressed my sadness at the cruel sacrifice of a first-class member of the House of Commons. David Steel agreed. I then, indiscreetly for a Speaker, expressed hope that he would get elected as the leader of the Liberal Party. A dedicated Christian, his radicalism had revealed itself over the years.

My feeling has always been that Jeremy Thorpe was destroyed by his parliamentary colleagues as much as by the press campaign against him. The Liberal MPs behaved very badly by showing disloyalty just when their leader needed it most. Jeremy had been in dire trouble for a long time and had a right to expect far greater loyalty from those around him than he received. In fact he had more friends outside the Liberal Party than inside.

Harold and Mary Wilson and their son Giles came to dinner that evening and inevitably we talked about Jeremy's resignation. Harold said he had been in touch with him all over the weekend and had wanted him to continue to fight, but the Sunday newspaper stories and the broadcast attack by Richard Wainwright, the Liberal MP for Colne Valley, had proved too much.

Those early months were probably the most difficult of my seven years as Speaker. Major trouble came at the end of May over the Aircraft and Shipbuilding Industries Bill, a jewel in the Government's crown. The bill had been considered line by line in the committee stage and had reached the report stage when Robin Maxwell-Hyslop, Conservative member for Tiverton and an expert on House of Commons' procedure, raised the question of whether the bill was hybrid or not. The rules of procedure meant that if it were hybrid, that is to say if it did not deal fairly and equally with every shipyard concerned, then the bill could not proceed. Maxwell-Hyslop asked me to give a considered ruling within the next few days and I undertook to do so.

Mountainous pressure began at once. Both Government and Opposition had much at stake and I received a powerful delegation from both sides. The Tories included Sir Michael Havers, the Shadow Attorney General, Humphrey Atkins, Chief Whip, and other frontbench spokesmen. Labour were led by Michael Foot, Leader of the House, Eric Varley, the minister responsible for the bill, other ministers, the Attorney General, Sam Silkin, and the government draftsmen responsible for drawing up the bill. Both sides argued their case with passion, but the meeting with Labour was particularly tense as they argued why I should rule in their favour. I think it was only then that they realised just how impartial I intended to be.

My advisers were the Clerks of the House led by Sir David Lidderdale. Maxwell-Hyslop drew my attention to the fact that in definitions to the bill the draftsmen had said, "For the purposes of this Bill a ship is anything that floats and has a hull." Maxwell-Hyslop gave me a picture of an oil rig that had a hull and certainly floated, yet oil rigs were not included in the bill, the shipyards which built them were not to be nationalised. My advisers wobbled and changed the advice they gave me. At first they sided with the draftsmen; later they strongly advised me that there was sufficient doubt for me to rule that the bill was hybrid.

The bill was hybrid, there was no doubt about it, but even if there was doubt, the ruling of Speaker Denison in the 1860s had been that, if there was any doubt, the bill should go to examiners. I was quite satisfied. I had been Speaker only about six weeks and it was a harrowing time for me. Not only did I have the representatives of the two big parties but I had a string of Labour people asking to see me. Eric Heffer, the MP for Walton, came to tell me that if I ruled against the Government I was going to make thousands unemployed. I told him that would be a grievous thing indeed but my decision could not be made on that basis. I told him it was simply a question as to whether it was right or wrong so far as the House was concerned. I had to keep to the rules of the House as it was the only way to be fair.

So Labour were aware that I was likely to rule against them. I think it was probably hurried legislation and that the bill was just not put together as carefully as it should have been. The incredible thing is that neither of the front benches had seen the difficulty earlier on – after all they had been through it line by line.

When I gave my ruling, Harold Wilson passed by the Chair to say, "The right ruling and a very courageous one." It gave me enormous reassurance but I knew that when he said it was courageous he meant there would be a tremendous row about it. I would have been dishonest if I had not ruled that the bill was hybrid and would always have been uneasy knowing I had not done the right thing.

The Labour people knew I was right but they expected me to save the party to which I had belonged for fifty years. However, once you put the Speaker's wig on your head, you feel differently. Selwyn Lloyd came to see me later and said that he thought the ruling was right. He too said it was very courageous but added that if he, as a Conservative, had given the ruling, the Government side would have got shot of him as soon as they decently could.

Just before I gave the ruling, Richard Barlas, then Lidderdale's deputy, said that he knew it would be distressing to rule against the Government but that eventually the House would appreciate that I had done the right thing, although it would cost me a lot of goodwill for a long time on the Labour side. I think the Party as a whole understood what I had to do but I am sure that Jim Callaghan and the rest of the Labour leadership never really forgave me.

Shortly after the row, Cardiff City Council asked for a picture of the two of us together and at first Jim Callaghan refused. I invited him to come to the state rooms at Speaker's House which he rejected and he insisted that if there was to be a picture at all I should go to Number Ten, where I would wear my normal working outfit of black gown and wig. It was only when I told him I would have to tell Cardiff that he was not prepared for us to have a picture taken together that he eventually agreed.

During my speech to the Commons when my re-election was proposed after the 1979 general election, I quoted a hymn and Jim said that it sounded like one of Mr Speaker's prayer meetings, a sop I am sure to the feelings of a small but vociferous crowd on the far left. He went on to say that he would support me as long as I made the right decisions – which meant the ones with which he agreed. There was a great shout of protest, so he quickly added, "Well, of course you always will be right, Mr Speaker."

Jim never forgot. Shortly after my retirement, I was at a dinner in Cardiff with our mutual friend Sir Julian Hodge, the founder of the Commercial Bank of Wales, when Jim suddenly crossed the room to us and said to Sir Julian, "It is you who should be the viscount, not him." I was so surprised that I had to point out that if he had really believed that, then it had been in his gift some years previously.

Even with the ruling on the Aircraft and Shipbuilding Bill out of the way, my troubles concerning the bill were far from over. Michael Foot, the Leader of the House, was obviously very angry that the ruling had gone the way it had and, in the discussions following it, Richard Barlas told him that it would be possible to move a motion that, notwithstanding Mr Speaker's ruling, the Government could go on and deal with the bill. And that is what was done. Even now I feel upset that my ruling was simply ignored. Looking back I know I would not have tolerated it in my later years. For any government to overrule the Speaker, as the Callaghan Government did, is really so offensive that the Speaker ought to resign once the motion is carried.

When the Opposition protested that Foot, in accepting the advice from Barlas, was ignoring my ruling, he told a crowded Commons that he was acting on my advice. In fact Barlas had drawn up the motion which he had passed to me to give to Foot. It was an unpleasant business altogether.

So on 27 May, the House of Commons met to decide the fate of the Aircraft and Shipbuilding Industries Bill. That night there was such tension as I had never experienced in the House before. There was bitterness on the Labour side because of my ruling that the bill was hybrid. There was bitterness from the Opposition that the Government was going to carry on regardless. When Eric Varley proposed the motion to set aside standing orders so that the bill could be proceeded with, there was a Conservative amendment to have the bill referred to a committee of examiners.

If tension was high at the beginning it was at fever pitch in the closing stages of the debate that had at times been rowdy and bad-tempered. I shared in that tension when I came to give the voting figures on the Conservative amendment. We had all of course been only too well aware that the figures would be close and both sides had come to me before the debate to ask how I would use my casting vote in the event of a tie, a decision that would be heightened by my earlier decision.

Fortunately a Speaker's greatest ally is precedent and there is very little that happens which has not happened before at some time in the long history of Parliament. I made it clear, therefore, that I would be following the ruling of Speaker Denison in the 1860s in both the amendment and the motion.

Different solutions applied to the various stages of a bill's passage through the Commons. Denison had ruled that if it was a Second Reading (this is a general debate on the merits of the bill – the First Reading is just a formality) he would vote in favour, to give the House time to look at it again. If it was in committee (where the bill is subjected to detailed scrutiny), and there was a tie, the chairman should vote to keep the bill as it was before it came to the committee. At the Report Stage in the House, the Speaker would vote to keep it as it left the committee. But if it was the Third Reading, the last chance the House had to consider the bill, and the House failed to give it a majority, the Speaker would go against it and the bill would fail to pass. This last principle applied to motions too. Denison had taken the very sensible view that it was not up to the Speaker to make up the House's mind for it.

The packed House that had been so noisy suddenly gave way to a deathly hush as I announced the voting figure on the amendment of 303 to 303. As I stood up to give the casting vote, Neil Kinnock shouted: "Vote Labour, George!" The House was roaring with laughter but

I turned sharply as giving a casting vote is always difficult and the House knew that my personal feelings did not enter into it at all.

As I stood in my place, I said, "I am following the precedent laid down by Mr Speaker Denison, which has been followed to this time. He said that the question upon which he was called to give his casting vote was one of great importance, and if affirmed by a majority of the House, it would have much force. It should, however, be affirmed by a majority of the House, and not merely by the casting vote of its presiding officer. For these reasons, my vote has to go with the Noes and I declare the Noes have it."

This meant of course that the Conservative amendment had been lost but it also meant that if there was a tie on the Government's motion to approve the bill, which followed immediately, then the bill would fall. Despite my careful explanation, my casting vote was criticised by some. As he was passing my Chair, Edward Heath rather huffily asked why I had voted with the Noes. I explained that I had done what I would always do, and that was to follow precedent. I also pointed out to him that it was one of the few occasions when the three Clerks and I all agreed.

Tempers ran high with many interruptions, and Michael Foot referred to the reputation of the House, adding, "Nothing could do more injury to the House of Commons than for the people outside to hear that the jobs of workers in the shipbuilding and aerospace industries are put in jeopardy by a semi-drunken Tory brawl." There was further uproar and John Peyton rose on a point of order to ask me to get Foot to withdraw. I said, "It is not in order to accuse anyone in this place of being drunk. To a man in my position, to be semi-drunk is as bad as being drunk." Foot withdrew, but added, "Yesterday many Opposition members tried to stop me speaking in the House when they were sober and tonight some have tried to stop me speaking when they are in a different condition."

So the House was in an extremely volatile state when I announced the votes on the Government motion to approve the bill. The same number of people were in the House as far as I knew and the two votes had been separated by minutes. So it surprised me as much as it did the House, when the Government won by 304 votes to 303. Somehow or other they had found an extra vote. Fortunately my only concern was to get the actual figures out of the lobbies. The complaint was that somebody had broken his pair and in the House it is a matter of honour that people do not break their word if they have given it. I believe in miracles but I think that extra vote was a well-organised miracle, whatever had happened.

As I announced the vote a group of Welsh MPs including Neil Kinnock started to sing the Red Flag, with a special emphasis on the word "here", when they got to the line "We'll keep the red flag flying here". Some Conservatives responded with Hitler-type salutes.

Scuffles, which threatened to become outright fighting, broke out among a few MPs from opposite sides. I shouted "Order!" but as everyone knows no Welshman will stop singing until he gets to the end of the song. I was about to suspend the sitting, when Michael Heseltine, who had been leading the fight against the bill, beside himself with anger, suddenly grabbed the mace and wielded it over his head. James Prior, then the Shadow Employment Secretary, took it from him and returned it to the table.

Heseltine told me later he was going to give it to Labour, but just how was never made clear. It looked to me as if he was going to crash it down on top of them. That was the moment I suspended the sitting for twenty minutes. I went to my rooms and sent for the Clerk. Adam Butler, the Conservative member for Bosworth, came with a message from Margaret Thatcher, the Leader of the Opposition, to say that Michael Heseltine would apologise immediately I went back in. I said I would not accept any apologies that night and Butler began to insist that Mrs Thatcher would like him to apologise then and there. Heseltine had committed a serious offence but if I had accepted his apology immediately the Labour side would undoubtedly demand that he be named and a vote on his suspension would have had to be taken. The House was frantic, and even worse scenes could follow.

What was also at the back of my mind, although I did not mention it at the time, was that it would have been grossly unfair to name only the man who picked up the mace, and not those who had sung the Red Flag. Trying to name people from both sides of the House in that atmosphere would have been almost impossible so I decided that the best thing to do was to wait for the next morning. When I went back at twenty minutes past ten, with only ten minutes of debating left, the House was crowded and greatly excited. They had all come pouring back in now. As I was approaching, I could hear the whispered message of my impending arrival go right round the Chamber.

I did not sit down. I just stood in my place which, according to the custom of the House, made it impossible for anybody else to do or say anything. I simply said that I was suspending the sitting until the following morning because of the scenes of grave disorder. Before they realised what was happening, I had left the chair. There was a great roar of laughter because members had expected more of the earlier antics. I felt that that night I had established that I could deal with a crisis.

In the morning, Heseltine made a point of saying he had tried to apologise the night before but had not been given the chance and said that he was taking the "first opportunity of apologising unreservedly". I still believed that the matter should rest there, but inevitably there were other views and Eric Heffer immediately rose to say he had hoped I would make some comment on the incident.

I told him: "May I tell the House that I gave careful consideration to whether I should make a statement this morning. I have been in the House thirty-one years. I have witnessed many occasions when tempers have become frayed and right honourable and honourable members have said and done things which they regretted afterwards. I hope that the House will remember that any action which undermines the dignity of this House undermines its authority both here and outside."

Willie Hamilton, the Labour member for Fife, then accused the Serjeant at Arms of using the most foul language he had heard outside the barrack-room and said that he had told him he would be raising the matter with me. It would have been most unfair to take any action against the Serjeant at Arms and I agreed with Andrew Faulds, the Labour member for Warley East, who said he had been near the Serjeant at Arms and had seen some "general swipes in his vicinity". Faulds added, "There was a lot of naughty language and equally a lot of unbecoming behaviour. However I think it is most unfortunate if the Serjeant at Arms is the only one who is called to account."

It had been a truly disgraceful night in the Commons but I still believe the action I had taken was the best in the circumstances, with so many members in breach.

CHAPTER NINETEEN

The Pressures Continue

That disgraceful night in the House of Commons led to all-out war between the two major parties. For a while the Conservatives abandoned the pairing arrangements as they were convinced that a Labour member had broken his pair in order to give the Government their one-vote victory. But from this point on, to the end of the Parliament in March 1979, tempers ran high and the pressures on me as the Speaker increased. It was almost inevitable, given their very shaky condition, that I would have more trouble with the Government side than I did with the Tories.

In the middle of June, Michael Foot and the Labour Chief Whip, Michael Cocks, came to ask me how I would cast my vote in the event of a tie on Mrs Thatcher's motion referring the Shipbuilding Bill to a select committee. They also wanted to know how I would cast my vote on a guillotine measure in the event of a tie.* Michael Foot was in a belligerent mood and it was clear that Cocks was there only to witness every word that I said. I told Foot I would be guided by precedent, at which he launched into a long harangue about the vital importance of the guillotine to the Government.

I undertook to consult the Clerks within half an hour, it being urgent for Foot to know the answer at once so that he could advise the Cabinet at its weekly Thursday meeting that morning on the possibilities of my casting vote.

When I saw Michael Foot again, I made it clear that following Speaker Denison's ruling, I would have to vote against Mrs Thatcher's motion if there was a tie and also against the Government on the guillotine motion. He at once started to challenge this by looking for other interpretations of the rules of the House but after half an hour

---

*A guillotine is a motion to limit the time devoted to a particular stage of a bill.

I stressed to him that I was going to follow precedent as other Speakers had. I was a servant of the House and the House alone.

It became clear to me then that whereas the struggle of my early predecessors had been to protect the rights of the Commons against the monarch, a modern Speaker's struggle is to be independent of the Government. In former days the monarch was the Government, for he was all-powerful. Now the Government is all-powerful and I believe passionately that the Speaker's role is to confine himself to protect the rules of the House and not to take sides in the battle. It was not an easy passage but I resolved to keep my integrity and to vote regardless of any old loyalties. And I felt a real sense of shock at the way Michael Foot had behaved in trying to influence my vote.

Government pressure was renewed the following month when Robert Kilroy-Silk, the Labour MP for Ormskirk and a member of the left-wing Tribune group, tabled an amendment to the Finance Bill, which would release war widows from tax on their pensions. His amendment had been defeated in the committee by the casting vote of the chairman, and it is long-standing practice in the House that at Report stage the Speaker always calls amendments that have been defeated in committee only by the vote of the chairman – that is to say he puts the amendment to the vote of the whole House.

Cledwyn Hughes came to see me and put the maximum pressure on me, saying that it would be highly embarrassing to the Government if I were to call the amendment. He insisted that he was not a messenger from the Government, but as the conversation unfolded it became clear to me that he had been present at a meeting in Downing Street, when my attitude to the amendments on the Finance Bill and on possible guillotine measures for other major bills had been discussed. Cledwyn clearly reported our conversation because at a quarter past two in the morning, when I was waiting to return to the Chair, Michael Foot and Michael Cocks both came to see me to renew the pressure.

They all knew that the practice of the House was quite clear and if I had not called the amendment there would have been an uproar both from the Conservative Party and from the Tribune group because they would know I was bending the rules to save the Government from a defeat. But the pressure continued.

Just before my normal noon conference for selecting amendments, Joel Barnett, the Chief Secretary to the Treasury, telephoned to add his pressure. He argued that it would be ridiculous to call an amendment that had been discussed at considerable length in committee. I gave a non-committal reply, but when I went to my conference for the selection of amendments, it was quite clear to me that my duty to the House would lead me once again into conflict with the Government benches. The Government believed that the House would support the amendment, a fact which I believed was all the more reason for me to give the House a chance to stand up to the executive. In the event the Government accepted the amendment to avoid defeat.

I had realised by now that whatever I did as Speaker there would be little chance of pleasing both sides and that the post with all its trappings and prestige was a very lonely one. No sooner had the arguments with Labour over the amendment died down than the Conservatives were upset that I had allowed a Government motion to approve the guillotine on five bills in one day. It is usual to include not more than two bills in the motion and there was uproar and anger in the House when Michael Foot revealed his plans.

The Opposition wanted me to rule that the motion was out of order and John Peyton, Humphrey Atkins and Sir Michael Havers came to argue that the Government motion should be overruled. John Peyton, a tough character in private interviews, made it plain that if my ruling went the wrong way from their point of view the Opposition would be very angry indeed. Once the deputation had left the room I told Richard Barlas that I would stand firmly by the ruling that I had given in the House on his advice.

I would worry a great deal before arriving at decisions on vital matters like this, but found I could relax once I had definitely made up my mind. It would be impossible to live as Mr Speaker if one worried about decisions after one's mind had been made up.

The Shadow Cabinet met to discuss the conversation I had had with Peyton, Atkins and Havers and was divided on the issue. I knew that Conservatives had been waiting for a guillotine measure to be introduced. Their only real concern was the number of bills to be included in the measure.

An indication of their disagreement came when a very senior member of the Opposition came to me when I was in the Chair and said he hoped I was not going to grant the fifteen-hour debate instead of the nine hours offered by the Government. Within a quarter of an hour, Reggie Maudling, the Shadow Foreign Secretary, said, "Why doesn't the Government give fifteen hours to save any further bother?"

This obvious disagreement among the Shadow Cabinet expressed to me privately was an indication as to the more serious arguments going on between them. Nevertheless, the Tories generally were a little sour when I ruled that the Government's timetable motion allowing only nine hours was in order.

It was nearly a month before Humphrey Atkins came to see me again. He had clearly been avoiding me and I guessed that the interview would not be very pleasant. In the event he was all smiles and charm and had his usual drink. After chitchat about unimportant matters, he eventually came to the point by reminding me that he had once said he would faithfully report any movement of opinion in the Chamber of which he thought I should be made aware. He then went on to say that several of his senior colleagues had told him that they thought I was too friendly with Cledwyn Hughes and the Prime Minister. I immediately asked whether the implication was that I was being unfair to the Opposition, for I knew that such a charge would not hold water. He hastily said, "No, no, no, there is no suggestion that you are unfair, but it is thought unwise for you to be so friendly with Cledwyn Hughes and the Prime Minister."

I told him that I rarely saw the Prime Minister, for indeed he had not honoured me by coming to Speaker's House for a meal or a drink since he was Prime Minister, but that I had been friendly with Cledwyn Hughes for twenty-five years, and that like my predecessor Selwyn Lloyd I had kept up my friendships. Selwyn Lloyd had Julian Amery and other leading Tories in his room, night after night, chatting with them and discussing matters of interest to the Conservative Party.

I think the mistake I had made was to tell Michael Heseltine, who had come to see me two nights previously, that I was going for a holiday with Cledwyn Hughes and his wife. What Humphrey Atkins did not know – and I did not tell him – was that, when Selwyn Lloyd had been to Spain for a holiday, he had taken among others the Tory MP Jonathan Aitken with him. Selwyn never made any bones about having the company of the Tories and I was anxious to keep my Labour friends. To begin with, I was perhaps too frank when talking to the Tories.

I did not tell Atkins either that I now felt that I had to be on guard with Cledwyn, who had been very close to me, particularly since I became Deputy Speaker. In those difficult days for Labour his first loyalty was understandably to the Party. I had talked very freely with him because I felt that we should confide in each other but it became clear that even he felt his loyalty obliged him to take messages back to the Prime Minister.

As the Callaghan Government limped along a real sense of crisis gripped the House and by October 1976 there was much talk of forming a National Government. Some Tories were the first to raise the matter with me and it fascinated me that not only did they put so much trust in me by revealing their hopes but that they considered a National Government a real possibility.

The financial crisis worsened during October with the pound under very serious attack and the trek of members to my door continued unabated with a long succession of leading members from both sides of the House discussing the need for a government of national unity. Some leading Labour members thought that if Callaghan was driven to seeking national unity he would have the support of three-quarters of the Cabinet. The great question was how many Labour backbenchers would be prepared to follow suit. The general opinion conveyed to me was that at least one hundred would do so – a feeling I shared.

In the event, the Government weathered the storm and carried on in power much longer than anybody could have anticipated. They did not even have the solid support of their own members in the House.

In December, a Conservative backbencher came to tell me an astounding story. It seemed that for some weeks a small group of Tories had been working on Reg Prentice, the Minister for Overseas Development, to try to get him to resign from the Cabinet to attack the left wing of the Labour Party. The fact that Reg Prentice, who resigned on 21 December, should go to the Conservative Party for advice at a time when he was feeling out of step with the left wing in the Labour Party is an indication that his roots in the Labour movement were very shallow indeed. Later in the afternoon Prentice contacted me himself, both to tell me of his resignation and to ensure that he was called early in the debate.

He told me he planned to stand as an independent candidate against the Trotsky people who had taken over his constituency organisation in Newham North-East, which we both knew would lead to his expulsion. I thought he would win, but told him that he should apply for the restoration of the Whip (that is, to rejoin the Parliamentary Labour Party), early in the new Parliament, or he would end up as another Dick Taverne, the member for Lincoln, who resigned from the Labour Party and stood as an independent member, was re-elected and then lost his seat at the general election. Prentice agreed with me and said that he thought any prospect of formation of a new group of moderates from all parties getting together had now receded. Quite clearly the Conservatives felt they could win on their own, and as long as this mood prevailed on the Conservative benches, there would be no move from their moderates to join with moderates in the Labour Party to form a separate group.

The more I talked with Prentice, the more I marvelled that Harold Wilson, still more Jim Callaghan, included him in their team. There were so many other people with higher ability on the back benches waiting for promotion. Prentice went on to become a Conservative and a junior minister in Mrs Thatcher's first government, which I found equally surprising.

The crisis finally came for the Government in March 1977, when Mrs Thatcher tabled a motion of censure and the minority parties began to make noises. If they combined with the Conservatives, the Government would be defeated. I knew that negotiations were under way to save the Government and that David Steel had said he would be delighted to meet the Prime Minister.

It seemed that David Steel did want to reach some agreement. Geraint Howells, the Liberal MP for Cardigan, was firmly against an election. It was also likely that Emlyn Hooson, the Liberal MP for Montgomeryshire, would take the same view. John Pardoe, the Liberal MP for Cornwall North, had already said he was against an election and Russell Johnston, whose Scottish seat was in danger, was also likely to be anxious to reach an accommodation. David Steel would have to persuade only another two of his group and the Government would be home and dry.

Callaghan had made it clear that any agreement with the Liberals would have to last for at least twelve months. In return, he was prepared to make certain concessions on the basis that they would undertake to support the Government on vital matters throughout the next twelve months.

That night in my room, Cledwyn Hughes told me he had been through the lobbies and the tea-rooms talking to members and right across the board on the Labour side they were anxious to reach an accommodation with the Liberals. Even extreme left wingers had joined with the moderates in saying it would be wise to reach an accommodation.

David Steel told me later that his conscience was absolutely clear that he had done the right thing. He was satisfied that he was acting in the national interest and although he naturally hoped to gain at the election, he was prepared to accept the verdict.

During the last few weeks, Cledwyn Hughes had emerged as Callaghan's chief confidant and obviously played a leading part as the liaison man between the Liberals and the Government. Cledwyn's power and influence with the Prime Minister had become enormous: out of office, he attained much greater strength than he had as a member of the Cabinet. So the Lib–Lab pact was concluded and the Government continued to limp along.

CHAPTER TWENTY

You Are Invited to Speaker's House

There were, of course, enormous compensations in being Speaker of the House of Commons and one in particular was the use of Speaker's House as my home.

One of my first guests was the actor Stanley Baker, a dear friend from the Rhondda Valley, who came to call on me the day after I was elected, and before he went into hospital for what was to be his last operation. We stood in my room overlooking the River Thames. He pointed out a large building and said with perfectly understandable pride, "That's mine, George." He went on to say that we had not done badly for two boys from the Rhondda and I replied, "No, but you have done better. I am only a tenant here."

At the time I became Speaker, the country as a whole really knew very little about the job, or about the history of the role; nor had it shared the magnificence of Speaker's House. The interest and the opening out of Speaker's House really began when in his last month of office, Selwyn Lloyd agreed that a television film about the work of the Speaker could be made. When the time came for filming to begin, I had become Speaker so it fell to me. If he had not given his permission, I would have been very nervous at becoming involved as the new Speaker.

Called "Mr Speaker, Sir", it showed everything connected with the work of the Speaker; it went round the world and led to other broadcasts on television and radio so that people came to know of the role of Speaker and of my own life as a Methodist local preacher as well as politician. They also saw the splendours of Speaker's House for the first time. In all my time in Parliament, Speaker's House had remained something of a mystery even to members, very few of whom had a chance to see it properly. There was an annual tea party but I did not like it as a member, and as Speaker I abandoned it after the first one because I believe it served no useful purpose.

Most members had attended out of a sense of duty rather than to enjoy themselves and I soon decided I would scrap it in favour of a more friendly and open approach. I much preferred to speak to small groups of members over the dinner table or take tea with them individually after Question Time when I left the Chair until the evening.

I passionately believe that the House of Commons belongs to the people and that therefore everything connected with the Speaker, the official embodiment of the House, also belongs to them. I was determined that Speaker's House and its magnificent dining-room would not be used just for formal official occasions. It was also my home and I entertained my friends there too. So a great cross-section from the Archbishop of Canterbury to Menachem Begin, from ex-President Nixon to Chairman Hua of China, from Penelope Keith to Sheik Yamani, from policeman to union leaders, sat at that table.

And the table was splendid, particularly when set with the Speaker's state silver. Speakers now receive a parliamentary pension but until the end of the eighteenth century, the Speaker took the state silver for himself as it was considered a perk of the job.

In my first month I gave a dinner for all the church leaders in the country. They were very distinguished people and had dressed for a state occasion in their various robes and cassocks of different colours. Basil Hume came in, also fairly new in his job, as Cardinal Archbishop of Westminster, wearing a black suit with a black stock and a white collar. He took one quick look around the room and whispered, "George, am I improperly dressed?" When I replied, "Not at all, Basil, you look like a Methodist minister," I think he took it as a great compliment. The dinner gave the church leaders the quite rare opportunity of talking together in a relaxed and informal way and encouraged me in my determination to give a lead in cementing the relationship between Church and State, while I was Speaker.

It was also in the early months of my Speakership that I invited all the party leaders to dinner in Speaker's House. There were eight of them and everybody accepted. I knew that this would be an historic occasion as never before had all the party leaders met in this way. The night before the dinner, I began to get anxious in case they spoke only to me and not to each other. In the event, I need not have worried as from the word go Harold Wilson and Margaret Thatcher were teasing each other with evident good humour and the conversation flowed easily. At 9.20 in the evening, I said, "Order, Order. We have

Arrival at Palam Airport, Delhi, with Dr Bal Ram Jakhar, Speaker of the Lok Sabha, September 1981

Meeting Speaker Tom McGee, in Mass., May 1979. I am wearing the Speaker's tie designed by Roy Mason

The Commonwealth Speakers' Conference, 1976

Left: Receiving life membership of the NUT at Scarboro, Easter 1976

Below: In Speaker's House on my first day in office with Harold Wilson, Mrs Eve Thomas (Secretary of Cardiff West Labour Party) and Mrs Marina Owen, the longest serving member of the Party in Cardiff West

Receiving my honorary doctorate at the University of Wales from Prince Charles — his first appearance as Chancellor. (Right) At the University of Southampton, 1977

Former Prime Minister Menachem Begin with Aliza, his wife, when they came to breakfast at Speaker's House and presented me with a Hebrew Torah

Entertaining Chairman Hua at Speaker's House, 1981. Roy Hattersley can be seen in the background

Entertaining Prime Minister Lee Kuan Yew of Singapore and his wife at a Speaker's House dinner held in honour of him receiving the Freedom of London

Rt Hon. George Thomas MP, Mr Speaker. A lifesize bronze portrait sculpted by
Robert Thomas which is on display in the City Hall, Cardiff, with a replica in the
Borough Council Offices, Rhondda

Their Royal Highnesses the Prince and Princess of Wales came to dinner at Speaker's House in the autumn of the year they were married

George Thomas as Mr Speaker in state robes, 1980

Greetings from our respective Houses to HM Queen Elizabeth The Queen Mother on the occasion of her 80th birthday *Back row, l to r:* Sir Christopher Soames, Most Rev. Robert Runcie, David Steel, William Whitelaw, Lord Aberdare, John Parker and Michael Foot. *Front row, l to r:* Margaret Thatcher, Self, The Queen Mother, Lord Hailsham, Lord Peart, Norman St John Stevas, Lord Byers and Lady Hylton-Foster

Admiring HM Queen Elizabeth The Queen Mother's Welsh corgis outside Clarence House on the occasion of her 80th birthday. Her Majesty suggested that I say something to the corgis in Welsh. 'But they've been brought up to speak only English!' I replied

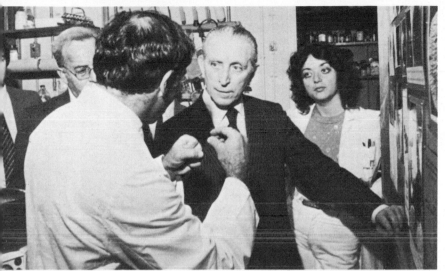

At the dedication of the George Thomas Laboratory at the Weizmann Institute of Science, Rehovot, Israel, December 1981

Self with Prof. Michael Sela, President of the Weizmann Institute, and Sir Isaac Wolfson

The Speaker's procession

With Lord Hailsham in Westminster Hall at the opening of the Nato Assembly

Joining the folk dancing at the Matlock Festival, 1981. Spencer Le Marchant, the local MP, can be seen in the background

Boy Scouts reunion at Speaker's House, January 1982

At the Speaker's Dinner held in honour of Lord and Lady Denning, July 1982

In conversation with Lord Denning earlier in the evening

George Thomas, Chairman and Treasurer of the National Children's Home, 1983

'This is Your Life'—just before the moment of truth at an afternoon rehearsal for the National Children's Home Gala in the Royal Albert Hall, October 1983

Left: Ready for The Wedding, 29 July 1981

Below: A reunion of three friends in Cardiff, July 1984: Sheik Yamani, Sir Julian Hodge and myself

My coat of arms depicting the open bible and miner's lamp flanked by daffodils and the leek

On the day of my introduction to the House of Lords, July 1983

had a good time together but now I must return to the Chair, while you can go downstairs and continue your battles there."

Jeremy Thorpe, the extrovert, declared, "Mr Speaker, this is an historic night for we have all met happily in this neutral place and we thank you for underlining the fact that although we are each seeking power for our respective parties, we can still respect each other personally." I felt a glow inside me as I heard the party leaders laughing and joking together on their way to the lift in my private quarters to take them back to the House. I felt very proud that it was my privilege to preside over a parliamentary chamber which showed such respect for democracy.

One of the earliest state receptions at the House was also the one that got off to the shakiest start. When President Ceauçescu of Rumania came, during his state visit to Britain, it was clear he did not like all the trappings of state and was particularly ill at ease at the state banquet in Buckingham Palace, which he left early to go to bed. And when he came to Speaker's House, it was obvious that he was still not at ease, so as I greeted him at the door I explained that he was coming to the house of the son of a coalminer. As soon as this was translated for him, his face beamed: perhaps he thought all our coalminers were treated as well as I had been.

Providence has smiled on me all my life and it was with me again early in my Speakership when the Commonwealth Speakers' Conference was held at Westminster, an event not likely to happen for another twenty years. There was much business to discuss but the twenty-eight visiting speakers particularly enjoyed the dinner at Speaker's House. It was a tremendous experience to meet my colleagues from Parliaments spread across the world and to realise the enormous respect they have for Westminster – I sometimes feel that its history and traditions are better known throughout the Commonwealth than they are by our own people. There is also a European group of speakers but the Commonwealth Speakers' Conference does have a special family feeling. And like all families there are quarrels.

This Conference began friendships which still endure with Sir Billy Snedden, Australia, James Jerome, Canada, who is now a Supreme Court Federal Judge, Sir Richard Harrison, New Zealand, and Speaker Ramjakar of India. In later years, friendships formed with Jeanne Sauve, Jim Jerome's successor in Canada and later Governor-General of Canada, Moses Quirionobati of Fiji and Alecos Michaeliades of Cyprus have enriched my life enormously.

Moses Quirionobati went on to serve Fiji as Foreign Secretary and could well move on one day to lead his country.

Alecos Michaeliades is probably the ablest of Cyprus' post-Independence politicians. He is a highly successful businessman whose integrity is matched by superb ability. His natural eloquence will ensure his continuous pre-eminence in the public life of Cyprus.

Shortly before the 1976 London conference we received a telegram from Speaker Nabulyato of Zambia protesting that there was not enough time for the speakers at the ceremonial opening of conference, and he definitely would not take part. When I met him at the airport later in the evening, I spent a half an hour persuading him of the importance of a speech from him. I realised all along that he wanted to make the speech but he also wanted me to make a fuss of him, which I duly did. The following morning I was handed a letter from him in which he agreed to share in the ceremonial proceedings.

But my difficulties with him were not over. He protested that the rules required us to choose the chairman of this conference at the first sitting of the conference, which he interpreted as the ceremonial opening. It took the assembled speakers half an hour to persuade him that the ceremonial was apart from the conference itself. When conference assembled in Grand Committee Room, Westminster Hall, I was duly elected chairman, but still Speaker Nabulyato was unhappy.

He protested that Speaker Colane from Lesotho did not have any right to be in the conference at all. Nabulyato explained that there had been an election in Lesotho, which the Opposition had won, but instead of accepting defeat the Government put them all in jail. It was a difficult problem but I did ask Mr Nabulyato how many parties there were in Zambia. He agreed there was only one but that was different and anybody could stand within the party and would not go to jail. Eventually my suggestion that we followed the rules of the Interparliamentary Union carried the day. Anybody entitled to join them could join us and, as they had admitted Lesotho, Lesotho could stay with us.

Many of the speakers used to look to Westminster for guidance and I was asked what I would do if I clashed with a minister who then refused to withdraw a remark that I had ruled out of order. They were obviously thinking of the incident in the Australian Parliament, where the Speaker had warned a minister that if he did not withdraw a remark and sit down he would name him, which should have led to his suspension.

The Labour Prime Minister Gough Whitlam had jumped up and said, "My God, Sir, you'll not name one of my ministers," at which the Speaker had no option but to name the minister. The Government refused to move the usual motion that the member concerned be suspended from the service of the House for a period of five working days, so the Opposition leader moved the motion, but naturally it fell and the Speaker resigned immediately.

I told my colleagues that if I was faced with a similar situation I would fight for time as there is no point in anybody making a sacrificial lamb of himself. I would suspend the sitting for half an hour for the people concerned to cool down and for them and the Speaker to have a chat so that hopefully when the sitting was resumed the matter could be settled amicably. If at the end of the suspension, they still were determined to resist the rule of the Speaker, there would be no option but to resign. But in going, I would say what I had said on more than one occasion privately in Westminster, that if I go my tongue is as long as my body and I will certainly make sure that the country knows my point of view. The Speaker is not without power, invisible power but very real. And no Government at the end of the day wants to pick a quarrel with the Speaker. In fact they have a vested interest in supporting the Speaker to ensure the business of the House is carried on and their legislation approved.

I came to know many of the speakers as personal friends and believed that the Commonwealth ties were strengthened by the conferences. In following years I visited many other parliaments and was able to compare them to Westminster, and I came to the conclusion that apart from India and Israel the House of Commons was the most difficult to control. In India, they even have a special twenty minutes every day when members can let off steam and just shout and bawl at each other. The Speaker sits with his arms folded and then, at the end of the twenty minutes, calls for order and they all sit down and behave themselves. In Israel, famous for its multiplication of parties, tempers often run high in what is anyway a fairly tense country. The House of Commons has no excuse for its regular tantrums.

The European speakers hold a conference every two years, but the role of the speaker in Europe is really quite different from that in Britain. In the European assemblies they find it almost impossible to understand that the British Speaker is outside the party battle. At the end of the conferences they all wanted to issue highly political communiqués, so I could never join in them. Then there would be another argument, but, despite that, one did make friends all over the continent.

Through being Speaker and the many dinners and receptions, both public and private, held in Speaker's House, I had an opportunity to meet many people from the broadest possible backgrounds. Now that I was free from party restrictions, I found people more willing to enter into more open friendships and I learned again the value of listening to others. Never before in my life had I had a better opportunity of listening to both sides of the question so eloquently put.

Through my friendship with Sir Julian Hodge, I came to know Sheik Yamani, the oil minister of Saudi Arabia, who became a frequent visitor to Speaker's House. He is my idea of a sheik, very cultured, courteous and possessed of great natural dignity. He is a deeply religious man but not in the fanatical, cruel sense of Ayatollah Khomeini, and like me he is a firm believer in the golden rule: do unto others as you would have them do unto you.

Sir Julian and I first went to his summer home in Taif, high up in the mountains, during the 1976 long recess. The first night we were there, King Khaled, the late brother of the present king, and the seven Royal princes came to dinner for what can only be described as an Arabian Nights' feast and, following local custom, the poor from the neighbourhood were invited to sit down with us.

Each night that I was there, distinguished, powerful people, who had their millions swirling around the market places of the world, were calling to see Yamani and I became even more convinced that his influence in Saudi Arabia was far greater than the British Foreign Office realises.

I went there again in the summer after I left the Speakership, when there was a mini-OPEC meeting. All the ministers came to his house, a hive of activity. It gave me the opportunity to meet the oil ministers who represented countries that were traditionally our friends but which we were in danger of offending. The Iraq/Iran war was obviously causing divisions but Sheik Yamani was doing his best to try to get some united front to protect the Arab nations. Saudi will not fall to the Communists; the real danger could come from the extremists on the far right.

I have friends on both sides of that troubled part of the world but when Prime Minister Begin first came to see me in Speaker's House, I was initially concerned that we did not have much in common other than a love of Israel. Having been brought up on the Old Testament, as well as the New, that country holds a very special place in my affections and I greatly admired the way the Israelis had in such a short time made the desert bloom.

But as I was waiting at the steps of Speaker's House for Mr Begin to arrive, I could not help but remember that not so many years before he had been a terrorist leader in Jerusalem, involved in the killing of British soldiers. So I was astonished at the effect which being in Westminster had on him. The Israelis, like the Welsh, are a very emotional people and he kept looking at me and the building and said, "Mr Speaker, Sir, to think that I have come to the Speaker's House of the Mother of Parliaments to whom the world owes so much." As we spoke, he invited me to visit Israel in Easter 1978 and, as he left, presented me with a copy of the Old Testament in Hebrew.

While in Israel I went to Yad Veshem, the memorial to the Holocaust. I was halfway through the guided tour of the museum when the memory of my visit to Auschwitz, just after the war, came flooding back and I just could not go any further. I turned to the man who was with me and told him I could not go on. I had tears running down my face as I thought of what the Jews had gone through during the war. There was a great throng of people behind us, whom I thought were parliamentarians. In fact they were journalists and the story appeared throughout Israel. In British public life, you are not meant to show emotion, but that does not apply in Israel and I like to think the people felt that I had some understanding of what the persecution had meant to them.

I believe there is always room for compassion, so when Jonathan Aitken, the Conservative MP for Thanet, asked me if I would receive ex-President Nixon in 1978, I had no hesitation in agreeing. The news soon got over to Number Ten and it became quite clear that, whatever else was going to happen, he was not going to be invited there. There was a general air of disapproval but I have always believed that if anybody has done wrong and been punished for it – as President Nixon undoubtedly had been – it was not for me to say that the punishment must continue. Sitting in judgement on other people is a very risky business.

When Nixon came, in 1978, he was obviously grateful to be received but had that battered expression of a man who had been knocked about. Two years later, when he came to address a group in the House on foreign affairs, he was a different man. With his confidence back, he even looked taller. Despite everything that happened in Washington, there is no doubt that he is one of the best-informed people in the world on foreign affairs and when he had finished speaking to the 200 or so MPs, they gave him a standing ovation. And who is to say they were wrong?

He was not such an expert on paintings though. While he was looking at the portraits of all my predecessors that adorn the walls of Speaker's House, he particularly liked one and remarked that it was a splendid picture in the style of the eighteenth century. Obviously he knew much more about portrait art than I did so I tentatively agreed. He turned and asked when I was going to have mine done. I had no alternative but to tell him that I already had, and he had just been looking at it. The whole question of portraits is fraught with danger. As Kingman Brewster once told me when he was the American Ambassador in London, "Remember this, if you say you like your portrait, people will say you are conceited. If you say you don't like it, they will say you are even more conceited."

Gradually as the years progressed, Speaker's House became a part of the life of Parliament in a way it never had been before and I think that the dinners held there did play a part in bridging Parliament and the world outside. I gave several farewell dinners but the one for Lord Denning, when he retired as Master of the Rolls, was really a sparkling occasion. I regard Tom Denning, a very great Englishman, with affection and respect, although one Labour politician, in accepting the invitation very gracefully, did rather stress that he was particularly happy that it was a farewell dinner.

I also opened Speaker's House for several charities but I had to be very careful. Sometimes members associated with various charities would ask whether I would allow them to use the rooms. Nine times out of ten I had to say no, but where there was a strong parliamentary link, I would usually agree. I was also highly sensitive to the fact that I must not drop my guard and give any party the chance to say I was allowing the rooms to be used for political purposes, so I was a little bit nervous about what the Tories might say when it was suggested that I should allow Amnesty International to use the rooms for a reception. I wrote to the Prime Minister, the Leader of the Opposition and the other party leaders to see if they had any objections. Indeed, when the reception was held, there were as many Tories there as Labour – but it was the only time I saw the GLC leader, Ken Livingstone, in Speaker's House.

I also tried to let the people in, and almost everywhere I went, even

if I was preaching as I did many weekends, I would always invite
people I had met to come to Speaker's House. They all came, so there
were visitors nearly every day, sometimes half a dozen at a time. Over
my seven years, many hundreds of people must have come to tea or
dinner.

It must have been the first time for many years that children could
be heard regularly in Speaker's House. As I came to know members
I used to invite their wives and families to tea. Members would always
tell me with great pride when they became parents or grandparents
and I allowed them to use the rooms for their christening parties.
Some of the great names and some of the lesser known had their
parties there after the christening in the crypt. Other members had
their wedding receptions there so Speaker's House became a part of
parliamentary life, both political and personal, in a way it never had
before.

Of all the memorable times there, the most historic was the visit of
the Queen who came to dinner to celebrate her Silver Jubilee. That
week in May was the happiest time I had experienced since becoming
Speaker a little over a year before. The trials and tribulations of
controlling the House were for the moment forgotten. The House of
Commons had voted to present a Loyal Address to the Queen to mark
her twenty-five years on the throne and I had to put into words what
I thought were the feelings of the House, which I would then read to
the Queen before both Houses of Parliament in Westminster Hall on
4 May 1977. The Lord Chancellor, Elwyn Jones, would do the same
on behalf of the House of Lords.

For six hundred years, whenever the Commons wanted to give a
greeting or a message to the sovereign, the Speaker did it in person.
But ever since Sir Thomas Hungerford in 1376, the Commons have
insisted that when the Speaker talks to the monarch on their behalf,
they should accompany him to see that he says the right thing.

So the Monday before the ceremony there was a rehearsal in
Westminster Hall and I went in wearing my heavy gold state robes.
Nobody knows how old they are but they were certainly made for a
taller man, which caused great difficulty when I had to go down on
one knee to give the Queen the address, then stand up and take three
steps backwards before I could walk normally back to my place. I
tried it four times and each time I stepped off the stool I caught my
foot in the hem of the robe. To the horror of my staff I decided we
would have to cut a lump off the bottom.

When Wednesday came, I got up early and said my prayers with deep feeling. I had rehearsed my speech aloud many times to make sure that my punctuation was correct, but after my prayers, I spent at least half an hour practising kneeling on the stool in my own state rooms, with the Speaker's train-bearer, Jim Green, a former marine, taking the place of the Queen, while I handed the Loyal Address across and then returned from the stool to my proper place. Again I stumbled, but eventually I discovered that if I clutched a great piece of the gown in my hand and threw it backwards as I rose, I could do it. So we did not cut the robes.

When I arrived at Westminster Hall, which was crowded to the door, and I heard an attendant call out "Make way for Mr Speaker," I felt a strange mixture of excitement, pride and humility. As we processed through the hall, the Serjeant at Arms carried the mace before me and then placed it in front of me in the great hall, where I waited for the Lord Chancellor. The audience of ministers, Members of Parliament, judges, ambassadors and people representative of our national life all remained standing with me until the Lord Chancellor came. We bowed to each other and took our seats.

The ceremony went without a hitch but when it came to the moment that I had to get off the stool in front of the Queen, there was an anxious look in her face. Somebody had told her that I could not do it and could well fall down the steps. It was surprising, but clearly she knew all about my problems.

When the Queen came to dinner that night at Speaker's House, it was the first time for 150 years that a monarch had dined there. Every one of her living former Prime Ministers was there: Harold Macmillan, Alec Home, Ted Heath, Harold Wilson and the then Prime Minister. Neither the Queen and the Duke nor the guests around the table knew that Jim Callaghan had almost failed to attend. He had received the invitation in February and the date was firmly registered in his diary but he had contacted me to say he had other engagements and could not come. I telephoned Number Ten saying that I was putting no pressure on him to come, it was for him to decide, but I thought that he should know that every living former Prime Minister would be there, together with the leader of every other party. He changed his mind. The Queen was relaxed and gracious and I believe she thoroughly enjoyed herself.

The Queen stayed at least half an hour over the time stipulated for her return but Harold Macmillan, who was holding court with

Margaret Thatcher and James Molyneaux, the Ulster Unionist leader, was reluctant to go, enjoying telling stories of Churchill as Prime Minister when he, Macmillan, served in his Government.

That night was probably one of the most glittering nights in Speaker's House and I was glad it happened in my time. I have often thought that the fact that the Queen herself came meant that everybody else realised that Speaker's House belonged to the country.

The jubilee celebrations continued through the summer and in June I thoroughly enjoyed myself when I rode in the procession to St Paul's in the Speaker's coach. The coach was pulled by magnificent Shire horses owned by Whitbreads, the brewers. More than 125 years earlier, Speaker Shaw-Lefevre had married Samuel Whitbread's daughter and so established the link between the House and the brewers. That morning, as the horses pulled the coach along with the mace sticking out of the window, was the first time it had been used since Speaker W. S. Morrison rode in it twenty-five years earlier for the Coronation.

The custom is that after the coach has been used, the coat of arms of the Speaker who has ridden in it is put on the doors. Whoever uses the coach again will have my coat of arms on the door, and I often wonder what they will make of the miner's lamp and the open Bible.

There was only one sour note during the jubilee and that came when the Queen paid her official visit to Wales. I was planning to wear the Speaker's state regalia as I had in St Paul's, when there had been no word of criticism. But before the visit to Wales, I was told that the Lord Chamberlain thought it would be better if I left my robes at home. Naturally I agreed but I have often wondered whether the real objection came not from the Palace but from the Government.

The idea for me to wear the robes was not my own; it was at the request of the people in Wales. It was the only possible chance they would have to see their own MP as Speaker wearing the state regalia. There may have been an element of personal vanity in it but they were my people and I thought I should wear the state robes on what was an official ceremonial occasion. But the message came back very strongly that state dress should not be worn. In accepting the advice from the Lord Chamberlain, I wrote to him: "I readily accept your judgement in this matter, though I would like it placed on record that I believe the Welsh people would like their service to be given the same significance as the service in St Paul's."

There are people who will say that I should not have paid so much attention to tradition and pomp, but again I think it is the politicians who are out of step with what the people like.

CHAPTER TWENTY-ONE

On a Point of Order

Among the early problems facing me in the new session of Parliament in November 1976 was yet another procedural point – though by no means the last – discovered by Robin Maxwell-Hyslop, who once told me that he read Erskine May, the parliamentary bible, every night before he went to bed. I rather dryly observed that we would perhaps all be better off if he read the real Bible. But yet again he had pinpointed a loophole that would be of great use to the Opposition and a major irritant to the Government.

John Peyton, the Shadow Leader of the House, came to tell me that Maxwell-Hyslop had informed him that the motion, which had, until then, automatically been passed unopposed at the end of a debate on a bill could in fact be challenged. In this case the Government had not specified it as exempted business that could be dealt with after the 10 p.m. guillotine so any motions could have the effect of holding up the bill. I had a difficult conference with the clerks who said that Maxwell-Hyslop was quite correct, although the motion, which was required in order to set up a committee to formulate the reasons to be given to the Lords for their amendments being rejected, had been part of the procedure of the House for centuries and had never been opposed.

Later that day, I received a message that Michael Foot and Michael Cocks wanted to see me. Michael Foot was in a belligerent mood, which was becoming increasingly common, and asked me outright what my ruling was going to be. As he was responsible for arranging Government business in the House, I told him I would rule in favour of the Opposition, at which he flared up and said such a thing had never happened before. I replied quietly that if it had not happened before, it was only because no one had discovered the loophole before.

Eventually Foot's attitude was so aggressive that I also began to speak sharply and told him, "You are not to come here to try to twist my arm: I am not going to be pushed around by anyone in this House. If the House does not like my ruling, they know what to do and you know what to do, but my ruling will be that the motion cannot be discussed if there is opposition to it." It was my responsibility as Speaker to guard the interests of the House and the rights of the House, and I had no intention of being shifted. Michael Foot came back very strongly, but I was not going to change my mind. I suggested that the Clerk of the House should be called in to hear the rest of the discussion and, when he arrived, Foot asked how the Government could deal with the situation that had arisen. Twice in the discussion that followed, the Clerk had to tell Foot that he must not put words into his mouth. The Clerk then told him he could propose a motion to ensure that all business motions for the rest of the session would be covered by the guillotine. Foot then asked me whether I would regard such a motion as a challenge to my ruling. I told him that I was not prepared for him to tell the House I had given him advice as it would give the impression that I had been in collusion with him. He clearly resented this and, from then to the end of the session sixteen months later, relations between us were always strained.

In the event, John Peyton proposed that Alan Beith, the Liberal MP for Berwick-upon-Tweed, be added to the list of names to serve on the committee. My ruling that this constituted an objection and that the matter could not therefore be discussed as it fell outside the time allowed by the guillotine was received with some cheers from the Conservative benches.

The Clerk of the House told me that Michael Cocks had spoken to him after our earlier meeting and had said that he agreed with my ruling: there was a state of war between the parties, the Opposition had caught the Government out and there was nothing to do but to accept it. Strangely enough, Dennis Skinner, the Labour member for Bolsover, had also been to the Clerk to say he thought I was correct to insist on the rights of the House being observed. I was delighted that this rebel should feel I was doing the right thing by the House.

There is always danger in quarrelling with the Government, but my job was to protect the House against the executive when it became overbearing and wanted its own way in everything: to regard any challenge as something to be crushed.

As tempers frayed so the use of unparliamentary language became more of a problem. It is often easier for the Speaker to rely on his legendary deafness but in November 1976 I was forced to warn the

House that in future I would take a firmer view, and would if necessary order members to withdraw from the Chamber for one day.

One of the difficulties facing the Speaker in running the Chamber is the vexed question of parliamentary privilege. It is largely undefined but falls into two categories. First, it allows members of parliament to speak freely in the House without any fear of being challenged by the law as they might be if they said the same things outside. Secondly, it protects MPs and the business of the House from any unreasonable interference or abuse from outsiders. If the members feel that a group or an individual has infringed this convention then they could accuse the offender of a breach of privilege and he could be called to the bar of the House to explain his actions. He could be admonished, fined or even sent to jail.

In the event there were negotiations and an agreement was reached. Arthur Latham, the MP for Paddington, and chairman of the Tribune group, raised as a matter of privilege a speech made by Ian Sproat, the Conservative MP for Aberdeen, in which he had alleged that a number of Labour members, whom he named, were agents for a foreign power. When I gave my ruling the following day that there was a prima facie case of a breach of privilege, Michael Foot, as Leader of the House, rose to move the customary motion that it be referred to the Committee of Privileges. An angry debate followed at once in which members below the gangway began to hurl insults at each other and for an hour and a half I had to call for order.

Twice I threatened to suspend the sitting and it was one of the worst scenes since the night Michael Heseltine lifted the mace. The matter was made worse when Sir Paul Bryan, the very respected Conservative MP for Howden, raised as a matter of privilege a statement issued by the Socialist Democratic Alliance, a breakaway group of right-wing Labour supporters in London, accusing thirty-three members of the Labour Party of being under alien influence.

To my surprise, Michael Foot asked to see me privately to advance reasons why I should not allow Sir Paul's motion to be referred to the Committee of Privileges. He said he was not seeking to bring any pressure to bear upon me, but I did not like anyone coming to advance private arguments when I had to deal with privilege, and I gave a non-committal reply. In the event, I ruled that Paul Bryan's complaint was justified and should go to the Committee of Privileges.

Sir Paul's move was obviously linked with Arthur Latham's own privilege motion and it seemed that generally the Labour Party was furious with Latham as it meant that the House would now have an opportunity to debate whether or not the Labour Party was under Communist influence. It really was one of the most stupid moves any party supporter could have made and it was highly embarrassing to the Government.

So the House was in a very tense mood and at the same time mindful of my warning to order the withdrawal of members guilty of unparliamentary language when the Home Secretary, Merlyn Rees, answered a private notice question from Judith Hart, the Labour MP for Lanark, about the proposed deportation of two Americans, Philip Agee and Mark Hosenball, alleged to have been engaged in activities hostile to British security. I allowed only one question from each side and there was a tremendous outburst from Tom Litterick, the far-left Labour MP for Selly Oak, who was held in his seat physically by his colleagues, who feared I would order him out of the House.

Tom Litterick and some of his left-wing friends, like Stanley Thorne, MP for Preston South, Dennis Skinner and Martin Flannery, MP for Sheffield Hillsborough, later signed a motion on the order paper regretting my curtailment of the discussion. It was the equivalent to a vote of censure, but since only six of the more extreme members had signed it, I had nothing to worry about.

In the normal running of the House, there were three main problems which usually arose every day: points of order, usually false ones; unparliamentary language, which it was very often better to ignore; and, as I have already explained, the question of parliamentary privilege. They frequently overlapped, but, separately and together, they were fraught with difficulties and unless a very firm line was taken, the actual business of the House would grind to a halt.

On one occasion, Eric Heffer described Mrs Thatcher as a "stupid woman" and Nicholas Fairbairn, the Conservative MP for Kinross and West Perthshire, raised a point of order, claiming that this was unparliamentary language. I let it go but pointed out that courteous behaviour was always required in the House and hurling abuse at one another which we would not like hurled at ourselves added nothing to the debates.

Nicholas Winterton, the Tory MP for Macclesfield, was often the target of attack for left-wing Labour MPs, and he once claimed that Russell Kerr, then the Labour MP for Hounslow, had described him as a member of the SS. In reply, Kerr said that he had not used Winterton's name, he had not said he was a member of the SS and in any case he took the letters SS to mean silly sod. I ruled that if the words complained of by Winterton had been used, then they would have been unparliamentary, which seemed to satisfy both sides.

I always came down very heavily on members calling each other liars or accusing their opponents of telling lies. I also ruled that blasphemy was unparliamentary after Eric Ogden, the Labour MP for Liverpool, had used the word "Christ" in the Chamber. Usually the matter could be dealt with then and there and did not waste too much time, but one morning I had an indignant telephone call from Edward du Cann, the chairman of the 1922 Committee (which comprises all Tory backbenchers), protesting at a statement made by Willie Hamilton the previous night, while neither du Cann nor I were in the Chamber. Hamilton had described the board of Lonrho, a company of which du Cann was a very well-known director, as a "bunch of crooks who should be locked up in Brixton prison".

Hamilton can be very rude and had I been in the Chair I would have intervened at once, so when the sitting began, I called on du Cann to raise his point of order. In forceful but extremely courteous language he protested that it was unparliamentary to cast any reflection on the honour of a member of the House. Hamilton accepted that he should not have used the words, withdrew them and apologised to du Cann.

Another most exceptional incident was when Reg Race, the Labour Member for Wood Green, used an offensive four-letter word when he was addressing the House while the Deputy Speaker was in the chair. Mr Race had said he was using the word in a quotation and the Deputy allowed the expression to pass. When I read Hansard the next morning I was horrified and told the Deputy Speaker I was not prepared to allow that word to be inserted in Hansard or accepted just because it was quoted. If we had accepted it, there could be all sorts of filth repeated in the House under the guise that it was being quoted. I made a statement to the House and ruled that in future language that was unparliamentary would not be included merely because the member maintained that he was quoting what someone else had said. I believe this was an essential step in maintaining standards in the House of Commons.

But I felt it necessary to say that although I deprecated any reflections on the personal honour of members of the House, I felt that they should be more careful about the words they used concerning people outside. There had been a growing tendency for members to use the privilege that permitted them to make accusations in the House for which they would be sued if they said them outside, in order to make attacks on individuals and companies when they had very little real evidence and would certainly not risk making such allegations outside the Chamber.

The House shared my view and was particularly angry the day Jeff Rooker, the Labour MP for Birmingham, Perry Bar, misused privilege to accuse a businessman of improper practices. The House turned on Rooker because privilege is something to be cared for, not abused. Anybody named by an MP in the House of Commons has no satisfactory way of clearing his name, unless the accusations are repeated outside. In Rooker's case, the Conservatives insisted that he either justified his claims or withdrew them.

He came to me to say he realised he must withdraw the allegations as he could not prove what he had said. My advice to him, and it was always the same in similar circumstances, was if you are going to withdraw, then do so wholeheartedly. If you make a wholehearted withdrawal, you will get the immediate support of the House. A half withdrawal could produce a worse position than saying nothing at all, because it could only mean that you wanted the smear to stay. The House as a whole disapproves of that kind of tactics – and I think the public do as well.

Parliamentary privilege exists to give members the right to raise genuinely serious issues in the knowledge that they cannot be sued. The most dramatic example during my time in the House was in 1955 when the Labour MP, Marcus Lipton, named Kim Philby, "the third man", as a spy in the Foreign Office eight years before the Government conceded that the charge was true. Privilege is invaluable but it has to be used carefully, thoughtfully and sparingly, and not to make a party political point.

In April 1978, I became involved in a very serious argument about privilege concerning an army colonel in the intelligence service who had been referred to in a criminal case only as Colonel B, following a court ruling that the man's name should not be used in newspaper reports of the trial. The problem arose when Jo Richardson, the Labour MP for Barking, asked for a debate on press freedom and at the very end of her question used the colonel's name. I had not been following the case in the newspapers and was unaware, as indeed were the clerks, of the court ruling so that when I heard a Conservative member shout "Disgraceful!" I had no idea why. The House was crowded and nobody raised any objections so I let the matter pass. Later, three other members repeated the colonel's name and still nobody rose on a point of order to remind the House of the court ruling.

In the evening, I began to receive messages from the newspapers asking whether they were free to publish the colonel's name. It had been used in the House of Commons and, therefore, they claimed, they were totally protected by privilege. Finally Jeff Rooker came to me to say he was going to raise the issue when I returned to the Chair in the evening. Just before I did, Humphrey Atkins, the Opposition Chief Whip, came to tell me that the Director of Public Prosecutions had issued a further warning that despite the fact that the name had been used in the House of Commons, the ban on publishing still applied. I think the lobby correspondents must have spoken to Humphrey as well as to my office because he appeared to be arguing that the press should be free to go ahead and publish the name.

At the end of normal business, there was a series of demands from the left wing, who, to my great surprise, were supported by Peter Rees, a Tory QC who represented Dover. He wanted me to summon the Director of Public Prosecutions to the Bar of the House to explain his action in apparently overruling the House of Commons. Throughout the various points of order, I took the line that it was not for the Speaker of the House of Commons to rule what was contempt of court and what was not, that was a matter for the courts alone. Another Conservative, Graham Page, a Privy Councillor and the MP for Crosby, raised the whole question as a matter of privilege and asked me for a ruling. I gratefully seized the opportunity to say that I would give a considered ruling the next morning, but that by no means pleased the Tribune group, who had to stop while in full cry.

I rose early in the morning to consider my ruling very carefully and it became clear that what I was really being asked to do was to rule that if a court ordered that a name should not be published and a member of the House of Commons rose in the Chamber and used the name, then I was to say that the court had no further jurisdiction.

I refused to give such a ruling but pointed out that in fact the House had been in breach of its own rules, which were that where a matter was before the courts, the House of Commons would not discuss it. I told the House: "The proper course for members who disapprove of the rule is for them to attempt to get it altered but not to flout it or even bend it. I must advise the House that I will not permit any further identification of the officer nor any reference to the criminal case in which he is involved."

It was a difficult situation and I felt very sorry for those in broadcasting and the newspapers, who faced a crisis as to whether or not they could publish his name. On the one hand, they had the responsibility to report faithfully what was said in Parliament, and on the other, they had to respect the court's ruling or they would be in contempt. It all arose from the unique situation where neither I nor my advisers were aware of the court ruling.

I could not understand at the time, nor can I understand now, why nobody stood in the House on a point of order to remind us of the court ruling. It is possible that there was not one person there who was aware of it, but that is unlikely. I can only believe that there were some members who were prepared to make as much mischief as they could for they knew the embarrassment it would cause.

Parliament's general attitude to privilege has undergone a fundamental change in the last twenty-five years with both public and Parliament now thinking MPs should be far less touchy. Reform was long overdue. When I was in the Chair, members would be on their feet nearly every day wanting to raise some matter that they thought was a breach of privilege. Technically it often was, and therefore, according to the rules, I had little option but to refer the matter to the Committee for Privileges. The rules have now been changed. Members must write to the Speaker explaining why they want to raise the matter. If he decides there is no case, the member either lets the matter drop or if he feels very strongly will table a motion on the order paper. But even then it will only be discussed if the Government gives time. If the Speaker has agreed to the application, the member concerned tables a motion which has precedence over everything else the next day the Commons will meet. By and large, the basis on which privilege applications are now granted is if there is a serious threat to the working of Parliament.

So the Speaker does now have some protection from the unreasonable use of parliamentary privilege by some members seeking to make a party point. But the point of order, the favourite way to challenge the Speaker, still exists. If a member shouts "Point of order!" it is customary for the Speaker to listen. It was a problem in my early days, but I soon was able to make a decision as to whether it was going to be a genuine point of order or not, usually just after one sentence. I would then interrupt and say that it was quite clearly not going to be a point of order but a speech, as some people tried to use points of order as a means of making a speech which they had been unable to make during Question Time or after Government statements.

Bob Cryer, the Labour MP for Keighley, was one of the worst offenders and I once told him, "It is very interesting that whenever the honourable member has not been called to ask a supplementary question, he gets up on a point of order which is not a point of order and it does not help him." I believed in meeting them head on and it usually worked as members came to realise that it was counter-productive. At the end of my time there were far fewer false points of order.

There were members of course who were great experts on parliamentary procedure and I knew that if one of them stood up on a point of order it was very likely going to be a sound one. Enoch Powell, for example, very rarely made a mistake and was a great defender of the rules of Parliament, which, if used properly, protect the rights of members. When John Stonehouse was on trial at the Old Bailey for fraud, he would come back to the House of Commons every day after the court had risen. On one occasion, after he had enjoyed the front-page headlines in the evening newspapers, he returned to the Chamber and wanted to speak. Under English law, he was innocent until found guilty and I called on him to speak. He was still a Privy Counsellor so I even had to call him "the right honourable gentleman".

At which point, the whole of the Government side stood up and walked out of the Chamber and were joined by two-thirds of the Conservative Opposition. Stonehouse reacted to the mass exodus by walking down from his seat across the floor, still making his speech, and stood at the Treasury Box. I ordered him to return to his seat, whereupon Enoch Powell stood up on a point of order to say that any member was entitled to address the House from any place they chose within the Chamber. I had to agree but added, "No honourable member is entitled, having been called from one place, to perambulate around the Chamber, and the right honourable gentleman will return to his place at once or I will order him to resume his seat." This would have meant that Stonehouse would have had to stop talking. He returned to his seat. On a strictly parliamentary level, he had challenged the authority of the Speaker. He had done it in a way that had never happened before and now will never be allowed to happen again.

While all this was going on, I could not help thinking of my mother and his, who were friends in the Co-op Guild. Both mothers were proud of their boys and that thought was very much in my mind then because I had received a letter from Mrs Stonehouse in which she had said that her son was a sick man or he would not have behaved as he had.

The House may have felt justified in the way it had treated John Stonehouse but I felt very unhappy at the way it dealt with John Cordle, the Conservative MP for Bournemouth East, and Reggie Maudling, the former Tory Home Secretary, in the aftermath of the Poulson affair. By the time the select committee report on the affair was to be debated by the House, John Cordle had already been persuaded to resign and so was unable to defend himself. There are times when the House of Commons becomes very emotional and excitable, when anything can happen. One of the worst was the day of that debate.

The select committee had concluded that Reggie Maudling, John Cordle and Albert Roberts, the Labour MP for Normanton, "had been guilty of conduct inconsistent with the standards the House is entitled to expect from Members of the House", and I went into the Chair knowing that the Opposition was going to join the Government in recommending suspension for a specified period. Before the debate began, I ruled that Maudling and Roberts could stay in the Chamber after they had made their statements to listen to the House debate what to do with them. It had never been done before and undoubtedly influenced the way the debate continued as there is a vast difference between criticising a man to his face and criticising him in his absence.

I was feeling terrible because it would be me who would actually suspend Reggie, whom I had always looked upon as a friend. Tradition meant that while a member was being suspended he would stand in his place and the Speaker would wear the three-cornered official black hat that reminded me of the death cap a judge used to wear when sentencing a man to death. I had decided I would not wear it, but I was so upset that when I came to call Reggie Maudling to speak, I called him Mr Reginald Amery, as Julian Amery was sitting in front of him. It was a genuine mistake but it did reduce the tension a bit.

Reggie, and therefore Roberts, was saved by a magnificent speech from Edward Heath who had been Prime Minister when Maudling had been in the Cabinet. He ended with a resounding, "Mr Speaker, Sir, my right honourable friend is a right honourable gentleman." He sat down to great applause as the Opposition front bench, led by Mrs

Thatcher, left the Chamber. They returned after a brief meeting in which they had decided not to support the select committee report after all.

John Cordle should not have resigned when he did. The House can be cruel and I think it was unjust to John Cordle, who had merely made an adjournment debate speech about a building project in Nigeria without declaring an interest. I was in the Chair at the time and I heard the debate. There were only two other people in the House, the minister who answered the question and Cordle himself. I felt at the time, and I have felt since, that this was one of the occasions when the House was unworthy of itself.

CHAPTER TWENTY-TWO

Order, Order

Nothing did more to open up the proceedings in Parliament and coincidentally focus attention on the role of the Speaker than the broadcasting of Parliament, which began on 3 April 1978. The House of Commons had taken the decision to allow the microphones into the Chamber during Selwyn Lloyd's last year of office. It seems ironic now but in fact I had been against it, believing at the time that it was a mistake to have too many extraneous influences in the proceedings of the House.

It was an enormous undertaking. The BBC had a capital outlay of £340,000 with running costs estimated at £275,000 a year and an additional staff of twenty-five. We were slightly misled, I think, by the BBC, who asked the House to agree to an experimental period of broadcasting before the regular permanent service. In fact we were on the air practically all the time during the experiment.

On the morning on which broadcasting was to start on a permanent basis, the BBC told me they were a little bit worried about the microphone by the Chair because my voice might not carry, so they very politely asked if I would speak loudly and throw my voice out for the first Order, Order of the day. I agreed at once, not realising what they were up to because that Order, Order – which even now seems to greet me wherever I go, even on buses – was the recording they used throughout my Speakership. It is strange how one word repeated began to get me known throughout Britain. Within months, wherever I went, some proud mother or father would come up and say their little girl or boy – usually about three years old – was always saying Order, Order, imitating my Welsh accent. Some of the examples I listened to were enough to make me cringe and I had visions of a whole generation of English children growing up with a Welsh accent.

It so happened on that first day of permanent broadcasting that Question Time dealt with Welsh questions, and I was staggered when

I reached the Bar of the House to see at least sixty to eighty members in for prayers on the day when the Secretary of State for Wales was answering questions. Normally I would be lucky to see a dozen people there, but I knew at once that broadcasting was going to have a major effect on our proceedings. My instinct was not wrong.

After a week, I found that the character of the House had changed. Members who had been silent ever since I had been elected Speaker suddenly came to life. It was as though the dead had been restored to life and had found a new aggressiveness. It became clear at once that both sides of the House were determined to use broadcasting to party advantage and the party political differences were much sharper and more angrily expressed than they had been before broadcasting.

The difficulty for me was that far more people wanted to ask questions and they were making longer and longer supplementaries. The pressure to speak in debates also rose by at least fifty per cent but there was an initial advantage in that members did not want their constituents to hear them involved in angry exchanges with the Speaker that they would inevitably lose. This was a restraint which some members found far less of a concern as time went on.

Inevitably there were the extroverts and exhibitionists who pushed themselves forward to grab the limelight. In the first week both Andrew Faulds and Eric Heffer clashed on points of order with the Chair, which were duly reported, but gradually the reporting of these noisy exchanges declined, particularly when it was not a point of order at all but merely an opportunity to be heard. I did my utmost to ensure that the steady, solid members received their fair share in being called both at Question Time and in debate. But there were some people like Dennis Skinner and Bob Cryer who would jump up to ask a supplementary question on almost every question and then give me black looks if they were not called before the end of the afternoon. In my judgement any member who got two questions in the same week had not done badly, considering that there were 535 members eligible to ask questions in the House, the other 100 being members of the Government, who provide the answers.

Broadcasting did also change some debates in the House in a way which nobody had foreseen. It had become customary, particularly in dealing with controversial Private Members' Bills, to allow speech after speech to be made in opposition in order to save time in getting the bill approved by the House. In the committee stage, it was quite common for nobody to speak in support but simply to wait for the moment to vote. It was Eric Heffer who pointed out to me that this would now have to change with the advent of broadcasting as nobody could afford to let only one side of the argument be heard.

It has always been a problem for the Speaker that there are more members wanting to ask questions or speak in debates than he can call. Speakers really have to accept the unfortunate fact that they invariably upset backbenchers who feel they should be called but are not. But with the start of broadcasting, the applications to speak leaped upwards. Members wished to be heard, not just in the House, but on the radio in homes and cars throughout the country. They were particularly anxious that their constituents would hear them and realise what a marvellous job they were doing for them.

Broadcasting also increased interruptions, people wanting to be clever and to be heard being clever. It has limited the time members can speak in the House because in an effort to give more members the chance to speak, the Speaker and his deputies are forever seeking shorter speeches. This does have an adverse effect on the standard of oratory in the House, which I believe has fallen over recent years. Oratory requires time – and that is one thing the House of Commons no longer has – and not the petty consideration of having to speak for ten instead of eleven minutes.

Winston Churchill was a great speaker rather than an orator because he usually read his very carefully prepared speeches. Orators are those who speak without detailed notes but from heart and head, a blend of emotion and intellect. David Lloyd George was an obvious example, but in my time so was Nye Bevan, and so too was Michael Foot at his peak. One of the great orators today is Enoch Powell, whose mastery of the language is superb and who rarely uses notes in the House, although his speech and the arguments are carefully prepared. He is a very courteous man and if he is interrupted he will always sit down and then get up when he can continue: no matter how long the speech or at what point the interruption occurred, he can continue at the point he was stopped. I have always considered Ted Heath to be an orator and strangely he became much better after he ceased being Prime Minister.

Broadcasting did little to help attendances either, other than at Question Time, which was one of the most regularly broadcast pieces of parliamentary business. The improvement did not help prayers: they were not broadcast. That may sound cynical, but it just happens to be true.

In fact the attendance in the Chamber became deplorable in the evenings because once members had found out whether they were likely to speak or not, those who knew they were not would be away. Time after time, the Whips on both sides had to scour the corridors looking for somebody to go in and talk to a particular motion to keep the debate going. This was sometimes necessary even when the debate had been heralded as a crucial one in which the Opposition was going to lambast the Government in a very big way indeed. Even then, there was not the response one would have expected, let alone hoped for. To keep up appearances, party managers would often come to me and say that they hoped I would not hold it against a particular member who was going to make a long speech only because he had been asked to keep the debate going.

The bawling and braying has become worse since broadcasting but it must be remembered that the BBC is as concerned to keep its audience as a newspaper is to keep its circulation and therefore chooses the lively periods for the broadcasts.

On one occasion, when there had been a major debate on the health service, that edition of "Today in Parliament" spent more than half the time on a scene I had had with one member. I do not blame them entirely but that kind of editorial decision can give the wrong impression to the public about how Parliament behaves, particularly during debates, which for the most part are quiet and orderly. Some members would ask me to rule on whether or not the BBC had given a fair report of a particular debate, but I always said that any complaints would have to be dealt with by the select committee set up by the House specifically to deal with any problems connected with the broadcasting of Parliament. In fact I think they were generally fair in their reporting.

I think there is some danger now that the broadcasting companies are moving away from the straightforward reporting of the debates and questions into a kind of parliamentary sketchbook. There is a place for that but I do believe that the day-to-day business of Parliament should also be reported in a factual way.

I was not in favour of broadcasting because I did not think that an extraneous influence that could change the nature of Parliament should be allowed to intrude into the Chamber. And there is no doubt at all that it did have an effect on Parliament. The good effect was the increase in public interest. My correspondence more than doubled with many people writing to tell me how to deal with the members.

The public were most concerned with what they considered to be the unruly and childish members of Parliament who shouted and bawled while others were speaking.

Broadcasting increased the public awareness of what was going on. There is no doubt in my mind that the long-term effect was beneficial and I was wrong to resist it. It did create a renewed interest in the business of Parliament among people who before were only really interested in what was decided, not necessarily in how the decisions were reached. Now they were able to participate in the workings of Parliament and have a much better understanding of the House as a whole and of individual members. Some of those impressions were probably not what the members would have wished, but perhaps those members should look to their own behaviour in the House, rather than to the way they are perceived outside.

On the whole I was happy that Parliament was being so widely heard and more and more people were taking an interest in its work. At the same time, of course, as people listened in their homes, or on their car radios on the way to work in the mornings, they began to realise the Speaker played a much bigger role in the running of Parliament than they had realised.

It had always been the case but until the broadcasting of Parliament the Speaker was the unheard voice, the unseen hand. They knew now that he controlled the debates, the extent to which insults could be exchanged and the parliamentary language required. The public had a new interest and within weeks of the broadcasts starting, there was an increase in the number of people actually visiting Parliament.

On the four main working days of the House, there would always be about four or five hundred people milling about in the central lobby waiting to see the Speaker's procession pass – a very simple procession with one of the attendants walking in his white tie and tails in front with the measured step and bearing of a guardsman, followed by the Serjeant at Arms carrying the mace on his shoulder, his sword at his side, followed by the Speaker in wig and gown and the train-bearer behind holding up the gown, followed by the Speaker's chaplain and secretary walking together.

When we got in to the central lobby, the police inspector in charge would shout "Hats off, strangers!" That is the only place in the country that I know of where police salute by taking their hats off. One of the odder traditions of the House of Commons is that it divides the world into members and strangers, so although those policemen were our friends, working there every day and we knew their names, they were still strangers.

In the first half of my Speakership, I used to look straight in front, never to the right or left, but then I relaxed a bit and if ever I saw young children in the lobby, I would look down as I was passing and wink at them. I even received letters after that from people thanking me for giving their son or daughter a wink they would never forget. I do not think the procession lost any dignity.

As the procession enters the Chamber, the Speaker stands at the Bar of the House and bows, then he walks forward with the Serjeant at Arms at his side and bows to the Chair from the table. When he is at the steps leading to the Chair he bows again before kneeling for prayers. There was inevitably a tiny handful of members who did not believe in acknowledging the authority of the Chair by bowing, but I told them I used to bow to the Chair three times a day and I did not think I lost any dignity by it. I believed I was bowing to the authority of the House and the greater authority that lies behind it.

Imposing that authority is now becoming even more difficult. One of the noisiest members was the Labour MP Dennis Skinner, known in the newspapers as the Beast of Bolsover, a term which I ruled unparliamentary in 1978 when Norman Tebbit said, "The Beast of Bolsover turns out to be a fossilised dragonfly." Skinner was less than gracious for my concern about him as he retorted, "He can say what he likes."

In the old days, Skinner's behaviour would not have achieved anything, yet he was elected to the national executive of the Labour Party, and that staggers me, as he seems to have become known more for his rudeness than for fighting for the people he represents in the House. He is capable of making a good speech but he appears to specialise in heckling to stop others from making a coherent speech. He tries it particularly with David Steel, because they sit by the same microphone, he tries it with David Owen and, of course, with Roy Jenkins. He and his kind are fearful of the Social Democrats and therefore try to deny them free speech in the House, a very dangerous trend which, if it is not curbed, could do untold damage, not just to the reputation of the House of Commons, but to democracy and to the very future of the country. I believe the situation is getting worse and the control of that little crowd, and to some extent our future, depends on the firm hand of the Speaker. He has to insist that they show respect to the House through him or throw them out. Skinner himself is a very able man with a good brain and a forthright style in debating, but I had to watch him because he could become very personal. He knew exactly how far to go and so for a long time kept out of serious trouble, often only by half an inch.

I had many a jousting battle with him – the first within days of being elected Speaker – but the day came when he was on his feet interrupting James Prior, the then Employment Minister, and shouting abuse at the Prime Minister, Mrs Thatcher. So I stood up and said very firmly, "Order!" In my judgement, he had gone too far. He was too excited to listen to me and carried on despite my own efforts and those of Mr Prior and Jim Callaghan to calm the situation. I was still on my feet and the custom is that if the Speaker rises, the member, whoever he is, sits down. I told him again: "Order, the honourable gentleman will resume his seat at once." He would not stop and went on to finish his argument and I suspended him for the rest of the day's sitting. He folded his arms and looked at me as if to say, "That's what you think." I tried again but he still kept his arms folded with a defiant look and so I called on the Serjeant at Arms to conduct him out of the Chamber, the first time that the Serjeant had been called for such action for a hundred years.

I had made up my mind that if Skinner refused to go peacefully with the Serjeant at Arms, I would suspend the sitting so that there should not be a scene with me in the Chair watching it. Here was a battle of nerves with high drama in the House, which knew that the crunch had come between that fellow and myself. He had really challenged the authority of the Chair this time, whereas in the past he had always managed to jump back to safety before I could do anything. On this occasion, the Serjeant at Arms stood up and walked up the floor of the House. You could feel the electricity in the air with everyone holding their breath wondering what would happen. Skinner was pale but not saying a word. He was shaken and looked around at the Serjeant at Arms, Colonel Sir Peter Thorne, a slim fellow, and said, "What, him? Get back in your chair." I was tempted to laugh but naturally did not because I knew there was a great issue on for me and for him. One of us was going to be broken that day and it was not going to be me. The Serjeant at Arms was within one yard when Skinner's nerve cracked and he stood up and walked out docilely.

I knew this was a very important turning point and after that, whenever I warned him, and there were many times, I never had to do that again. Some time later, I had a message asking me to call

Dennis Skinner at his home where he was recovering from an accident and to my surprise, he wanted me to arrange a ticket for his son to visit the House of Commons the following day. I said I would, but even then he was argumentative, questioning whether or not I could really arrange this if the House was full. But I assured him I would and went on to say that I would invite the boy to have tea with me in the afternoon. Skinner was outraged: "I don't want him to have tea with you."

I arranged one of the best seats in the House for the boy under the gallery on a level with the Opposition members of Parliament. When I looked down from the Chair at him, it was like looking at Dennis Skinner. I sent down a message asking him if he would like to join me for tea and naturally enough the boy said he would like to come. When he came into my room, I said, "Oh no, not another." He laughed and said, "My old man's given you a lot of trouble," to which I replied, "Yes, and I've given him some trouble too."

On the question of discipline, it is a very nice question to know when to assert authority, when to try humour or when to play the follow-on rule. I remember on one occasion a member clearly getting on the nerves of the House because, in asking his question, he kept repeating the beginning over and over again. The House can be very cruel when it wants to be and the other members began to shout, so I stood up to give him a chance to collect himself and said, "The honourable gentleman is taking almost as long as I used to take and that's very unreasonable so he must come to the point." That calmed the House and the poor man asked his question – but you have to be careful even with the use of humour. I tried never to make a joke at the expense of a member. It is easy to make a person look small in front of everyone and although everybody else might forget the incident, the individual concerned never would.

There was one very strong character, James Wellbeloved, the Labour MP for Erith, who switched to the Social Democrats and lost his seat at the next election. He got up in one debate and asked was I sure that I was not deaf in one ear. I wish I had remembered at the time, but later as I was going back to Speaker's House, I remembered he had said exactly the same thing to Selwyn Lloyd. The fact is that Speaker's deafness is often a blessing. It really is a matter of choosing when it should strike you.

Sometimes of course I really did not hear. There was an occasion when Andrew Faulds insisted that he had referred to the Prime

Minister as "that bloody woman" and I had not heard it. None of us heard it in all the hullabaloo. I asked the Government front bench, the Opposition front bench – nobody had heard it. Hansard had not heard it either until Faulds told them he had said it. Eventually Hansard said that by playing over the tape of the proceedings and listening very carefully, they could pick out the words. That is when I gave a ruling to the House that I was not going to be guided by what the radio said but by what I had heard and by what Hansard had heard, not what they were told had been said.

The main disciplinary sanction the Speaker has is to name a member. The Leader of the House or the most senior minister present then proposes that the member who has been named be suspended from the service of the House for five days. It was something I never liked doing but it was necessary from time to time in order to keep control of the House. On the day I named Ian Paisley, I had been told there was likely to be trouble from him that day. News does travel fast in the House; one member only has to tell another something and it is not long before the whole House, even the Speaker, gets to know about it.

Irish questions were being asked and at the very first question, Gerry Fitt, quite a character and a very brave man, suddenly rose on a point of order and said he had distinctly heard the honourable member for Antrim South, Mr Paisley, say that the Minister, Humphrey Atkins, the Secretary of State for Northern Ireland, was a liar. And Gerry, with that innocent look he could put on his face, asked if that was in order. He knew as well as I did that it was not in order, but not having heard the remark I turned to Paisley and asked him if he had used that term, still, of course, describing him as an honourable member.

He replied in that unforgettable voice, "Yes, I did, Mr Speaker, and he is a liar." And with that he ran down the steps hoping to get out of the Chamber before I could take any action. Once he was out of the Chamber, there was nothing I could do. So without any more ado, I named him and as I did, so he shouted, "No," which meant that the motion to suspend him would have to be voted on. But as no other member of the House was prepared to act as a teller for the Noes, he was duly suspended. Paisley came to me later on to tell me how surprised he was that I had taken that action: "I didn't think you would do that to me." There was only one reply: "And I didn't think you would behave like that, Ian."

Paisley is a strong character and in the House of Commons weakness gets nobody anywhere. That is why I always believed I had to stand up to the strong characters because if they had won, the job of Speaker, to ensure the smooth running of the House, would be impossible. To maintain discipline the Speaker needs the support of the House. If the House refused to carry a motion to suspend a member, after the Speaker had named him, then I believe the Speaker would have no choice but to resign. This never happened and there was only one occasion when the motion was not fully supported.

During the third Falklands debate on 14 April, Andrew Faulds felt that I should have called him to speak and he jumped up shouting. He had done the same at a previous debate and I felt I could not call him in the next debate as it would appear that I was giving in to bullying, a precedent I could not afford. When he got up that day, he was most abusive, asking if I was aware that he had stood in the three debates and he had not been called in any of them. I pointed out that he was not alone as at least 100 members had also been standing without being called in either debate. He would not stop shouting so I ordered him to leave the Chamber for the rest of the day's sitting.

The House was crowded and all this was being broadcast across the world, so Andrew Faulds, the actor, walked down the centre of the floor of the House. The sense of occasion overcame him and he could not resist the drama. He turned round and started to wave his hands and shout at me. This was the only time I named anyone without the Opposition giving full support. Michael Foot had very mixed feelings about his sacking of Faulds from the Shadow Cabinet after Faulds had publicly disagreed with the official Labour policy on the Falklands and advised the Opposition not to support the naming It was the only time during my Speakership that the motion to suspend a member was voted on, but it carried easily as many Labour members abstained.

Broadcasting has worked but I do think that the recent attempts to shout down other members must damage our reputation for fair play, free speech and decency right across the world, where the proceedings are heard on the BBC World Service. I think that some members of the House of Commons too often forget the responsibility they have to maintain the deservedly high reputation of the House, built up over the centuries, which could be lost by a few selfish words or a bout of stupidity that is heard on the radio. To prevent a point of view from being heard just because you personally do not agree with it is undermining the basis of parliamentary democracy.

There is only one thing to do and only the Speaker can do it: that is to exercise a firm hand and throw out the people who break the rules. My own view is that to suspend a man just for five days is not sufficient. When I was young, it was a terrible disgrace if anybody was thrown out of the Commons for misbehaviour, but it seems to me that, with some of these extreme constituencies, a man gets a medal if he has challenged the authority of the House, an authority which has stood us in good stead for 300 years.

He does not lose any pay and as the act of suspension does not seem to make him suffer, he and perhaps his party should be made to suffer in some other way. Discipline is breaking down in the House and in the parties too, largely because the Whips have lost control, particularly in the Labour Party.

The Chief Whip in the Labour Party has no sanctions to exercise on his backbenchers who ignore parliamentary decency and who behave like shouting hooligans. There was a time when the Chief Whip's threat to report a member to his constituency was sufficient discipline to ensure co-operation. But now there are constituency parties that seem to revel in their MPs being involved in a parliamentary scene and that sanction is no longer effective.

Now that Parliament has accepted broadcasting, with all its attendant difficulties, as part of its life, the next question to decide is whether to allow in the television cameras. The Lords has already agreed in principle and I believe the televising of Parliament is inevitable and desirable. But if the cameras do come in, they must be allowed to move around the Chamber so that everyone can see how people are behaving. It is one thing to be just a voice shouting and bawling, quite another to be seen to be doing it. I know from experience in the Chair that the rowdy few try to intimidate their opponents by glowering, scowling and shouting. As I sat there, I very often thought of the old saying that it was empty vessels that make most noise. It is a view that should be seen by the cameras. The bully boys deserve to be shown up on television.

The introduction of television would put a brake on the excesses that we have been hearing in the Commons by showing the public the faces of those people who are shouting and snarling while others are trying to make a point. There is an anonymity in radio, which there would not be on television provided the cameras are allowed to operate freely and are not just focused on the man who is speaking. The camera acts as the eyes of a visitor and their eyes would be roaming all over the place, not just looking at the people who are on their best behaviour.

The House would become better behaved overnight, and attendances would also improve, because if members were never seen there, it would be noticed in the constituency. An always empty seat would send a powerful message. But all that depends on the all-seeing eye of the camera. If it is allowed only to peep through the keyhole, then that is not Parliament. It could almost be misleading.

There is a Trades Description Act to ensure that what is described on a packet of beans is indeed in the packet. To claim the televising of Parliament and yet show nothing of the more unpleasant side of the proceedings would infringe the Trades Description Act. Let the country see who is shouting and misbehaving. Let the public know that it is usually the same twenty or thirty members who are particularly active during Prime Minister's Question Time. You can depend on them shouting and shouting abuse but the Speaker cannot stop for every one. If he did, the business of Parliament would come to a standstill and I sometimes think that is what they want. And that is why a Speaker cannot be stone deaf all the time.

CHAPTER TWENTY-THREE

Limping to an Election

Life became no easier in the House either for me or for Jim Callaghan's Government. Perhaps it was because I literally sat in the centre of things, but I soon realised that to be Speaker was to be in the eye of the storm. Members on both sides, some quite senior ones, would come to me to tell me their views of the current politics and even after more than thirty years, I was surprised by what I saw and heard in the last years of the Labour administration.

Jim was clearly under considerable strain throughout 1977 and it may have been this that led him to the very strange decision in May to appoint Peter Jay, his son-in-law, to the plum diplomatic posting as Ambassador in Washington. If the Tories had tried something similar, there would have been uproar in the House. It was bad enough that the post was going to somebody without any experience in Parliament, let alone any diplomatic background. That he was the Prime Minister's son-in-law added injury to the insult caused to our ambassadors and diplomats across the world. Peter Jay was very fortunate. The Washington Embassy can open many doors for you. The opportunities were there to be taken but, unhappily for Peter, he went through the wrong doors. His appointment did, however, provide a way out for Brian Walden, the Labour MP for Birmingham Ladywood, who took Jay's job as an ITV current-affairs presenter. Walden, a very capable man, had been deeply concerned with the way the Government had been behaving and had let this be known.

There were many other Labour MPs on both wings of the party who were far from happy with the way things were going and seemed to lose no opportunity to shoot into their own side. In February 1977, Alex Lyon, the Labour MP for York, and a former junior minister at the Home Office, demanded an emergency debate into the proposed deportation on security grounds of the two Americans, Philip Agee and Mark Hosenball. My refusal led to a tremendous outcry from Lyon's friends on the left.

Earlier in the day, Merlyn Rees, the Home Secretary, had told me he was going to make a statement to the House announcing the proposed deportation of both Americans. He was desperately anxious that there should not be a debate on the question of the deportation itself; although he made it clear he would welcome a debate on the procedures adopted in such cases. I told him quite firmly that while I had been glad to see him and hear his account, I would of course give my decision in the House itself if there was an application for an emergency debate.

Immediately I had rejected the application, Alex Lyon, a difficult man, came down to speak to me in the Chair, accompanied by about six civil-liberty campaigners and left-wingers. I explained that I never gave reasons for rejecting an application for an emergency debate, but I reminded him of what usually happened when national security was involved. This proved to be a mistake on my part.

He renewed his application the following day and pointed out that I had granted only four emergency debates in my year as Speaker and these had all been on the Tory side. I had to object strongly because the clear implication was that I was biased. When I objected, Lyon withdrew that suggestion, but renewed his demand for an emergency debate. I indicated that there were at least four weeks before the men would be deported, and that the responsibility for granting time for a debate did not lie with me.

During Question Time, Michael Foot (then Leader of the House) was pressed to grant time for a debate on the deportations but said that although he could not give time for the debate he recommended that the members pursue the other means open to them. Since the only other course was the granting of an emergency debate, he was clearly putting the responsibility on me. I immediately told the House that the responsibility was not mine, and there were cries of "Michael Foot!" There had been no conversation at all between the Leader of the House and myself on this important issue but the following day, to my great surprise, Foot announced that he was finding time for a debate on the deportations after all. It was quite clear that his second thought was linked with the question of the guillotine on the Devolution Bill, which had to be decided the following week. Foot gave way after left-wing members threatened not to support the Government on the guillotine unless they had the debate on Agee and Hosenball.

Throughout my experience of Michael Foot, his ability as a political acrobat never ceased to surprise me. He could stand on his head with the greatest of ease and reverse his firmly announced decisions within twenty-four hours. It always astonished me that he survived for so long at the top of the Labour Party. One thing was very clear. If he felt that he could escape from any difficulty by planting his responsibilities on to me, he never hesitated to do so.

The Agee–Hosenball incident highlighted one of the most difficult areas for the Speaker. There were requests for emergency debates nearly every day but I rarely granted them, and when I did, particularly during the Callaghan Government, I was always unpopular.

Jim was very angry in March 1977 when I agreed to the request from Hal Miller, MP for Bromsgrove and Redditch, for an emergency debate on the toolmakers' strike at British Leyland, which had led to nearly 30,000 men being out of work. I had initially refused the request, causing obvious disappointment on the Opposition benches, and later I asked Francis Pym, the Shadow Leader of the House, whether the Opposition were officially supporting the application for an emergency debate. As a result, he discussed the matter with the Tory leadership and returned to report that the Conservatives were very serious in their demand for a debate on the strike.

This altered my view and shortly before the House was due to sit, I sent a message to Michael Foot and the Opposition Front Bench to tell them I proposed to grant the emergency debate if Miller made the request again, as he had already told me was likely. For my first hour in the Chair, both Michael Foot and Michael Cocks came to me urging me not to grant the emergency debate because it might endanger prospects of a settlement. This had caused me deep anxiety, but since there appeared to be no prospect of a settlement, I felt that the House of Commons had a right to discuss what was an important issue. I had been guided by precedent, for when there was a strike amongst the nurses, the Labour Opposition demanded and obtained a debate on that strike – a very clear comparison with what was happening at British Leyland.

When I granted the emergency debate, the Prime Minister slammed his papers down and muttered something which I could not hear, but as he passed my Chair he said in a loud voice, "Bad, bad." By the time I had left the Chair and returned to my room, there was a letter from him telling me in rough language that he thought I had made a bad decision.

It so happened that for the next hour, I was alone in my room and I must say it is very difficult when there is tension in the air to sit alone with one's thoughts on the question whether the right decision has been taken. I am convinced that I took the right decision, but I hated the thought that the Prime Minister and my former colleagues were as angry as they undoubtedly were that I had allowed that debate.

I knew that every time I granted an emergency debate, I hurt them, but we were on the brink of anarchy and I passionately believed that the House of Commons had the right to discuss the issues which I was convinced were of major importance – like the firemen's strike, where I had visions of Britain's cities being engulfed by fire. The Prime Minister and I discussed the matter quite forcefully before the dinner given by Mr Begin in December 1977, after I had granted an emergency debate on the Crown Agents' loss of £212 million, immediately following my granting of the fire debate.

He made it quite clear that he thought I had been wrong to have granted the debate on the Crown Agents' loss and he was clearly agitated about the course the debate itself would take. I was not a bit surprised by his attitude because I have not met a Prime Minister yet who liked an emergency debate, which will inevitably criticise the Government. When things are going well or calmly, nobody wants an emergency debate; it is only when things go wrong, as they did for Labour, that they are demanded. I remember very clearly saying to him, "You want to be a good Prime Minister, I presume. I want to be a good Speaker. History will judge who did best but my job is to look after the interests of the House, not of the Government."

He was clearly very concerned that the Crown Agents' debate could result in a demand for the inquiry into the loss to be held in public rather than in private as the Government were planning. Jim emphasised that the reason the inquiry was to be held in private was solely to protect innocent people. He reminded me that when Lord Justice Salmon had considered the question of inquiries, he had made the very point that the old style of public inquiry damaged innocent people.

The Prime Minister turned to me rather sharply and said, "You should use your influence, because I understand that the Tories are meeting to consider whether they want a public inquiry. This is not a party political matter, it is merely one to protect the innocent people who serve us in public life." I told him I thought the House might well defeat the Government when it came to the vote, because there was strong feeling in favour of a public inquiry.

Later, as I sat next to Mrs Begin, with Jim on her other side, we spoke about the current wave of wage demands and the firemen's strike, and Callaghan insisted that even if he was defeated, he was not going to give way. He kept referring to the fact that he was sixty-five, and he told Mrs Begin that the advantage of having a Prime Minister at that age was that he was not worried about his future and could just do what he believed was absolutely right for the country. I could feel that Jim was rather tense and he was obviously full of anxiety as he said, "I have to stiffen my Ministers' resolve these days."

The day following the dinner, the debate on the Crown Agents went as I had anticipated with clearly an overwhelming feeling in the House that a public inquiry was preferable to the private inquiry proposed by the Government. The Government was defeated by a majority of more than thirty – a clear vindication of my ruling. I felt that I had fulfilled my historic role as Speaker in upholding the rights of the House against the will of the executive, who would have preferred silence from the Members of Parliament. Once again it had been made clear that the Commons is indeed the guardian of public standards as well as of public liberties.

The pressures on Jim came from every quarter. As he was fighting the financial crisis, the growing industrial unrest and disloyalty from his own supporters, trouble was brewing on the Devolution Bill. In November, there were stormy scenes in the House when Michael Foot announced that there would be only one day's debate each for the second reading of the Scottish and Welsh Bills. The time given for such a major constitutional issue was ridiculously short. It was quite impossible for me to call every point of view represented in the House and I believed that the House had the right to expect more time. During the exchanges between Foot and Francis Pym over the time allocated, it was clear that Pym, a forceful speaker, clean and fair, emerged as the winner.

As I sat listening to the debate, I felt for the first time frustrated that I could not join in. I was fearful for the future of the United Kingdom and felt I ought to join the battle. As it was, I had to sit and listen for nine hours with two short breaks of twenty minutes in the Scotland debate and seven hours in the Welsh debate. On both nights, I did not get to bed until three in the morning. But the Government won the day, although it was clear that there had been an enormous amount of arm-twisting to ensure that they did. The Devolution Bill was one occasion when brutal tactics certainly paid off.

The Government plans had a serious setback at the Report Stage in February of 1978, when the House was discussing an amendment that would mean that at least 40 per cent of the electorate, and not just a straight majority of those who voted in the referendum, would have to be in favour of devolution in Scotland before the assembly could be set up. In the event this amendment stopped devolution in Scotland as the referendum did produce a small majority in favour – but not 40 per cent of the electorate. It was one of the very few occasions when one speech turned the mood of the House. Michael Foot and the Government believed they had the necessary votes in the bag to defeat the amendment but this proved to be an error of judgement. Michael Foot allowed the last speech to go to George Cunningham, the Labour MP for Islington, who later switched to the Social Democrats and lost his seat at the next General Election by only a few hundred votes.

George, an abrasive man with a first-class intellect and a superb understanding of parliamentary procedure, quickly sensed the feeling of occasion. He spoke without a note for half an hour in a magnificent and convincing way that persuaded a great many Labour members to vote against the Government. It is not often that one speech can be so decisive but it certainly was that night: that speech stopped devolution in Scotland.

It still astonishes me that the Government should have been so out of touch with the feeling in the House and in the country on devolution, which would have opened up the possibility of the break-up of the United Kingdom. From the very beginning, the Cabinet had sought to force devolution on an unwilling Party, in order to outwit the Scottish Nationalists at the general election. At every stage of the Bill and of the ill-fated one that was withdrawn by the Government in the previous session, it was clear that there was a good majority in the House against granting a legislative assembly to Scotland, but none are so blind as those who do not want to see. The Cabinet, having made up their mind, thought they would be strong enough to force their will on the House. I believe that we saw the House at its best that night, when members followed their conscience and their instinct rather than give in on a major constitutional issue.

Immediately after the Government had been defeated, a senior

Labour politician came to tell me that the Prime Minister wanted Denis Healey to follow him as leader of the Labour Party. As Denis was then already sixty-two, it seems as if, even then, Jim was considering retirement.

Those years were not a good time for the House or Labour. The damage done then and later, under Michael Foot's leadership, will take a great deal of repairing and it remains to be seen whether the present leadership, without much experience of government or party management, will be able to achieve what must often seem the impossible dream. It might have been so very different if Denis Healey, one of the most powerful of modern Labour politicians, had taken over as Jim had wanted.

Election fever began to grip Parliament in 1978 and even in the late spring, there was talk of an autumn general election. By the summer, there was hardly a member of the House who did not believe that Jim was going to call an election in October. Even after he publicly warned the TUC Conference in Brighton that it was by no means certain, nobody believed him.

I was in Australia for the Commonwealth Speakers' Conference but left after a week because my advisers and I were certain that an election was about to be called. The decision to return home meant that I spent almost more time in the air than I did at the conference, but we were all certain that I would be needed for the dissolution of Parliament for an election on 28 October.

Like the rest of the country and most of its politicians, I was staggered at the Prime Minister's decision to plod on and I thought then it was probably one of the great political mistakes of the century. A senior minister said to me at the time that the Government could "limp along", but limping is not very good for anybody, let alone a government. The future for Labour could have been so different if Jim had gone to the country that October. It would have been a gamble but one I think Labour might well have won.

So Callaghan did limp along into 1979, with the pressures growing all the time. In the dying weeks of the Government, Michael Cocks came to see me at the request of the Prime Minister to say that the Cabinet had complained that I was allowing too long for the questioning of ministers after they had made their statements to the House. The truth was that ministers were under such stress that they had come to feel it necessary to make a long political argument every time they were asked a question. It was up to the ministers to be more brief in their replies and not to provide such a wide target for supplementary questions.

Finally in March, a motion of no confidence was tabled by Mrs Thatcher. With the numbers so close, and the future of the Government depending on the voting of the minority parties, there could be no room for mistakes at the close of the debate on 28 March. With so much tension in the House, either party might well have used any device at all to claim that the vote had been improperly taken, or that the members had been given insufficient time to get into the Lobbies to place their votes. Both the Clerk, Sir Richard Barlas, and I were determined that if there were any slip-ups, they would not be laid at our door. So I was very careful at the start of the debate to remind the members what time the division would take place and point out to them that it was their responsibility to be in the Chamber at the right time.

As always before a crucial debate, particularly when a tie is a real possibility, both the Opposition and the Government wanted to know how I would use my casting vote. I was able to tell them once again that I would rely on Speaker Denison's ruling, which in this case, would mean that I would vote with the Government.

As so often happens in the House of Commons, history repeated itself. In June 1841, on a motion of no confidence, Speaker Shaw-Lefevre announced the voting figures, 312 to 311. On 28 March 1979, I announced the figures, 311 to 310. Callaghan stood up immediately and said that as the Government no longer had the confidence of the House, Parliament would be dissolved, once all outstanding business had been cleared in the next few days.

We were soon to have a Conservative Government and the first woman Prime Minister in our history. But first she, the Conservative Party and the House were to be dealt a shattering blow when Irish terrorists booby-trapped the car of Airey Neave, the Shadow Minister for Northern Ireland and one of Mrs Thatcher's closest aides.

I had been in the Chair that Friday morning, 30 March, but left to go to Wales. As soon as I had arrived in Cardiff, there was a telephone call from my secretary to tell the dreadful news of the explosion at Westminster in the underground car-park. It was thought that the car belonged to Mr Airey Neave. The news of his death was not confirmed, although it was clear that whoever had been in the car would have been killed.

During the election period, the Speaker is in sole charge of the

House of Commons. He is the only one left and stays in office until a new man is elected, so with the power I had, I decided that Airey Neave's coat of arms should be put up inside the Chamber to mark the fact that he had been assassinated on the premises.

His death was a stunning blow. Not just because of the awful personal tragedy for the Neave family, who had lost a father and a husband, nor even because Airey himself was on the brink of becoming a powerful figure in the country, but for the inescapable realisation that even the seat of democracy was vulnerable to the bombers and madmen.

CHAPTER TWENTY-FOUR

Nation at War

As soon as the Conservatives had been elected, I told Margaret Thatcher that if the new Government wanted me to retire, I was willing to go at any time, but she refused to discuss it, saying that she and the Cabinet wanted me to continue. Retirement had been in my mind for some months and I had even told Michael Foot when he was Leader of the House that I intended to go at Christmas 1979. To my surprise, he became quite excited and insisted that both sides of the House wanted me to stay and that I must not give retirement another thought. I accepted what he said and let the matter rest but the thought of freedom from the strain of Parliament did have an enormous appeal.

The convention has been that at a general election the Speaker does not campaign on a party ticket and the main parties do not oppose him so when I was negotiating with the local Conservatives and Liberals in Cardiff, who along with the constituency Labour Party contributed to my election address, I did tell them privately that I would certainly not be seeking re-election at the next general election. I was thinking about my age even then as I had a dread of being the last person to realise that my faculties were failing and I was determined to leave the Chair of my own accord and not when others wanted me to leave.

On a personal level, I had always got on well with the Conservatives in Cardiff West but there was a faction there who felt after the 1979 election that they should prepare the ground for the future and wanted to select a prospective parliamentary candidate to oppose me at the next general election. When the Government Chief Whip, Michael Jopling, came to tell me in July 1980 that the local party was putting great pressure on Conservative Central Office for permission to select a candidate, he said he was greatly embarrassed by their demands.

I told him he had no need to be and that I would not be standing at the next election, but that I did not want to announce that yet. I also told him that the Conservative Party would not be helping themselves by announcing they were going to oppose me as it would look as if the Parliamentary Party had lost confidence in me and that could make things difficult in the House.

I was already aware of the pressure from the Cardiff Tories as Edward du Cann, the chairman of the 1922 Committee, had told me that Lord Thorneycroft, the chairman of the Conservative Party, was sympathetic to their claims but that he had told Thorneycroft that under no circumstances should he agree to an announcement being made. Du Cann insisted that I should not announce my retirement until I was ready to go as he said this would undermine my influence in the House, but in the event, in March 1981, I announced it was my intention to retire.

I felt that if the Cardiff Tories were going to select a candidate it was only right that I should give the Labour Party the same opportunity to choose a man who could nurse the seat. But as soon as I made my announcement, the leaders of the main parties made it clear they wanted me to stay. I was pleased the air was now clear and that I could leave the Chair in my own time and I really began to enjoy myself as my experience grew.

The pressures of the minority Government were no longer present, although the Labour left were no less active in the House, clearly believing that noise would win the battle they had lost at the ballot box. There was also a noticeable change of style under the Conservative Government and strangely I met with far more courtesy from Mrs Thatcher, who had for so long been my political opponent, than I had from Jim Callaghan, whom I had known and worked with for thirty-five years.

When the Labour Party had their reception in Number Ten the night before the State Opening of Parliament, it was always a very informal affair. Ministers stood to be served drinks before the Prime Minister asked the Secretary to the Cabinet to lock the doors so that the PM's reading of the Queen's Speech could be heard in private. We would all be away by eight o'clock. But when the Tories came to power, you put on a black tie and were invited to dinner after the reading of the speech. Every member of the Government would be present and I always sat on the right hand of the Prime Minister with Willie Whitelaw on the other.

As the speech was read out, people waited to hear their favourite bills announced. Harold Wilson had a habit of looking in the direction of the people whose bills were being introduced and I clearly remember hearing him say "A measure of leasehold reform will be introduced." And he bowed in my direction. As Speaker, I was always on the lookout for what I thought might produce some fairly rough weather in Parliament. Harold and Jim never asked me for my opinion but I used to talk to Mrs Thatcher about how I thought various measures would be received.

One of the changes that came about in that Parliament was the huge increase in the number of research assistants, many of them from America, attached to MPs. They were young and they were curious and naturally liked to look around Westminster, but we did have to issue a warning that members would have to exercise more control over them as there was some concern over security.

In the Chamber, their presence was felt in the rise in the number of parliamentary questions, as the research assistants spend their time delving into all sorts of subjects to provide questions for people who until then had not been asking any at all. None of this does anything for our democracy and is only a cheap publicity stunt which has demeaned the order paper of the House of Commons and lowered the prestige and dignity of the members, many of whom are not even there to hear the answer. Most of them are questions just for the sake of it and are not intended to provide real knowledge. Questions are important but the system was abused and we had to limit members to two questions a day to the same minister. There are now usually about 100 questions on the order paper every day, all of which have to be answered orally or in writing, which means that civil servants are stopped from doing their proper work to answer what in many cases are obscure and wasteful questions.

That Parliament was, of course, marked out from all the others by the Falklands War, which caught us all by surprise. On Friday, 2 April 1982, I had gone to the Polytechnic of Wales in Treforest to receive their honorary fellowship. Speakers were not supposed to leave the House if they were not going to be in immediate contact and I had been given special permission to be absent.

I arrived at the college about ten in the morning and within half an hour there was a telephone call from my secretary to say that it was believed that the Falkland Islands had been invaded, although the information was very confused throughout the day.

During that day, my secretary telephoned me three times and there were also calls from Michael Cocks, the Opposition Chief Whip, John Silkin, the Shadow Defence Minister, and Francis Pym, the Leader of the House. All were anxious but also confused, not knowing what was happening, not even knowing what had happened. Francis Pym left me in no doubt at all that I would be very unwise not to return to London on the Friday night to take the unprecedented Saturday debate, for which I had to give permission.

Before I went into the Chamber, Humphrey Atkins, the Lord Privy Seal and Lord Carrington's number two at the Foreign Office, came to see me in a very agitated state. I had never seen him like it before but I understood why when he told me that he wanted to make a personal statement in the House to correct some of the things he had told them the previous day. As Speaker, I had to approve any personal statements which in that case I did in every detail. He told the House: "Following my statement at eleven o'clock yesterday, I said that we had been in touch with the governor of the Falkland Islands half an hour before. That was inaccurate. We had in fact been in touch earlier, at 8.30 a.m. our time. No invasion had then taken place, and when I made my statement I had no knowledge of any change in the situation." It was not a good start for the Government.

From the moment I entered the Chamber it was obvious that the debate was going to be one of the most dramatic in recent times. It was, incidentally, the first time that the House had been crowded for prayers. Normally the members wait to rush into the Chamber immediately prayers are over, no matter how dramatic the events that are to follow. But that day, everybody was anxious, even rather frightened, at what might happen now that those small islands so far away had been invaded by the Argentine dictator Galtieri.

During the course of the debate, I saw Mrs Thatcher's Parliamentary Private Secretary, Ian Gow, talking to the right-wing Conservative MP Ray Whitney, a former diplomat. It was therefore obvious that the Government wanted him to speak in the debate. He explained to the House the negotiations that had taken place and warned of the dangers of any military action. He did not get a good reception, unlike Michael Foot, who was considered to have made his best speech as Opposition Leader. His theme was that Britain could not allow dictators to invade our territory and I can even now hear his voice going higher and higher as he pointed his hand upwards to say, "It's deeds we want, not words."

I thought at once of the Suez debate, when Hugh Gaitskell had begun by supporting the Government and then backtracked later. I could not help but feel there would be a change of course in this case too. As the Task Force was assembled and began to sail to the South Atlantic the demand came from the Opposition in increasingly shrill tones that Britain should return to the United Nations and talk. So now it was words rather than deeds that were called for.

In each of the six Falklands debates, there were high passions, and I had to make sure that those who were opposed to the Government's action were given the right to be heard. I also had to bear in mind their number in relation to the rest of the House, who were in favour, and overall I think the balance was maintained.

The first voice to be raised against retaking the islands by force was the Scottish Labour MP George Foulkes, who wanted to let the islands go, but I am quite convinced that if this view had prevailed, Belize would have gone, trouble in Gibraltar would have been inevitable and in a number of places across the world the bully-boys would have moved into action knowing that the democracies were afraid to respond.

Lord Carrington was an enormous loss for the Prime Minister and the Government, which was weaker from that moment on, and I have never understood why he felt obliged to resign as Foreign Secretary. The Government was desperately anxious that he should not resign and Willie Whitelaw spent the whole of the Sunday after the emergency debate trying to persuade him to stay.

Some people say that John Nott, the Defence Secretary, should also have resigned, but I think he showed moral courage by staying on, particularly after his very rough time in the first debate.

To my surprise, David Owen also emerged as a considerable politician, growing in stature throughout the Falklands debates. He proved to have inner strength and refused to be deflected, not at all afraid to take on the Government, but it was obvious his first loyalty was to the country. He took the quite correct view that any political points could be scored when it was all over.

Towards the end of the war, President and Mrs Reagan paid a state visit to Britain and came to the Royal Gallery, where the President addressed Parliament. So for a few hours we escaped from the tension of the fighting to give the President and his wife a ceremonial welcome. The Lord Chancellor, Lord Hailsham, and I stood together, dressed in our state robes with the black embroidered gowns, knee-length trousers and stockings, waiting for the Reagans. The American contingent came in before their President and sat in their seats at the side of the hall, just as if they were in the choir, with Secretary of State, Alexander Haig, whom I had never met, sitting at the end. Quintin and I were just looking into space, when I was suddenly aware that Haig was looking at us as if we were something out of a museum. He had a quizzical look as he stared at the top of my wig and then went all the way down to the silver buckles on my shoes. He started again but this time I caught his eye and winked at him. He burst out laughing, for until then I do not think he believed we were capable of winking.

During the proceedings I had seen an American carrying the black box, which is never away from the President, and I thought how mad it was to think that they might want to start a nuclear war in the middle of our ceremony.

The Queen later gave a state banquet for the Reagans at Windsor Castle, where I renewed my acquaintance with Mrs Reagan, whom I had met at the wedding of Prince Charles and Lady Diana the year before. When we met again at Windsor, she held out both her hands to greet me and I caught them just at the moment Prince Charles came up. He said jokingly to Mrs Reagan, "Be careful with him, don't you listen to what he says." She would have none of it and said, "He's the darlingest," a word that Prince Charles had never heard before. I did not let on, but neither had I.

The banquet itself was a considerable strain for Mrs Thatcher and those of us who knew that there had been very heavy losses in Bluff Cove as Welsh Guardsmen were being landed prior to the taking of Port Stanley. The news had not yet been released and that was the only time I saw Mrs Thatcher show any real sign of strain during the whole Falklands campaign.

I think that had a man been Prime Minister, he would probably have lost his nerve long before. Any man would have gone back to the United Nations to make sure he was not going to be ostracised by the world community, in much the same way as the Opposition were putting themselves in the clear if things went wrong. Britain would have lost all influence in international affairs if Mrs Thatcher had submitted to the pressures and gone back to the United Nations. It would have meant that never again would Britain take any decisive action to defend her people. The Prime Minister showed remarkable courage and determination throughout the whole of the tragedy, and she knew tragedy was inevitable once the islands had been invaded by Argentina. But by her action she saved the good name of Britain.

The whole exercise showed that British youth, who never thought they would have to do that sort of thing again, could respond magnificently to the challenge. The Falklands affair reinforced my belief that the British character has not really changed, despite all the troubles that we face with violence and sometimes appallingly selfish behaviour. We are still a tough little race, and now the world knows it.

CHAPTER TWENTY-FIVE

A Question of Religion

Throughout my public life I have never made a secret of my Christian beliefs, and nobody had ever objected until a few months after I had been elected Speaker. The day after I had given a lecture at Radcliffe College, Leicester, in which I had stressed the necessity for Christian teaching in our schools, I heard Geoffrey Edge, a Midlands Labour MP, on the radio, calling for my resignation because he claimed that the speech had shown I was not impartial. I was in favour of Christian teaching in schools and he was against it. Therefore I was not impartial. I sent for him to come to the State Rooms in Speaker's House – if I wanted anything to be strictly formal, I always saw people there. He was embarrassed of course when I told him that I understood he wanted me to resign. These early days were difficult times for me anyway and I wanted everything to be quite clear to everybody.

I told him that his view seemed to be that I should not express opinions on anything, particularly something with which he disagreed. I pointed out that he knew my views when he was among those who voted for me in the election for Speaker a few weeks earlier. I made it plain that neither he nor any other member had bought me body and soul just because I was Speaker, and that I would go on saying those things – maybe even more so. I would keep my mouth shut on party political issues but teaching the scriptures was not a mere party issue, rather one on which I would have thought all parties would have agreed.

Towards the end of that Parliament, another Midlands MP, Bruce George, asked me if I would receive a vicar from the constituency who was riding down to London on a sponsored bicycle ride. Lo and behold, when he came in, Geoffrey Edge was with him. I could not resist saying, "Hello, have you been converted then?" He lost his seat shortly afterwards.

People like that make the mistake of underestimating the strength of the spiritual belief in our country. Not so many people go to church now, but they do want their children to grow up knowing the difference between right and wrong – that at the very least our society has an undercurrent of Christian ethics. Far from hiding my own beliefs, I became actively involved in two Christian groups in the House of Commons.

Michael Alison, a Yorkshire Tory MP, and his wife Sylvia came to see me to say they wanted to form a Christian wives' group in the House of Commons. I did not need time to consider this proposal and agreed at once that they should meet in Speaker's House. I really was moved by the number who came, which showed that through the years there had been a need for this sort of thing, because the wives of MPs can become very isolated, even if they are with their husbands in London. Once in about three months, they would invite very distinguished speakers like the Archbishop of Canterbury. They would also invite their husbands so that sometimes as many as 120 people would crowd round in the Speaker's dining-room. The wives would all make special dishes for these meetings – never was so much food seen in Speaker's House. I am very proud of my part in forming the Christian Wives' Fellowship and the only request I made to my successor was that he should continue to allow the Christian Wives' Fellowship to use Speaker's House.

One of the leading figures in the group was Alec Douglas-Home's wife Elizabeth, the daughter of Dean Alington, a former head of Eton. She is a tower of strength to many of the other wives, who, by the very nature of their position as MPs' wives, with all the uncertainties and difficult hours, were often under stress. One wife who had had a terrible bereavement told me at one of the meetings that it was only being in that group and being able to talk and share her experience with women like herself that had helped her to keep her sanity. The one with the gentle touch to bring them all together was Elizabeth Home. She was also able to bridge the gap between those who, like any Christian group, wanted to specialise in Bible study and prayer and those who really just wanted to talk to each other in a Christian setting, which is what most of them preferred.

MPs themselves had a prayer group, which met for breakfast once a month. This was the British section of an international Christian leadership movement which had started in America and had been going long before I was Speaker. I was a little bit anxious about it to start with, because I was afraid that the CIA was behind it, using Christians who were obviously anti-Communist as part of their foreign policy, but I was soon persuaded that it was a genuine Christian movement and, as soon as I became Speaker, I invited them to meet in Speaker's House.

The MPs who were members did not like their names to be known as they did not want it to be thought that they were courting the Christian vote, and there were many good Christians in the House who were not members of that group. The membership grew to cover all shades of political and religious opinions in the House and the numbers who came to breakfast of coffee and toast grew to about twenty-five. The fact that Tory, Liberal, Labour and Nationalists can meet together in prayer does not in any way affect their ability to fight for their cause in the House, but it does strengthen the place when there is an undercurrent of common belief. The custom grew that we would take communion at St Margaret's Church before breakfast. The Roman Catholics did not come to St Margaret's of course – they made the toast.

We were a happy family party united by our Christian beliefs and many times I wished the day would come when I would be able to get all the Ulster MPs to share a meal in Christian fellowship, but I never felt that I could issue the invitation until I was satisfied that both sides would respond favourably. Unhappily that day never arrived.

I also played a part in one of the most historic religious events in the House, when early in 1978 Kevin McNamara, the Roman Catholic Labour MP for Hull, came to ask if the Roman Catholic members of the House could celebrate mass in the crypt of the House of Commons to mark the 500th anniversary of the birth of Sir Thomas More. I immediately gave permission without consulting any of the House authorities, although I told him that he would have to gain the agreement of the Lord Chancellor and the Lord Great Chamberlain. The fact that I had said I had no objection at all to the mass being held would make it very difficult for them to refuse. I can still see the look of astonishment on his face.

He was kind enough to point out the significance of the decision as there had not been a Roman Catholic mass in the crypt since the Reformation. And I could understand his delight because my first twenty years in the House had been spent campaigning for the rights of Nonconformists to hold a service in the crypt. I felt that the crypt belonged to all Christians in the Commons and not merely to the Anglicans.

McNamara could not wait to tell the world of his great achievement but before he went he told me that Cardinal Hume would probably conduct the mass. I offered to come myself, while realising that I could not participate in the Holy Communion. In the event I read the lesson. The Roman Catholic Church inevitably publicised the fact that permission had been given and equally inevitably this angered some Protestants in Northern Ireland.

The Reverend Ian Paisley came to see me in a very indignant mood saying, as he hit the table, "This is blasphemy, Mr Speaker." I quietly pointed out that blasphemy was illegal and that I did my best not to break the law. Paisley made it clear he considered I had committed an error of judgement in agreeing to the mass being held. He said he understood how difficult it was for me to say "No" after the Lord Chancellor and Lord Great Chamberlain had agreed. I immediately corrected him to make it clear that it was I who had given permission in the first place, and that I was going to share in the mass by reading a lesson.

He then told me he felt he would have to make a public protest and his first inclination was to protest when the Host was being raised, the most sacred moment in the service. We argued about this and finally he accepted that if there was to be a protest, it should be at the beginning of the service and after that, he would disappear. I contacted Cardinal Hume and every Roman Catholic MP in the House and told them what I expected to happen and suggested to them all that they ignore the interruptions from Dr Paisley and carry on quietly afterwards.

When I went down to the crypt for the mass in July, I found police everywhere because the new Black Rod was a former general of the forces in Ulster and was very security-minded. I recognised plain-clothes policemen in the crypt, which was crowded to the door. When Cardinal Hume came in, there was a hush and Paisley stood up in the middle of the congregation loudly proclaiming his protest. He turned and walked out followed by a Special Branch man guarding him against personal attack. There was only one MP who did not respond to my appeal to ignore him. For reasons I will never understand, Robert Mellish, a former Labour Chief Whip, who should have known better, had to shout and make a fuss despite the general feeling that those taking part in the service should behave with dignity. As a result, far more publicity was given to the demonstration than would have been the case otherwise.

It was more than 500 years since Catholics had been allowed to worship God according to their beliefs in that crypt and I found the service most moving. I believe that God used me on this occasion to provide another step forward in religious freedom in Britain: the bigotry of 500 years ago should not decide the way we behave today.

CHAPTER TWENTY-SIX

A Time for Reform

During my years as an MP and minister, I had watched clerks at the Table of the House turning around to the Speaker and giving advice like a clerk in a court who supplies the magistrate with answers to questions that are being put to him. I told the clerks when I took over that under no circumstances would I require a clerk to turn around to advise me. I was determined that if I made mistakes that would have to be subsequently corrected, I would explain that to the House the next day. In the event there proved to be two or three times when I had to tell the House that I had given further thought to a matter raised the previous day where I thought I had been wrong. The House always appreciated this straightforward approach. The Speaker survives only if the House believes that he wants to be fair and that all his actions are aimed at achieving that against all the pressures.

In the early days I found that I had to insist quite firmly that the clerks were indeed the advisers of the Speaker not his masters. Sometimes I would discover that the clerks had given some advice to a member agreeing to a motion or giving guidance to Party leaders on what decisions I would be likely to reach without consulting me. When I disagreed with the judgement of the clerks and would reverse the decision I could always tell if they had advised members differently. I was very pleased to get a letter on one occasion from Sir Richard Barlas, the second of the Clerks during my time and probably the best of all the postwar Clerks, saying that the clerks liked the Speaker to make his own decisions. Indeed whenever there was major trouble even Richard would say to me that of course the clerks were there only to advise and not to decide. I understood very well on those occasions that it was my head that was on the block and it was their advice that I should put it there.

In any case a Speaker who allows clerks at the Table to feel that they are running Parliament and that the Speaker could always be relied upon to accept their advice, would soon lose the respect both of the clerks and of Members of Parliament. Party leaders in the Commons always seemed to know when I gave a ruling contrary to the advice of the clerks but that fact never worried me.

It is the custom for Government and Opposition alike to go to the Clerk to seek advice as to what rulings were likely to be made and I fear that all too often in the past they were able to treat the Speaker as a cypher. When I overruled the clerks, I never minded people knowing because I passionately believed that the Speaker should be able to take his own decisions, bearing in mind all the advice that was available. And there was plenty. If they wanted the Clerk to be Speaker then they should appoint the Clerk as Speaker. When I made my decisions based on their advice, I had to use my sense of judgement and my feel of the House, not just the letter of the law. Quite often if I wanted to make a decision, the Clerk would say there was no precedent for it and I would point to Erskine May and ask who made the precedents. The answer was of course previous Speakers, so I did not hesitate to make a few precedents which others could use.

One of these that will live on was the decision on private rulings, which I made against the advice of the clerks. I decided at the request of Robin Maxwell-Hyslop, the Tory MP for Tiverton, that the Speaker's private rulings could no longer be given in secret. A member can write to the Speaker asking for his advice on an issue. The Speaker's reply is a ruling and on one occasion in Mrs Thatcher's second administration, Maxwell-Hyslop had been told by the clerks that something he wanted to do was out of order because of a private ruling given by Mr Speaker FitzRoy years before the war.

Maxwell-Hyslop did what any sensible member would do and asked for a copy of the ruling. He was told that it had been lost and he quite reasonably said that, if it was not recorded, how did he know the ruling was made at all. The clerks pointed to a footnote in Erskine May, saying only that the Speaker had ruled but the terms of the ruling were not given. I felt this was a gross injustice and gave far too much power to the clerks and, anyway, why should the Speaker rule privately without telling the House he had done so. Members could get caught out, possibly years later – in this particular case it was fifty years later. It was wrong that a member trying to do something should be blocked because a Speaker had written a letter which nobody could find. The arguments were so strong that I suggested to Maxwell-Hyslop that he should raise the issue on a point of order, which he did. I then ruled that in future all private rulings would be listed in the back of Hansard. If it was not published in Hansard, it was not a ruling.

The House of Commons has many different departments, all of which are answerable to the Speaker, but the Clerks, having been the senior members of the establishment for generations, had drawn a lot of power to themselves. By long tradition the Clerk of the House had regarded all other departmental heads as junior to him. I was unhappy about that and believed that the other departmental heads should be made to feel that they really were in charge of their departments. The Clerk would always sit in the chair of the management board and I did not really see why that should be. It could have been the librarian or the general manager of the catering department or the editor of Hansard. It should not automatically always have to be the Clerk.

The whole organisation needs changing and I would like to see the introduction of the Canadian system where there is a chief executive who supervises the actual running of the House. There the Parliament has decided that the Clerk should no longer be the head of administration, to deal with the trade unions for example. The clerks are experts in parliamentary law and procedures but are not trained to be managers. Madame Jeanne Sauve, who was then the Canadian Speaker, had realised the need to introduce a system of having a general manager to co-ordinate the running of the House and to deal with all staff matters. I think this is a giant stride towards democracy and it is something that the Canadians can now teach the Mother of Parliaments.

One of the reforms that had been introduced towards the end of Selwyn Lloyd's time was the setting up of the House of Commons' Commission of senior members representing all parties to act as a sort of cabinet advising the Speaker, who is the chairman, on how the House should be run. Most importantly, it took on the task of making the appointments to the staff of the House.

Promotions within the department of the Clerk of the House had been very much in the hands of the Clerk himself and the practice had always been for the Clerk Assistant almost automatically to become Clerk. The Clerk's recommendations would be accepted without any question for every job in the department. It was his department and it was right and proper that he should run it but if he is claiming powers in other departments, then the whole House has a vested interested in who is appointed Clerk.

On my advice the Commission decided that when it came to choosing a successor to Sir Charles Gordon, who announced that he would be leaving in July 1983, it would be wrong simply to go on the principle of "Buggins's turn". Even the civil service do not say that the deputy should automatically get the top job. So the Commission decided to invite applications from a certain level of clerks within the House. There were four applicants and a vote was taken which resulted in the job going to the deputy, but the principle is now firmly established that promotions are not automatic.

The head of every department has direct access to the Commission, which is really a great improvement for before this, everything had been dealt with by the Clerk of the House alone. If any member of the staff has a complaint about his conditions of service, he is free whether he is in a union or not to make his protest to the Commission through his head of department. The Commission gives an annual report to Parliament and has certainly made the life of the Speaker easier because he used to carry the ultimate responsibility for the running of the House. That now rests with the Commission.

Once we set up the Commission some members of the staff were worried about how it would affect them and there was renewed interest in joining unions. Many members of the Clerk's department for instance decided to join the First Division Association, the union for senior civil servants.

There had been an understanding that the staff of the House would never seek to have a strike to prevent Parliament meeting: when the Commission was set up the unions felt that the right to strike should be given to them. There was a major crisis and I met all the union leaders in the State Dining-Room of Speaker's House. I was really surprised at the number of unions and their officials who were in the House. They all turned up.

I discovered there was a world of difference between those who were union leaders outside the House and those who worked in the House. Those who worked outside only wanted to use Parliament when they had a quarrel with the Government and to call all their members out of Parliament to make a political point, not to improve conditions. It was rather a sharp meeting because it had to be made clear to them that I was not prepared to give them the right to decide whether or not Parliament should be allowed to meet.

They calmed down when I said I would tell the House that I was not prepared to allow that small group of union leaders to determine the workings of Parliament. They asked for further time to consider it and that consideration went on for two years. But just before I finished, they did agree that they would not seek to prevent the House from meeting and on those terms it was immediately agreed to recognise the unions. I felt that democracy itself was at stake. It was for the members of the House to decide when Parliament should meet, not people who were answerable to their own members, but not to the country as a whole. I felt that what they really wanted to do was to broadcast to the nation that Parliament had been unable to meet because of a union dispute. That was something to which no Speaker could ever agree.

While we have made some progress in reforming the staff side of the House, I believe there should also be sweeping changes to Parliament itself. We are the largest Parliament in the world but that does not necessarily make us the best. The time has come for the House of Commons to face up to the fact that it needs reducing by a third to about 450 seats. The only real question to be answered is whether or not the House could do its job as effectively with that number as it does now with 650 (increased from 635 after recent boundary changes).

The answer must be yes, provided members are given the secretarial facilities to deal with the increased correspondence and paper work connected with constituents' problems. There is already free postage and telephone service to the constituency so only a small amount of extra financial help would be needed. Even if the constituencies grew to 100,000 votes each, it would not be an unreasonable figure. The argument that with larger constituencies the member would lose the personal touch with his constituents is humbug. I like to think that I had a close relationship with the people of Cardiff West but I doubt if during the course of a general election campaign I met more than 5,000 of them. Over the years, I came to know many people but that sort of contact would also build up if the constituencies were larger.

It does not make sense for the House to go on making itself bigger and bigger until it could be a thousand or more as though there was something more democratic in having a large number of MPs. Other democracies manage perfectly well with smaller numbers and I see no reason why we should not do so too. Nobody is going to pretend we are more democratic than Canada or Australia or India – we may be a bit more democratic than the United States of America, but that has nothing to do with numbers. For our small country to have the largest Parliament in the world is ridiculous.

One reform I would not like to see is the proposal that we should have a written Bill of Rights. I am strongly opposed to that suggestion because it transfers power from Parliament to the judges, who would inevitably be called upon to rule just what was meant by a particular phrase of any written constitution. In America it is not Congress that is supreme, nor is it the President. It is the court that interprets what is meant in the written constitution, even though that interpretation might not have been the intention of those who drew it up originally.

It is like an Act of Parliament in Britain. Once it leaves Parliament, the judges take over to decide just what it means, never mind what was actually intended. The only possible justification for a Bill of Rights would be if we were threatened by a Marxist takeover. But does anybody really think a piece of paper would stop that? I prefer Parliament to be supreme, where the members can be kicked out if the public no longer approves of what they are doing. The judges are not so accountable.

There is a stronger case for some change in our voting system than there is for a Bill of Rights. Our British sense of fair play is outraged by the fact that Social Democrats and Liberals may gain almost as many votes as the major parties in the House and yet get a mere handful of seats. This is clearly a frustration of the will of the electors but it is not easy to rectify. There is an even more dangerous frustration of the popular will when proportional representation results – as in Israel – in a tiny group of extremists wielding power that properly belongs to majority parties or to the bigger parties. However, it should not be beyond the skill of parliamentarians to find some formula to deal with this situation. What is absolutely clear is that the present system is grossly unfair and needs rectifying.

The last two days of my Speakership were really much more emotional than I had anticipated. The motion paying tribute to my seven years' service was on the order paper on the Thursday and there was a highly charged atmosphere in the House. Some other members, like me, were retiring after many years and had their own memories. Most were off to fight a general election and many knew they might not be returning; but if they did not, the decision was not going to be theirs.

After the tributes, in which Mrs Thatcher was particularly kind, I announced to the House that on the Friday, the last day of that Parliament, I intended to suspend the sitting after prayers so that I could shake hands with all the members before immediately leaving the Chair to the deputies for the rest of that day so that I could look around the House for the last time.

That day began as usual when I said my prayers before leaving Speaker's House for the walk to the Chamber, hoping that all would be well and that I would be guided in what to say. Making the walk for the last time, I approached the policeman who heads the line-up of attendants in the Members' Lobby for the Speaker's procession to pass through a guard of honour. This policeman had volunteered to be on duty for my last day and when I saw him my thoughts went straight back to the Rhondda.

I could see Mam, my sisters Ada and Dolly, my brothers Emrys and Ivor. They were all dead now but I knew how much I owed them all and I could feel them with me. As I passed the policeman, as I had so many times before, I said for the first time and the only time, "Thank you, Ken" – he was the son of my brother Emrys.

CHAPTER TWENTY-SEVEN

The Viscount Tonypandy

It came as a real surprise to see the Chamber so full. I took prayers and then suspended the sitting to shake the hands of all the members and the servants of the House. Members came along, several very senior members, with tears streaming down their faces. It was very moving, it caught me and I could not talk – perhaps the first time that had ever happened to me in the House since 1945. I just held them by the hand.

They were led by the Prime Minister, and I remembered that when she was Secretary of State for Education I had been one of her strongest opponents as one of the NUT's sponsored MPs, but it never stopped us being friends.

When I stood up to leave the House finally, the whole House stood up and started to cheer, waving their order papers. I think if I had spoken to anybody then I would have burst into tears. Even as I walked down the corridor I could hear them still cheering, which was a tremendous experience and I count my blessings that I went on a wave of goodwill and not bitterness caused by the inevitable clashes with Parliament.

Sir Hugh Fraser, who had come into Parliament with me in 1945, followed me down, walked behind the procession and said he wanted to see me. He came into my study straight away before I had taken my gown off and he put his arms around me to thank me for my time as Speaker. He went out and I sat there looking around for the last time in my Speaker's gown, sitting in it for the first time, as before I had always taken it off straight away. I decided that the best thing was for me to go to my flat and have a strong coffee and change. It was the end of the Speakership and the break was clean.

It will be for others to assess the weaknesses and any strengths of my seven years in the Chair, but I enjoyed them and did my best to preserve the historic role of the Speaker. I think some people may have misunderstood my efforts to make sure that the Speaker was given all the dignity and honour that the office was due. It was not for myself, but for the office and through the office, for Parliament itself. I had a long correspondence with the Home Office over the arrangements for the Remembrance Sunday service at the Cenotaph. The first time I went there I discovered, to David Steel's embarrassment as well as mine, that the Home Office, the guardian of protocol, had put the Speaker way down the procession behind David Steel, the leader of the Liberal Party. I decided after a great deal of correspondence, firstly with Merlyn Rees and then with Willie Whitelaw, that if they wanted to make it a party occasion with the party leaders having precedence over the Speaker of the House of Commons then I would not attend it but go to the ceremony in my own constituency in Cardiff. This is what I did.

I believe firmly that the status of the Speaker should never be reduced and he certainly should never have to walk behind anybody who serves in the House of Commons. The Speaker's place is in the front. For 200 years the Speaker was the first commoner in the land and I recall Sir Winston Churchill, when he was Mr Churchill, saying to Speaker Clifton-Brown, when he was re-elected in 1945, "You are the first commoner in the land." Even Winston had overlooked the fact that at the end of Speaker Lowther's period in 1919 it had been changed so that the order of precedence was the Prime Minister, the Lord President and then the Speaker. In the House of Commons the Speaker is the embodiment of Parliament on all official occasions, so he should never have to take a subordinate position to the various political parties who, often for the wrong reasons, want to be represented at occasions like the Cenotaph ceremony.

There should be one wreath laid on behalf of Parliament by the Speaker so that a party political row could not develop over who should be allowed to take part in the ceremony. The Speaker is outside the party battle and represents the House regardless of party considerations.

I thought I had finished with party politics, but not many weeks later, I was visiting the home of Fergus Montgomery MP when I had a telephone call from Number Ten indicating that it was proposed to offer me an hereditary viscountcy, as had already been done for Willie Whitelaw. I have to confess it did not take long for me to decide that I would accept happily, because if you are going to the Lords anyway – and I had made up my mind years before that I would go, if asked

– there seemed no reason at all not to accept what had been the traditional honour for retiring Speakers for 200 years.

The House of Commons has never decided to abolish the hereditary system; in fact it has never even debated it in recent years. It was the personal decision of Ted Heath as Prime Minister that in future he would offer only life peerages. Wilson and Callaghan had followed Heath's precedent. Horace King was the first Speaker not to become a viscount and I know that when his time came Selwyn Lloyd was disappointed that he was not given an hereditary title. He felt quite deeply that he should have had the same honour as his predecessors stretching down through history.

It was put to me recently by an hereditary peer that it was very reactionary for Mrs Thatcher to have gone back to hereditary titles in the case of Willie Whitelaw, Harold Macmillan and myself. Neither Willie nor I have a son to inherit the title anyway but surely the answer to that is either to abolish the system entirely or to continue it to introduce new young blood into the House of Lords.

There is no doubt in my mind that although we could manage without the House of Lords, we could not manage without a second chamber. In my judgement, it would be a terrible gamble. Our second-chamber system works. It gives the Government and even the Opposition the chance for second thoughts. It prevents legislation being pushed through without proper consideration and it also prevents any administration prolonging its own life. There is already a handful in the House of Commons who only want to use democratic procedures to destroy parliamentary democracy and I do not think we can be too careful when it comes to protecting democracy. The House of Commons needs the restraint imposed by the second chamber.

My short experience in the House of Lords has convinced me too that there is not the slightest doubt that the debating level in the House of Lords is much higher than in the Commons, and bills are examined with much more care. There is not the same vested party interest, with people looking for votes. There is an independence of mind and considerable scholarship that serves the nation well.

In the Lords, people will listen to a point of view even when they disagree profoundly with every word that is being uttered and they wait their turn to make a directly opposing speech, which is also listened to politely. There is no reason at all why it should not be like that in the Commons. It is no more democratic bawling like animals rather than to listen in silence. There is a tradition of noise in the

Commons and that in itself is no bad thing as it adds to the atmosphere, but I believe we are now beginning to get members there who do not believe in the system, who would not care if they pulled the pillars down.

These are people who use free speech to stop others speaking. Instead of giving a reasoned reply to an argument with which they disagree they resort to mindless abuse and bullying shouting. Their real target is the denial of free speech to their opponents and this is against everything that the Commons has stood for. In my view these people are the weevils working remorselessly to destroy the fabric of our parliamentary democracy. If ever they gained a majority in the Commons the only safeguard for our people would be a vigilant House of Lords.

The second chamber also helps to maintain the quality of legislation. The guillotine, which can be applied to a bill in the Commons, sometimes results in rather scrappy legislation, which could end up on the statute book if it were not for the very careful scrutiny applied to the bill in the Lords. The second chamber is a guarantee of democratic consideration of Government measures, which would be impossible in a single-chamber system. It would be all too easy for a government with a big majority to force through any measure it wanted without proper debate. Britain could then suffer the tyranny of an elected majority who could, if they wished, pass legislation to prolong their years in power.

There is a great deal wrong with the hereditary system but I have been very impressed by the number and quality of young men in the House of Lords who may be there only because a distant ancestor was rewarded many years ago, but who take their roles in the parliamentary machine very seriously indeed. I hope some way can be found to keep them if the hereditary principle in government is finally abolished. There are, of course, many more who do nothing, save enjoy the privileges of rank, and these people should certainly not be allowed to take part in the process of government.

The Labour Party has been opposed to the House of Lords all my life and in the past I have often spoken against it myself. The Party wants the House abolished and has always fought against the right of hereditary peers to tell the rest of us what to do. Their right has usually not been earned but has been passed down to them by some long-forgotten ancestor who had been rewarded for a good deed to the monarch or some heroic deed on the battlefield.

There is one thing that annoys me even more now and that is the tax-exile peers, who have the nerve to dodge their responsibilities to the country and then to exercise their right to come to the House of Lords on the days when they visit Britain from their tax havens. They avoid their obligations to Britain, but are willing to take the privileges that are available to them.

The current proposal for single-chamber government is out of character with Britain and I do not think it will come about. I believe it would expose Britain to power-mad people whose first interests would not be the country at large, but rather to get their legislation through at all costs, whatever the Opposition or even the country said. The continuation of a second chamber is essential for the maintenance of democracy in these islands.

The second chamber should not be an elected chamber. If it is elected, it would have to be given financial sanctions and that would take away the essential power of the Commons. Both America and Australia provide us with examples of how two elected chambers in one legislature plunge the country into crisis when they disagree.

The second chamber needs almost to be an advisory chamber for tidying up legislation, which could be appointed in proportion to the strengths in the House of Commons and be made up of people from a cross-section of the country, who have proved their ability. People from the trade unions, business, the universities, the professions, public life, even retired politicians could all play a part.

They could have real powers but their appointment could be limited to the life of one Parliament. They would not behave recklessly because they would presumably wish to be reappointed with a new Parliament, though I think they would show sufficient independence to be of real value.

But today we still have the House of Lords, which, despite everything, works smoothly, and eventually when I went there, I had to decide whether to follow tradition and sit on the cross-benches to show that I had kept the custom of strict impartiality maintained in the Upper House by my predecessors. And that is what I did, despite pressure from my Labour colleagues to join them. I believe it would be unfair on my successor for me to resume the party mantle because people would look at him and think that the impartiality was really only skin deep and that as soon as he had the chance he would return to the Tory fold, where his true loyalties lay.

There is no point in the Speaker stepping out of the Party battle if he is going to go back into it at the first opportunity. It is therefore a very big price that is paid for being Speaker of the House. To have to make one's ideals subordinate to the traditions of the House of Commons and to serve all parties is a very great sacrifice indeed.

Even after I had made it clear that I would sit on the cross-benches, there was still some subtle pressure from my former colleagues who said that, although they understood that I had to sit on the cross-benches, they would assume that I would in fact always support the party line. I had to tell them that I would not. I felt myself free to speak on any issue that I chose and to make up my own mind on the position I would take. To do otherwise would be humbug.

I have not changed my ideals or my values but I am determined to remain independent. I entered politics as a Christian Socialist, and I went out of the House of Commons with the same belief that there is no unimportant person in this land and that our parliamentary system is devised to help everyone to grow to their full stature.

We still have a long way to go but much has been achieved since every adult was given the vote. It is a remarkable story of achievement based on vision, ideals and common sense. It has been our strength in industrial disputes, where in the end a compromise and sensible solution is found, and in international affairs, where British common sense so often prevails.

Inevitably when a man reaches my stage in life, he "looks before and after and pines for what is not". I am grateful for the memories I have and I believe the more the House of Commons changes the more it remains the same. We get anxious because some of the people there do not have any respect at all for its traditions but the House has never lacked such people and it would not have the same colour and character without them. Parliament remains our only hope of Britain staying a democracy.

Looking at the state of democracy in Britain today reminds me of the man of eighty who, when asked how he felt now he had reached such an age, replied, "Very well, especially when I consider the alternative." And I believe there is no alternative to Parliament if we are to remain a democracy.

So as I look back I count my blessings. God has been good to me and I remember those days in Tonypandy when my mother said God would open doors for me. I was not to know that the doors would open to lead me in to the Speaker's Chair at Westminster. I can only say now what I thought as I left Speaker's House for the last time and looked at the portraits of my predecessors: "I hope I didn't let you down."

Index